ALEXANDRA

The *Alexandra* (another name for Kassandra) of LYKOPHRON, a Greek poem of 1,474 lines, is probably a pseudonymous work composed in the first decade of the second century BCE. It is attributed to a tragic poet called Lykophron of Chalkis, who lived in the first half of the third century BCE, and worked in the great cultural centre, Alexandria; only a very few genuine fragments of his plays survive, and little is reliably known about his life. But this attribution of the *Alexandra* is disputed, and has been since antiquity; it is rejected in the present edition. It follows that a conventional biography of the author is not possible. But (on the hypothesis of pseudonymity) the best guess is that the poet of the *Alexandra* lived and worked in S. Italy. The attractive notion of female authorship should be rejected on present evidence.

SIMON HORNBLOWER held teaching and research posts at Oxford and UCL until retirement in 2016. He is a Fellow of the British Academy. His books include a large-scale scholarly edition, with commentary, of Lykophron's *Alexandra* (2015), and a monograph, *Lykophron's* Alexandra, *Rome, and the Hellenistic World* (2018), both Oxford University Press. His most recent book is a co-authored edition of and commentary on Livy Book 22, Cambridge University Press.

OXFORD WORLD'S CLASSICS

*For over 100 years Oxford World's Classics have brought
readers closer to the world's great literature. Now with over 700
titles—from the 4,000-year-old myths of Mesopotamia to the
twentieth century's greatest novels—the series makes available
lesser-known as well as celebrated writing.*

*The pocket-sized hardbacks of the early years contained
introductions by Virginia Woolf, T. S. Eliot, Graham Greene,
and other literary figures which enriched the experience of reading.
Today the series is recognized for its fine scholarship and
reliability in texts that span world literature, drama and poetry,
religion, philosophy, and politics. Each edition includes perceptive
commentary and essential background information to meet the
changing needs of readers.*

OXFORD WORLD'S CLASSICS

LYKOPHRON

Alexandra

Translated with Introduction and Notes by
SIMON HORNBLOWER

OXFORD
UNIVERSITY PRESS

OXFORD
UNIVERSITY PRESS

Great Clarendon Street, Oxford, OX2 6DP,
United Kingdom

Oxford University Press is a department of the University of Oxford.
It furthers the University's objective of excellence in research, scholarship,
and education by publishing worldwide. Oxford is a registered trade mark of
Oxford University Press in the UK and in certain other countries

First published as an Oxford World's Classics paperback 2022

Impression: 1

Published in the United States of America by Oxford University Press
198 Madison Avenue, New York, NY 10016, United States of America

British Library Cataloguing in Publication Data
Data available

Library of Congress Control Number: 2022942487

ISBN 978–0–19–886334–2

Printed and bound in the UK by
Clays Ltd, Elcograf S.p.A.

CONTENTS

PREFACE AND ACKNOWLEDGEMENTS

I AM delighted that Lykophron has been admitted to the Oxford World's Classics (OWC) canon, alongside those two other great Hellenistic poets, Apollonios of Rhodes and Theokritos. This edition naturally draws on my large-scale Oxford University Press edition of Lykophron's *Alexandra*, with thematic Introduction, Greek text, translation, and detailed commentary (Hornblower 2015, corrected paperback reprint 2017). But it is far from being a mere reduction for a mainly non-specialist readership. Every passage and every problem has been revisited and rethought. (I have also silently made a few small further corrections and clarifications, and have changed my mind on some points.) If the resulting treatment is more obviously literary in approach than my earlier edition, that is in part because of the aims of the OWC series (it needs to be shown what makes it a 'classic work of literature'). It is also in part thanks to the appearance since 2015 of two outstanding literary monographs: those of Charles McNelis and Alexander Sens (2016), and Emily Pillinger (2019). But I have also, on the historical side, exploited a later monograph of my own, Hornblower 2018. This assumed the correctness of an early second-century BCE composition date for the poem, and argued that the then recent Roman war against Hannibal (218–201 BCE) has left traces on it. For all these recent books, see *Select Bibliography*.

The *Alexandra* calls for an unusual amount of explanatory comment, because it does not present its characters or its material straightforwardly (that is an understatement). I am therefore grateful to Luciana O'Flaherty, the editor of the OWC series, for allowing me, exceptionally, a double system of annotation. The footnotes on each page of the translation, keyed by line numbers, tell the reader in a word or two the familiar names of obscurely designated individuals or places (but if a name's interpretation is seriously disputed or ambiguous, discussion is reserved for an endnote). This is to avoid the constant need for readers to keep a finger in the back of the book to find out who or where is being talked about. The fuller explanatory endnotes are keyed to the translation in the usual OWC way, by asterisks at the end of the most relevant verse of the translation. In Introduction and endnotes, cross-references in the form 'see 71n.'

refer to these endnotes. As in that example, and as in my 2015 edition, numbers in **bold** refer, for clarity and to save space, to lines of the *Alexandra*. (This system applies only to the explanatory notes, not to the Introduction.)

It is a notable feature of the poem that gods, male and female, are almost invariably referred to not by their names but by cult-epithets, sometimes in clusters. (For modern explanatory theories, see 206–15n.) These are often of great interest individually, and can sometimes be illuminated or corroborated from inscriptions. But for reasons of space I have in the endnotes discussed such epithets only very occasionally, where they seem to me especially important for the understanding of a passage's implications. (For full treatments, the curious reader is referred to my 2015 commentary.) I have nevertheless retained the original form of the epithets in my translation, while providing in a footnote—see above—the familiar name of the god referred to. On the rationale for this non-simplifying procedure, see the *Note on the Text and Translation*.

Several friends and colleagues have helped me in various ways with this edition (references, offprints, corrections, advice, encouragement, good questions). I warmly thank them all, from A to Z: the late and much-regretted Jim Adams, Alessandro Barchiesi, Esther Eidinow, Denis Feeney, William Harris, Anna Sherman, Skye Sherwin, Peter Thonemann, Stephanie West, and Emilia Zybert. At OUP, I thank Henry Clarke, Project Editor, and Meghan Watson, Senior Production Editor, for valuable help at different stages; and finally I am grateful to Juliet Gardner for her excellent and meticulous copy-editing of a complicated typescript.

S. H.
Islington, London

INTRODUCTION

The Main Myth

THE *Alexandra* of Lykophron[1] is crowded with Greek myths, often given in unusual versions (86–9n., and see below on Penelope); this Introduction cannot list, let alone describe, even a few of them. Only one myth must be summarized briefly at the outset (more detail will be supplied later): the ten-year Trojan War,[2] in the literary tradition a prolonged siege of Troy (Ilion)—a fabulously rich city in NW Asia Minor—punctuated by fighting. One crucial episode, but not Troy's actual fall, is narrated in Homer's *Iliad*.[3] The Greek invasion was undertaken by a Greek coalition force led by King Agamemnon with the aim of recovering Helen, wife of Agamemnon's brother Menelaos, king of Sparta. She had been abducted from Sparta by Paris, son of Priam, king of Troy. The Trojans were led by Hektor, another of Priam's many sons. The Greek army included the best fighter in either army, Achilles; also Odysseus, and two very different men called Ajax, distinguished as 'Lokrian' and 'Telamonian'. Troy was captured after a wooden horse full of soldiers, left by the Greeks as a trick, was brought by the Trojans into their city, despite the warnings of Apollo's priest Laokoon. By then Hektor had been killed in a duel with Achilles, who until then had shunned the fighting, after a quarrel with Agamemnon. Troy was now sacked, and Priam's family, including his wife Hekabe (Latin Hecuba), either killed or (the women) taken as slave concubines. During the sack, Priam's most beautiful daughter Kassandra was raped in the temple of the goddess Athena by Lokrian Ajax; she then became the property of Agamemnon. Kassandra possessed prophetic powers conferred by Apollo, and most of the *Alexandra* purports to be a prophecy delivered by her shortly before the Trojan War. Outside the frame of the *Iliad*,

---

[1] The usual opening 'Life and career' section is impossible for a poem whose century is disputed, and which will be argued to be pseudonymous.

[2] Wholly mythical, or in some weak sense historical? See A. Bowie, *Iliad* Book III (Cambridge, Cambridge University Press 2019), 21–31.

[3] See the OWC edition, translation by A. Verity, introduction and notes by B. Graziosi, 2012.

Achilles was killed by Paris with an arrow; Paris was in turn killed by another archer, the Greek Philoktetes. Other Greek heroes returned home, but their returns (*nostoi*) were often long or unhappy; the most famous such *nostos* is that of Odysseus to Ithaka, a ten-year epic in itself, the subject of Homer's *Odyssey*.[4] After twenty years in all, he came home disguised and had to fight to regain his kingdom and his faithful wife Penelope from the suitors installed in his palace. It is typical of the *Alexandra* that she is represented, contrary to tradition, as having been promiscuous and spendthrift in Odysseus' absence. Agamemnon returned safely, but was immediately murdered together with Kassandra by his wife Klytaimestra and her lover Aigisthos. Trojan Aineias (Latin Aeneas) led survivors to Italy, where he founded Rome and other places in Latium. Homer merely hints at a future career for Aineias; the full story would be told most famously in Virgil's *Aeneid*.[5]

Kassandra features in both the *Iliad* and (for her death with Agamemnon) in the *Odyssey*, but she is nowhere explicitly said to have the gift of prophecy. There is one possible exception. Near the end of the *Iliad* (24.699–700) she climbs to the topmost tower of Troy to watch for Priam's return from the Greek camp with Hektor's corpse, and is the first to see it coming. Why did she do this unless she had some supernatural awareness that it was near?[6] Later sources developed this hint; or Homer knew more than he chose to tell. But the first definite allusion to Kassandra's foresight occurs in a mostly lost post-Homeric epic from c.600 BCE, the *Kypria*, where she is said to 'reveal what will happen'.[7] She certainly has prophetic powers in poetry and drama of the fifth century BCE: Pindar *Pythian* 11; Aeschylus, *Agamemnon*; Euripides, *Trojan Women* (and its now fragmentary companion tragedy, *Alexandros*, i.e. Paris). Aeschylus was first to add that because she refused sex to Apollo after promising it, he ensured that her prophecies would never be believed. Lykophron's Kassandra sometimes envisages alternative outcomes for familiar myths; see 768–78n. for such 'future reflexives'.

---

[4] See the OWC edition, translation by A. Verity, introduction and notes by W. Allan, 2016.

[5] See the OWC edition, translation and notes by F. Ahl, introduction by E. Fantham, 2008.

[6] See Pillinger, 2 n. 1.

[7] West 2003, 69. For the Epic Cycle, including the *Kypria*, see *Sources*.

The Poem and its Literary Qualities

Lykophron's *Alexandra* is a pseudonymous Greek poem dating from the 190s BCE. That, at least, is the view preferred in this edition (see *Authorship and Date*). It is one of the most extraordinary, and most intriguing and rewarding, works of ancient Greek or Roman literature to have come down to us. The title refers to Kassandra, whose Spartan name was 'Alexandra'. In the metre of the non-choral parts of Classical tragedy (iambic trimeters), the poem gives, for most of its 1,474 lines, a prophecy put into Kassandra's mouth, reported to Priam by a guard, who delivers two short speeches at beginning and end. It is a pseudo-prophecy, a prophecy *post eventum*, 'after the event'. This ranges from mythical to historical times, from before the fall of Troy to the famous 'prediction' (1229) of Rome's acquisition of pan-Mediterranean dominion by what I take to be the early second century BCE. The alternative composition date is a century earlier. On either of the two main views, the poem is an important document about Greek attitudes to Rome. But its historical interest does not end there, nor does it depend entirely on dating. Its key episode occurs a quarter of the way through: at the fall of Troy, the odious Greek Lokrian Ajax assaults Kassandra sexually in Athena's temple, and this outrage will cause unhappy or failed *nostoi* from Troy for all the Greek heroes, not only the individual perpetrator of the crime (365–6). This is the prompt for a long series of *nostoi* narratives, which provide foundation myths for many historical Mediterranean settlements. The most moving and effective of these is the story of Diomedes and his homesick companions, turned into birds (592–632). Fleeing Trojans are also treated as 'returning', mostly to S. Italy (see 1236–41n. for this extended sense of 'return'). Greek colonization was among other things a religious business, and Kassandra gives details of cults[8] and rituals, often connected loosely to the main narrative; sometimes these can be corroborated from inscriptions; see e.g. 206–15n. and 459n. The most important such example is the story of the 'tribute' consisting of the Lokrian Maidens (horrific civic

[8] In particular, the poem regularly registers posthumous hero- and heroine-cult for both Greeks and Trojans (see *OCD* 'hero-cult'): 3on. and 1123–40n. (Agamemnon at Sparta); 180–210n. (Achilles); 564–8n. (Dioskouroi: divinization); 599n. (Diomedes); 732–7n. (Parthenope); 927–9n. (Philoktetes); 1047–55n. (Podaleirios); 1183–8n. (Hekabe); 1189–1213n. (Hektor); 1123–40n. again (Kassandra in Daunia).

atonement for Ajax's sin), described in one of the best and most sombre—and lucid—passages of the poem (1141–73) and remarkably confirmed as a genuine historical ritual by a prose Hellenistic inscription published in 1912.[9] The later part of the poem narrates, with heavy but reworked indebtedness to Herodotus' *Histories*,[10] the struggles between Asia and Europe, from the mythical age to the poet's own time.

But the *Alexandra* is more than a quarry for political and religious historians. It is a literary achievement of high quality. The author, who-ever he was—I reluctantly reject the attractive notion of female author-ship (see p. xxii)—created a complex architectural structure whose climax is a military victory by a Roman commander, whom Kassandra regards as her kinsman, because of the myth that Rome was founded by Trojan Aineias. The poet was phenomenally learned and well-read, like many poets of the Hellenistic age (the period from Alexander the Great to Augustus, 338 to 31 BCE). The *Alexandra* draws on many prose and verse predecessors, but often with deliberate differences and ingenious reductions in scale. Two examples, one long, one short: first, 648–876 narrate, in the future tense which is Kassandra's prerogative as prophet, the wanderings first of Odysseus (Lykophron's '*Odyssey*') and then Menelaos in search of his wife Helen. Much of this pair, the longest *nostos* section,[11] depends on, but rethinks, rewrites, and up-ends Homer's *Odyssey* from Kassandra's Trojan point of view. Second, the most tangibly historical episode in the poem is the account of the Achaemenid Persian king Xerxes' invasion of Greece in 480 BCE (1412–34). Here Lykophron is, as often, indebted to Herodotus; but with notable succinctness redirects the implications of the original.

We have noticed that the human 'tribute' of the Lokrian Maidens, and the homesickness of Diomedes' bird-companions, are two extended highlights of the poem. Individual powerful or succinctly expressive lines are many; two examples are the tremendous line 71, enacting the rapid conflagration which destroyed Troy, and 566, a neat rewriting of Homer on the half-immortality of the Dioskouroi, Kastor and Polydeukes (Latin Pollux).

---

[9] *SVT* no. 472; Greek text, English translation and commentary at Hornblower 2018, 179–86.
[10] See the OWC edition, translation by R. Waterfield, introduction and notes by C. Dewald (1998).
[11] The two together form a distinct thematic unit: see *Structure*.

Difficulty: the 'Lykophron Epigram'

'In our much-twisting labyrinths
   you will not easily come to the light, if you can manage it at all.
For such are the tales which Priam's daughter Kassandra uttered,
   and which the emissary, the messenger of crooked utterances,
   reported to the king.
If Kalliope [a Muse] loves you, take me into your hands; but if
   you are ignorant of the Muses, you are carrying a heavy load in
   your hands.'

                                                    (*Anth. Pal.* 9.191)

This clever, anonymous Greek epigram[12] neatly encapsulates the
qualities of Lykophron's *Alexandra* which have always made it a challenging read; this aspect is best confronted straight away. Many epigrams in the ancient *Anthology* are about authors and literary texts,
but this is the only one about the *Alexandra*. The epigram closest to it
in phrasing and message is also anonymous, and is about another
difficult author, the historian Thucydides: *Anth. Pal.* 9.583.

The Lykophron epigram can serve as an introduction to the dis-
tinctive features of the poem which it so warily celebrates. (a) It packs
much into a small space; this recalls the *Alexandra*'s ingenious brevity
of literary allusion (see *The Poem*). (b) Although it is obviously about
Lykophron's *Alexandra*, neither author nor poem are named. This is
mimetic of the *Alexandra*'s systematic allusiveness: gods and individual mythical figures are almost always referred to periphrastically and
indirectly (but animals are named! 152–67n.). In particular, gods are
routinely designated by cult-epithets or titles, often piled up together
(discussion at 206–15n.). The record is at 355–60, six (perhaps seven)
separate epithets for Athena; this plurality is designedly emphatic, at
a climactic moment: Kassandra appeals in vain to Athena to save her
from Ajax. (c) The poem's essential structure is conveyed by just two
lines of the epigram (3–4): the *Alexandra* begins and ends with short
speeches by a guard or 'messenger'[13] sent by Priam to report on his
daughter's utterances (1–30, 1461–74). See *Structure*. (d) 'Messenger

[12] For a full study see S. Hornblower and E. Zybert, 'An epigram about Lycophron's
Alexandra (*Anth. Pal.* IX 191', *Eos* 106 (2019), 55–84, arguing that it is late Hellenistic,
and correcting a common error of identification in line 4: see n. 13 below.

[13] 'Messenger of crooked utterances' is obviously the guard. It has been repeatedly
misunderstood as referring to Kassandra herself, starting with the bad entry *loxotrochis*
in LSJ, and W. R. Paton, Loeb *Greek Anthology (Anth. Pal.)* vol. 3 (1917), 101.

of crooked utterances' (line 4) is a single compound Greek word, found nowhere else: a so-called *hapax* word. This is the epigrammatist's way of drawing attention to a marked feature of the *Alexandra*, its recondite vocabulary: it has several hundred *hapax* words.[14] But the epigrammatist goes even further: the halves of the word are both taken from the last few lines of the poem, which use two out-of-the-way words for 'crooked' (1467) and 'messenger' (1471, the guard describing himself). (e) The epigram's first two lines echo two metaphors favoured in the poem's preamble (1–15): darkness and twisting paths. Lykophron was called the 'dark poet' in antiquity (n. 70). So 'dark' is after all a hint at the poet's identity, cf. (b) above. (f) The epigram's allusions to the Muses correctly acknowledge the high literary quality of the original; the Thucydides epigram does the same for its subject, again correctly.

The poem's difficulty can be exaggerated. Obviously, some of those listed above fall away if the poem is read in translation only, as in this edition. But even so, the persistently indirect and even riddling references to gods, mythical individuals, and places (even the simple Greek words for 'Troy' and 'Trojan' never occur) would make for a slow and frustrating read without immediate help.

In other respects the poem deals with its material straightforwardly and logically, providing clear transitional formulae derived in part from early 'Catalogue' poetry such as that attributed to the Archaic poet Hesiod. This is particularly true of the *nostoi* sections. 'Five (heroes) will settle. . .' places on Cyprus (447–9); each is then identified in turn and their foundational activity described at varying lengths and with some elaborate but clearly signposted excursuses. Again, after a section about Philoktetes' Italian activity, Kassandra moves without obfuscation to that of Epeios, builder of the Wooden Horse by which Troy was captured: 'the Horse-builder will enter the embrace of. . .' a named Italian city (930). About anonymous groups of returning Greeks we are told that, for example, 'others shall settle. . .' (951, 1027–8), or 'many will settle. . .' (978). Short, usually two-line, recapitulations can break up the narrative and signal the departure of

---

[14] See however 318n.: a compound word believed until as recently as 2018 to be *hapax* has now turned up in a long Hellenistic verse inscription from Asia Minor. Many of the *hapax* words in the poem, and words used there for the first time (*primum dicta*), are compounds. For a thorough study of such compounds (seventy-nine and twenty respectively in these two categories), see now Pellettieri.

one theme and the arrival of another: 909–10n., 1281–90n. More subtly and slyly, a casual remark or comparison in one episode can anticipate and prepare for the next; so in the pathetic story of Diomedes and his metamorphosed homesick bird-settlers, the comparison of the birds' activity with Zethos, who built the walls of Boiotian Thebes (602), looks forward to the next section, about Boiotians on the Balearic islands—the crab-like 'others' of 633; see 633–47n. In this way the abruptness of a transition is softened.

Within sentences, word-order is unproblematic (unlike the 'hyperbaton' or dislocated word-order of the famously difficult poet Pindar); and there are none of the dense abstract terms which made the speeches in Thucydides hard going even for readers in antiquity, still more so for us. The metre is simple and strict: few elisions, and an avoidance of 'resolution' (long syllables divided into two short ones).[15] The prophecy's actual content—myth after myth—resembles the choral parts of a Classical tragedy, whose metre is often complex and hard. Kassandra, by contrast, sticks to plain iambics.

But there are many interpretative challenges. Here the poem's very difficulty comes to our aid, because ancient and Byzantine commentators, with access to far more other ancient works of literature than are available to us, and to now lost or now fragmentary mythological handbooks and lexica, tackled the poem's intricacies and allusions, and much of their work survives. (But not the earliest commentary of all, by Theon of Alexandria in the first century BCE.) In particular, there are two no-nonsense prose paraphrases of the whole poem; excellent *scholia* (ancient explanatory notes); and a full and valuable commentary by the Byzantine scholar John Tzetzes.[16]

Structure

As we have seen, the *Alexandra* consists of a long prophecy by Kassandra, book-ended by short speeches by the guard who has been ordered by her father King Priam to report what she says. So the poem folds a speech within a speech; or to put it another way, the prophecy is a 'messenger-speech', of a kind familiar from Classical tragedy.

[15] For the strict metre of the *Alexandra*, see M. L. West, *Greek Metre* (Oxford, Oxford University Press, 1982), 159.
[16] See *Select Bibliography* under *Ancient Commentaries*.

Beyond this, two organizational principles operate in alternation: chronological and (within the long *nostoi* section) geographical. The first quarter is presented chronologically. When the poem begins, Priam is alive and the Trojan War is in the future. Kassandra begins by going even further back in time, to an earlier destruction of Troy, and to Oinone, Paris' first wife. His abduction of the Spartan queen Helen leads to a more or less sequential but episodic and highly selective account of the Trojan War and the deaths of Achilles, and of Hektor and Kassandra's other close kin (202–372). Her rape by Ajax and his almost immediate punishment by drowning on his *nostos* lead to the long *nostoi* narrative (417–1282), whose arrangement is essentially geographical (below). The chronological principle is resumed in the last two hundred lines: the struggles between Asia and Europe begin with mythical abductions of women, familiar from Herodotus (1.1–5): Io, Europa, Medea, the Amazons (1283–1368), and (1369–73) the Trojan War again. But Herodotus' order is followed only approximately. This introduction prompts a semi-mythical, semi-historical account of Greek colonization of three areas of Asia Minor, treated as acts of aggression by Europe against Asia: the Aiolid in the NE Aegean, Ionian Miletos in the central coastal zone, and the area of Dorian settlement in the SE Aegean, the Dodecanese islands and the mainland opposite Kos and Rhodes. Midas (1397–1408) is a fully historical figure who led Phrygian i.e. Asian migration into Macedonia and Thrace; but picturesque myths were attached to him, as to Kroisos of Lydia. Kassandra then jumps to the Persian wars, singling out Xerxes' invasion of 480 BCE for detailed treatment (above). Then she jumps again, to Alexander the Great's conquests, and finally the defeat of Alexander's eventual successor Philip V of Macedon in 197 BCE by a 'kinsman-wrestler' of Kassandra, the Roman commander Titus Quinctius Flamininus. (These last identifications are contested: no individual is actually named.)

The *nostoi* narrative as a grand whole is arranged geographically. It forms a roughly clockwise circuit: east Mediterranean, especially Cyprus–Libya–Italy and the west.[17] As we have seen, the prime cause of unhappy Greek returns is presented as Ajax's sacrilegious crime, but another agent plays a role too: Nauplios, father of Palamedes, took revenge on the Greeks, especially but not only Odysseus, for the

---

[17] McNelis and Sens, 83–4.

death of his son, who had exposed Odysseus' attempt to avoid the Trojan War by feigning madness: 384–5n. He comes in useful again as a structuring device much later in the prophecy.

The early *nostoi* (417–632), starting with that of Phoinix who raised Achilles (419) and continuing with those of the seer Kalchas, Sthenelos, Idomeneus, Teukros the brother of Telamonian Ajax,[18] and Diomedes, are thematically connected by imperfection and failure: 417–23n. The fortunes of Diomedes and his companions and successors in east central Italy are split into two widely separated narratives, 592–632 and 1056–66, part of the Italian series which close the *nostoi* (below). Boiotian colonization of the Balearic islands (633–47) is prepared for in the Diomedes section (see *Difficulty*). The Balearics are the destination of the westernmost *nostos*.

The longest *nostoi* are those of Odysseus and Menelaos (see *The Poem*). This pair of wanderings forms a single thematic unit in many respects (820–76n.). Kassandra's '*Odyssey*' is well aware of the Homeric ordering of the hero's adventures, but she often departs from it, for her own reasons. Menelaos' journeys reflect in miniature the clockwise[19] arrangement of the *nostoi* section as a whole: the east Mediterranean from Cyprus to Phoenicia and Egypt, then eventually to the west, Italy and Sicily. Italian and Trojan *nostoi* close the main sequence: Philoktetes, Epeios, Asklepios' son Podaleirios, the Trojan woman Setaia, and groups of anonymous collective Greeks in Italian Bruttium and Lucania. Also in the west Mediterranean, anonymous Greeks settle Malta, south of Sicily, and Elephenor leads Euboian islanders to the Adriatic region (911–1089). The murders of Agamemnon and Kassandra, brutally carried out by his wife Klytaimestra, are introduced at 1090 by a resumption of the Nauplios theme (above): his revenge took two forms: he wrecked the ships of homecoming Greeks, and made their wives unfaithful, conspicuously Agamemnon's. But Kassandra's future cult in Daunia (east central Italy) attaches this section to the many Italian *nostoi* previously described by Kassandra. This passage is linked thematically to the immediately following account of the tribute of the Lokrian Maidens: both reflect premarital

---

[18] That is, 'son of Telamon'. This Ajax, the subject of Sophocles' play, is so-called to distinguish him from Lokrian Ajax, Kassandra's rapist.

[19] See McNelis and Sens, 156 (but I take 'counterclockwise' to be a slip for 'clockwise').

initiatory rituals (1123–73). Kassandra's narrative of her own future and posthumous fate leads naturally on to those of her brother Hektor (whose bones will be moved from the Troy region for heroic re-burial at Boiotian Thebes, a cult of relics) and their mother Hekabe (1174–1213). Despite the eclipse of Priam's line, Troy will rise again: this is the prompt for an account of the Italian wars and city-foundations of Trojan Aineias, precious lines because they are the earliest fully surviving version of the traditions about early Rome (1226–80). Then the organization becomes chronological again.

An important feature of the poem's structure, shared with Kallimachos' Hymn 6 *to Demeter* and some Latin poems, is an internal architecture, or 'numerology': the 1,474 lines are divided up at key points. Most conspicuously, the exact halfway milestone is 737, the culmination of the long section about the three Sirens, and in particular about the Italian city of Naples and its patron Siren, Parthenope. Given the literary importance of the Sirens, and the historical importance of Naples to Rome (see *Historical Implications*), this is surely deliberate.[20] Again, the Roman prophecy at 1229 is five-sixths of the way through the poem; and the lengths of the twinned sections about Odysseus and Menelaos are in an almost exact 3:1 ratio. There are other, less striking examples. One important consequence of this is to reduce the likelihood that the poem contains passages interpolated later (see *Authorship and Date*).

Themes

One main theme of the latter part of the *Alexandra* is the rebirth of defeated Troy and Trojan glory, *kleos*,[21] in the form of Rome, founded by the refugee Trojan Aineias. The word *kleos* itself occurs only three times (1174, 1212, 1226), but always about Troy and Trojans; and there are other expressions with much the same force, notably *kudos*, a word which has entered the English language (1226–35n.). A sub-theme is destructive Trojan fire: 71n.

[20] The importance of this central passage is emphasized by a linguistic feature: certain words are repeated just twice, first in the half leading up to the centre, and again in the half after it. For this acute observation, see (with lists of words) E. Zybert, 'Symmetry and verbal parallels in Lycophron's *Alexandra*', *Eos* 106 (2019), 215–44.

[21] Trojan *kleos* is emphasized, as a dominant theme of the *Alexandra*, by McNelis and Sens, esp. ch. 8, 'Death and the restoration of Trojan glory'.

Second, we have seen that the main organizing principle and theme of the long central *nostoi* section is reciprocity or requital: the Greeks will pay, by unhappy or failed *nostoi*, from Troy, for the injury done to Kassandra and the impiety of its temple location. An important and recurrent sub-theme of the *nostoi* narratives is homesick colonial longing, Greek *pothos*. For this, and for 'place attachment', see 644–7n.

Third, the metamorphosis theme runs through the whole poem: 28 separate metamorphoses). See 171–7n.: Troy is itself metamorphosed into Rome.

A fourth theme is also ubiquitous: the ill-treatment and sufferings, often violent and sexual, of innocent and mostly young women at the hands of men or gods. Kassandra herself is naturally the chief of these, but the list of other female victims is long: Hesione (Priam's sister); Oinone (Paris' deserted first wife); Helen (abducted by Paris as an adult and sexually abused as a prepubertal girl by Theseus, 847–51n.); Iphigeneia, sacrificed by her father Agamemnon; Priam's abused relative Killa (316–22n.); Kassandra's sisters Laodike and Polyxena; the daughters of Anios of Delos (reduced to magical mechanisms for providing Greek soldiers with food and drink); Kassandra's mother Hekabe; Phoinodamas' daughters; Myrrha; Andromeda; Trojan Setaia; the Lokrian Maidens; Io; Europa; Medea; the Amazon Antiope; Neileos' unnamed daughter; Mestra daughter of Erysichthon. (The Sirens come to a bad end at Odysseus' hands, but are hardly innocent victims.) Odysseus leaves both Kirke and Kalypso, but we do not feel very sorry for them, and anyway their abandonment is a motif in Homer not Lykophron.

Fifth and finally, the poem systematically undermines the claims to heroic status of two of the central figures of the Homeric *Iliad* and *Odyssey*: Achilles and Odysseus.[22] Both are represented as cowards and would-be draft-dodgers (258–80n. for Achilles and 815–19n. for Odysseus). Achilles is mercenary (269–72n.) and brutal; there is no mention or hint of his humane reconciliation with Priam at the end of the *Iliad* (266–7n.). Similarly, Kassandra erases Odysseus' slaying of the suitors and his happy reunion with Penelope (768–78n.). But if she writes down Achilles, she writes up her brother Hektor (281–306n., 1189–1213), so her antagonisms express a purely patriotic Trojan as

---

[22] Tragedy had already treated them (and Menelaos) less favourably than did Homer, but Lykophron takes this to extremes.

well as a female viewpoint. Nevertheless the treatment of Achilles in particular anticipates modern feminist readings of the Troy story (see again 266–7n. and *Reception*).

Authorship and Date

The poem is attributed, in the ancient tradition, to an attested early third-century BCE tragic poet called Lykophron from Chalkis on Euboia. No play of his survives in more than fragments,[23] none of which resembles the *Alexandra*. But they are all short (many are no more than one-word play-titles), so this proves little. The main problem with this 'early' date for the poem is that the pseudo-prophecy of Roman 'sceptre and kingship over land and sea' would be astonishing, even as conventionally flattering hyperbole,[24] before the victorious close of the first of Rome's three wars against Carthage ('Punic Wars'): that is, after 241 BCE. Only then did the Romans acquire their first overseas possessions, Sicily and Sardinia.

It is also difficult to find a plausible candidate other than T. Quinctius Flamininus (consul in 198 BCE) for the 'kinsman-wrestler' of 1447. He defeated Philip V of Macedon at Kynoskephalai in 197 and imposed a settlement which purported to free the Greeks; this won him huge popularity and even cultic honours (cf. 1449). But this has not gone unchallenged.

By proponents of the early dating of the poem, the Roman kinsman has sometimes[25] been identified as Gaius Fabricius Luscinus, and his opponent as Pyrrhos, king of Epirus, who had invaded Italy in 280. It was not however—as is sometimes asserted—Fabricius who defeated Pyrrhos at Beneventum (275), but the consul Manius Curius Dentatus. In that year Fabricius was censor, a position with no military authority (*imperium*). Curius himself would be no better: there was no peace settlement with Pyrrhos after the battle, as 1448

---

[23] Collected (with *testimonia*, i.e. evidence for life and works) at *TrGF* 1 no. 100; translated by Kotlinksa-Toma, 74–86.

[24] Fraser 1972, vol. 2, pp. 1065–7, n. 331 still stuck to the 'early' date, but with qualms about taking 'land and sea' as a merely conventional formula. He finally abandoned this position in favour of an early second-century date: Fraser 1979; more briefly in *OCD*, 'Lycophron (2)'. He was converted by the presence, in the Cyprus section, of material from Eratosthenes, active in the later third century: 447–591n.

[25] As by Holzinger, 383–4.

requires.[26] And the language of 1449–50 suits the glamorous Flamininus much better than either Fabricius or Curius, who were often paired in antiquity for their old-style frugality. Some scholars nevertheless continue to hold to the 'early', third-century dating for the poem.[27] Since they cannot come up with a plausible early third-century candidate for the Roman 'kinsman-wrestler', they sometimes resort to the old and desperate expedient that the phrase denotes no individual (as 1449–50 clearly require), but the Roman people personified.[28] On this view, the 'agreement of reconciliation about sea and land' (1448) is argued to be the Roman treaties with certain S. Italian states, concluded after the Pyrrhic War (*SVT* nos. 473–5). But two of these are doubtful as to either date or content, and none of them suit Kassandra's majestic and far-reaching language, so the argument is weak. By contrast, *SVT* no. 617, the settlement after Kynoskephalai, suits perfectly.

By the end of the 190s, the Romans had defeated both Philip V and the Seleukid king of Asia, Antiochos III (at the battle of Magnesia, 190).[29] Roman 'kingship over land and sea' was by that date no more than the truth. One must choose (merely to list the alternatives without adjudication, as some editors and commentators do, is feeble), and the 190s are my preferred date.

Another argument is less compelling, but has some weight: a literary argument that Lykophron knew the great poems of the third century, especially those of Kallimachos, Theokritos, and Apollonios of Rhodes.[30] A telling example[31] is the compound word 'horse-builder' for Epeios (cf. above) at 930. It is not quite a *hapax* word, as claimed by Ciani in her usually impeccable Lexicon to Lykophron: it is also

---

[26] So, rightly, Hurst/Kolde, 316.

[27] Most recently A. Rozokaki, *The Negative Presentation of the Greeks in Lycophron's Alexandra and the Dating of the Poem* (Athens, Koralli, 2019): in Greek, followed by English translation.

[28] First advocate: H. Reichard, *Lycophronis Chalcidensis* Alexandra (Crusius, Leipzig, 1788), 227 (*populus Romanus*); latest: Rozokaki (previous n.), 80.

[29] K. Jones, 'Lykophron's *Alexandra*, the Romans, and Antiochus III', *Journal of Hellenic Studies* 134 (2014), 410–55 sees this battle, rather than Kynoskephalai, as the primary reference. The dating implications are much the same.

[30] For a cautious assessment of these poetic affiliations, see A. S. Hollis, 'Some poetic connections of Lycophron's *Alexandra*', in P. J. Finglass and others, *Hesperos: Studies in Greek Poetry Presented to M. L. West* (Oxford, Oxford University Press, 2007), 276–93.

[31] Not mentioned by Hollis (previous n.), who confined himself to Kallimachos' *Hekale*, *Hymns* and *Aitia*, 'Causes'.

attested in Kallimachos (frag. 197, from one of the *Iambi*), but *nowhere else in all Greek*. If the choice is between Kallimachos borrowing from Lykophron or Lykophron from Kallimachos, the second is far like- lier, given the *Alexandra*'s small impact at any period until Virgil and Ovid. (For another example, a rare word for 'mice', see 1296–1308n.) But the reply of the sceptic who retains the third-century date is that a group of contemporary poets were engaging in a kind of competi- tive and sophisticated literary conversation. That cannot be decisively disproved, any more than the view it discards.

A third approach is to accept that the prophecy of Roman great- ness cannot be the work of Lykophron of Chalkis, but to suppose that these lines were added by another, much later, poet. This, the 'inter- polation theory', had already occurred to an ancient commentator, and was developed most cogently in recent times by S. West 1984. It is not accepted here, partly because the poem is a tightly organized unity: its author paid strict attention to the number of lines of his work as a whole, and of its component elements (for 'numerology', see *Structure*). The words '*his* work' must now be justified.

If the poem's author was not Lykophron of Chalkis but a century later, it follows that it was pseudonymous. That leaves open the theor- etical possibility that the author was female, like the Hellenistic epic poetess, *poietria*, Aristodama of Smyrna, who gave performances of epic poems written by herself, and was honoured for it at Delphi (*Syll.* 532). This is an attractive idea, given that the speaker of most of the *Alexandra* is female, and narrates the fates of many other wronged women. But two considerations make it unlikely. First, there is no certain example from Classical Antiquity of a female author adopting a male pseudonym.[32] If an example could be found or new evidence discovered, the question would be well worth re-opening. Second, the poem is learned, and female education, even in the Hellenistic period, was at a lower level than that of men. (But a priestess might be an exception.) We have no idea why the poet chose to conceal his true identity. For his choice of a minor tragedian as pseudonym, see *Genre*.

As for his origins and domicile, a similar argument—that is, from distribution of attention—can be used for one of the cities of S. Italy:

---

[32] I owe this point to the late Martin West in conversation. For his annotated catalogue of female Greek poets, see M. L. West, *Hellenica* 3 (Oxford, Oxford University Press, 2013), 315–40.

nearly a third of Kassandra's prophecy (457 lines) is about the western Mediterranean, and the author is specially well-informed about the traditions of S. Italy. This argument is not vulnerable to the objections which can be raised against female authorship. Certainty cannot be claimed for it, and that is true of much else about the *Alexandra*. But for details indicating that the poet was at least bilingual in Greek and Latin, see *Rome and Italy*. S. Italy was a culturally lively place in the Hellenistic period: in particular, it produced a female epigrammatist, Nossis.

Historical Implications

If the case for a composition date in the 190s is accepted, and given that Roman military success is celebrated in what for this poet is exceptionally plain language which apparently refers to very recent events, it is natural to ask what historical implications follow. One detail has already been mentioned: the dead centre of the poem (737) is positioned at the climax of a long section about Naples, Greek Neapolis. This city, an old Greek foundation and re-foundation, was a faithful and valuable naval ally of the Romans. In the Second Punic War (218–201 BCE, the 'Hannibalic' War), the Carthaginian general Hannibal tried to capture Naples after his victory at Cannae (216 BCE), because he needed a good harbour on the west coast of Italy (Livy 23.1). But the Neapolitans stayed loyal to their long-standing Roman alliance. There are many other details in the poem which arguably acquire extra point if recently topical at the (assumed) composition date. Four further examples: first, Malta was settled by Greeks (1027–33). Why should Trojan Kassandra have been interested in this tiny and remote island? Livy (21.51.1–2) may supply an answer. Malta, which has throughout history possessed strategic importance out of proportion to its size, was seized from the Carthaginians by the consul Tiberius Sempronius Longus in 218 BCE, at the start of the Hannibalic War, and absorbed into the Roman province of Sicily. Second, in his last years as a hostile presence in Italy in the late third century, Hannibal fixed his military base at the Kroton region in the south, and in the 190s the Roman Senate was notably active in the same region, sending drafts of colonists to places named in the *Alexandra*, including but not only Kroton. Third, Kassandra has plenty in her '*Odyssey*' about particular sites in Campania, further north, some of which were visited both by Odysseus in myth and Hannibal in reality; see e.g. 704n. for the oracle of the dead at Avernus. Finally, see 615–29n. on the Dasii. It is always worth asking whether a place or episode in the poem might resonate with the poet's own experience.[33]

Sources

The poem's identifiable range of sources is exceptionally wide, even for a learned Hellenistic poet, and many lost works of Greek literature must be factored in; for example, Ion of Chios (see *Genre*) wrote a now fragmentary tragedy *Agamemnon*. It is usually assumed that these sources were all literary. But if the poet lived in a S. Italian city with recent traumatic memories of Hannibal's invasion, we should reckon also with oral informants and even the poet's own memories and travels. Some of his knowledge of Italian cults, cult-epithets, and foundation myths could have been so acquired, rather than from predecessors or mythographical handbooks.[34] For the possibility that Lykophron had seen a long inscription from Ilion (Troy) about immunity for tyrannicides, see 1172–3n.; and he could have paid for his shopping with Roman silver coins depicting the wolf-suckled twins Romulus and Remus, see 1232–5n.

Of literary sources, Homer (the *Iliad*[35] as well as the more obvious *Odyssey*[36]) is a constantly adapted and redirected presence. We have seen that Hesiod, and poems ascribed to him, influenced the 'Catalogue' style of the *Alexandra* generally, and supplied specific mythical material (see e.g. 1388–96n.: Mestra). Lykophron certainly used a mostly lost series of post-Homeric poems, the Epic Cycle,[37] especially *Sack of Troy*, *Kypria*, and *Nostoi*.[38] In particular, *Sack of Troy* narrated Ajax's rape of Kassandra and the Greek attempt to

---

[33] For the full argument see Hornblower 2018.

[34] For labour-saving recourse to such handbooks even by top-rank poets, see A. Cameron, *Greek Mythography in the Roman World* (New York, Oxford University Press 2004).

[35] Especially at 232–372, see *Structure*; but the *Catalogue of Ships* (*Iliad* 2) often supplies lists of place-names, especially in the *nostoi* sections.

[36] 'More obvious' because the long Odysseus and Menelaos *nostoi* narratives often represent a conversation with the *Odyssey*.

[37] West 2003 (fragments), and 2013 (commentaries).

[38] For discussion see West 2013, 260–2; G. Danek, 'Nostoi' in M. Fantuzzi and C. Tsagalis, *The Greek Epic Cycle and its Ancient Reception, A Companion* (Cambridge, Cambridge University Press, 2015), 355–79; and R. Fowler, 'The *nostoi* and Archaic Greek Ethnicity', *Returning Hero*, 43–63.

stone him for it (348–72n.). But we have only plot summaries of and quotations from these epics.

The Archaic poet Stesichoros, another 'fragmentary' author,[39] was a native of Sicilian Himera and provided Lykophron with western Mediterranean material. Alkaios (also an Archaic poet) first expressed an important, long-lived idea: the returning Greeks were shipwrecked through one man's fault: they should have persisted with Ajax's punishment (365n., also citing Euripides, *Trojan Women*).

We saw that Pindar and two of the three great Classical tragedians knew of Kassandra as prophet (and as much else),[40] and that the *Alexandra* has detailed parallels with the 'Big Three' Hellenistic poets: Kallimachos, Apollonios, and Theokritos. That is also true of Greek epigram (31n.; 387–407n.).

Lykophron had a thorough knowledge of Greek prose writings also (for Eratosthenes[41] see n. 24). The most important are two histories; the first survives complete, the other in fragments. The influence of the fifth-century BCE Herodotus on the *Alexandra* is profound.[42] That of the fragmentary Timaios of Sicilian Tauromenion (about 300 BCE) is also extensive.[43] It is hard to know how much of the Italian and Roman sections has a Timaian origin, but Lykophron was much more than a mere excerptor. Certainly Timaios was an excellent choice of source. Because of his pioneering attention to early Rome and Italy, not least their cults, it has been well said that Timaios 'was to the west what the Alexander-historians were to the east'.[44]

Genre

Ancient writers, at any rate before Plato and Aristotle in the fourth century, were not much bothered by considerations of genre; and when ancient literary critics do address the topic, their categorizations

---

[39] See M. Davies and P. Finglass, *Stesichorus, the Poems* (Cambridge, Cambridge University Press, 2014).

[40] For the third, Sophocles, see 450–69n. (Telemonian Ajax).

[41] On whom see *OCD* (Fraser).

[42] See S. West, 'Herodotus in Lycophron', *Eclats*, 81–93.

[43] Translation of the fragments: *BNJ* no. 566, with commentary by C. Champion. For a brilliant sketch see A. Momigliano, *Essays in Ancient and Modern Historiography* (Oxford, Blackwell, 1977), 37–66.

[44] J. Geffcken, *Timaios' Geographie des Westens* (Berlin, Weidmann, 1892), 177.

often differ from our own, and are not necessarily the worse for that.[45] In the Classical period, one author stands out for his generic versatility: Ion of Chios in the fifth century wrote history, poetry of various sorts including tragedies, gossipy biography, and philosophy. Kallimachos (frag. 203) defended himself against accusations of *poly-eideia*, writing in (too) many genres, by citing Ion's precedent.[46] Lykophron's *Alexandra* went one better, or at any rate further, by mixing several genres in a single daring work. (The possibility that he also wrote tragedies of a traditional sort is here disregarded.)

The *Alexandra* has features in common with another unusual, pseudonymous, and experimental Hellenistic poem, the *Exagoge* of Ezekiel, a Jewish-Greek author's versification of chapters 1–15 of the biblical book of Exodus, including the miraculous crossing of the Red Sea. This looks more like a tragedy than it looks like anything else. Only a long fragment (269 lines) survives of this extraordinary work, consisting of genuine dialogue,[47] and containing a messenger speech and a speech of prophecy (delivered by God, therefore unusually authoritative), all in iambic trimeters; it is unclear if there was a chorus.[48] The play's exact date is as uncertain as is the *Alexandra*'s, so it is useless to speculate on influence, one way or the other. The same is true of another pseudonymous Jewish-Greek literary production, the hexameter Sibylline Oracles.[49] Kassandra's laments for cities are (like some epigrams, see *Sources*) comparable to parts of the Third Oracle, the most important and the earliest in date of the set, composed about 150 BCE. (There is a lament for Troy in particular at *Oracle* 3.414, cf. 206.) But the genre is much older than that. The similarities have even caused the *Alexandra* itself to be classed as a Sibylline Oracle. This goes too far. Similarities of presentation are clear but superficial: the Oracles are violently anti-Roman, whereas

---

[45] See *OCD* 'genre' (G. B. Conte and G. Most).

[46] See J. Henderson in V. Jennings and A. Katsaros (eds.), *The World of Ion of Chios* (Leiden, Brill, 2007), 15–44.

[47] The *Alexandra* has no dialogue. The only speaker is the guard.

[48] Text, translation, and commentary: H. Jacobson, *The* Exagoge *of Ezekiel* (Cambridge, Cambridge University Press, 1983); cf. *OCD* 'Ezekiel'; P. Lanfranchi in Liapis and Petrides, 124–46.

[49] Translations in R. H. Charles, *Apocrypha and Pseudepigrapha of the Old Testament* (Oxford, Clarendon Press, 1913). These Oracles are not the same as the Sibylline books which the Romans consulted in crises.

the author of the *Alexandra* appears to welcome Roman dominance.[50] That is not to deny the interesting possibility[51] that Lykophron intended Kassandra to be seen as a sort of precursor of the vatic Sibyl most familiar from Virgil, *Aeneid* 6.

The *Alexandra* is often called a 'monodrama', as if that explained anything. It does at least hint at the important tragic element in the poem. After all, the anonymous author (if that is what he was) chose to write under the name of a genuine earlier tragedian, and this must say something about how he saw his project. (See *Authorship and Date*.) As we have seen, the prophecy is a gigantic messenger speech. The language throughout is often that of tragedy. The metre is tragic; there is no chorus and therefore no lyric interludes. (The guard to some extent performs the commenting role of a tragic chorus.) The author is fond of iambic lines consisting of only three outsize words; this takes to characteristic extremes an imposing feature already found in (especially) Aeschylus. There are fifty-four in the *Alexandra*, which is, as it happens, exactly as many as in all seven of Aeschylus' surviving plays (the *Alexandra* is roughly the length of a tragedy such as Sophocles' *Philoktetes*). Above all, the *Alexandra* draws some of its central themes from Aeschylus' *Agamemnon* and Euripides' *Trojan Women*, in both of which Kassandra has an important role (see *Themes*). The great German scholar Wilamowitz denied that the *Alexandra* was a tragedy; he was thinking of the near-absence of a plot: to put it at its lowest, a soldier reports that an excited young woman came out of a stone cell, prophesied, and went back in again. It would be better to say that the plot is huge and complex, but is all contained in the prophecy.

The vast and ambitious scale is epic. So too is much of the language—but that is also true of tragedy, especially Aeschylean. The final line evokes yet another genre: hymns (see 1474n.); and the *Alexandra* can be seen as in dialogue with lyric poetry, especially Pindar (Kolde 2018).

A serious argument can be made[52] that the *Alexandra* is a work of history. Naturally, much depends on one's definition of history (not

---

[50] See Hornblower 2018, ch. 5, also discussing the papyrus *Oracle of the Potter* (Austin no. 326).

[51] See Pillinger; McNelis and Sens, 207.

[52] See, for the full argument, S. Hornblower, 'The Hellenistic poets as historians', *Scripta Classica Israelica* 37 (2018), 45–67.

acknowledged as a separate genre until Aristotle's *Poetics*). Edward Gibbon[53] described history as 'little more than the register of the crimes, follies and misfortunes of mankind'. History need not be in prose: the *Lusiads* of Luis Vaz de Camões is a Portuguese epic poem which narrates a fully historical event, the voyage of discovery made by Vasco da Gama in 1497–8 CE.[54] Nor need it use past tenses: the future tenses of the *Alexandra* are a narrative device for a pseudo-prophecy culminating in historical episodes: Xerxes' invasion of Greece and Rome's defeat of Philip V. It is no objection that Xerxes was already treated by Herodotus, or that Timaios had covered some of Lykophron's Italian episodes: that would rule out categorizing Livy as a historian because he used Polybius for Trasimene and Cannae. It might even rule out Thucydides, who drew on his near-contemporary Antiochos of Syracuse for his own account of early Sicilian settlements. The subject-matter of the bulk of the *Alexandra* is mythical, to be sure; but the anyway debatable borderline between the two is often crossed. Thus in the Sirens section, Lykophron follows Timaios in referring to a visit to Naples by the fifth-century Athenian general Diotimos, known from Thucydides and an inscription (732–7n.). If, with the Roman historian Sempronius Asellio (*FRHist* 20 frag. 1), we insist that history should investigate causes—not just *what* was done but *why*—then the *Alexandra* operates with the reciprocity principle no less than does Herodotus. Polybius (Book 12) demanded that history be 'pragmatic', meaning written by men of affairs or with military experience. Thucydides, Xenophon, Hieronymos of Kardia, Sallust, and Tacitus all qualify. We have no idea whether Lykophron held public office or had a military career. It does not seem likely. But then nor, as far as we know, did Herodotus, Timaios, or Livy.

The Greek and Roman historians just listed are 'big name' authors who wrote about high politics and international warfare. But there were always smaller-scale historians as well, patriotic authors of '*polis* histories',[55] most of which survive in fragments. Often these historians

[53] E. Gibbon, *Decline and Fall of the Roman Empire* (ed. J. B. Bury, London, Methuen, 1896 [originally 1776]), vol. 1, 77 (ch. 3).
[54] See the OWC edition, translation, introduction, and notes by L. White, 1997. Some ancient Greek geographers wrote in verse, and provide much valuable history.
[55] See R. Thomas, *Polis Histories, Collective Memories and the Greek World* (Cambridge, Cambridge University Press, 2019).

are known only as the recipients of inscribed honours. Lykophron surely drew on such historians of *poleis* (individual Greek or Greek-influenced city-states), and can himself be regarded as one, for his well-informed and perhaps orally derived attention to the traditions and cults of individual communities, especially those of S. Italy.

Rome and Italy

That a Roman commander fought and won a great battle against a Macedonian king in the Hellenistic period is not news to modern historians of ancient Rome. But if the battle was Kynoskephalai, the *Alexandra* is the first fully surviving source for it: our main authority Polybius wrote several decades later on any compositional dating of the two authors. The more intense historical interest of the poem[56] lies elsewhere, in its account of Aineias' wanderings and his foundations in Latium, supported by his 'frenemy' Odysseus with an army, 1242, also two other immigrant leaders, Tarchon and Tyrrhenos. These last two came from Mysia in Asia Minor (or Lydia: Kassandra contradicts herself), and their military alliance with Aineias is emphasized by Lykophron, as also much later by Virgil (*Aeneid* 10.153–6): see 1242–9n., 1351–60n. The word 'military' is important: in Kassandra's presentation, the Trojan-led coalition was engaged in a war for Italy, what would nowadays be called violent 'settler colonization', resulting in displacement or annihilation of indigenous peoples.[57] (She narrates the Greek colonization of the Aeolid, Ionia, and the Dorian SW of Asia Minor in similar terms, stressing in particular the force and deception used against women: 1369–73n., 1378–87n.).

Kassandra knows about Romulus and Remus, 'twin lion-whelps' of outstanding 'strength' (*rhome*, two syllables) who founded Rome: 1232–3.[58] This is the first time a Greek author played on the city's

---

[56] Recognized by A. Momigliano, 'The origins of Rome', *CAH* 7 (1989), 52–112 at 60–1, discussing Aineias at Lavinium (cf. below).

[57] By contrast, McNelis and Sens, 205 regard conflict with the indigenous community as 'at most very glancingly evoked' compared to other accounts of Aineias' Italian activity; they cite only 1271 ('martial praise').

[58] Kassandra ignores the chronological and other difficulties of reconciling this with the Aineias story: D. Feeney, *Caesar's Calendar* (Berkeley, University of California Press, 2007), 95–100; cf. 1232–5n.

name in that way.[59] And she foretells the 'martial praise' to be won by a 'new fatherland' (1271, cf. 1230, Rome the new Troy). So it is surprising that she has so little to say about Rome itself, and never mentions the Tiber, despite her fondness for rivers. Her focus is on Latium, home of the Latins. After travelling from Troy to Etruria via Macedonia and Thrace,[60] Aineias founds a new 'place' in Latium (1253). This was probably meant to denote the important Latin cult centre of Lavinium. A later source (a commentator on Virgil) says that Aineias' first settlement, probably just a camp, was actually called 'Troy', but if Lykophron knew this tradition he would surely have exploited it. Aineias was led there by an oracle telling him to settle where his men 'ate their tables' (*mensae*); the story is in Virgil, but is found here for the first time in a fully extant author (see 1250–2n.). It depends on word-play of an opposite sort to *rhome*: it makes sense only in Latin, in which *mensae* can also mean a kind of food, whereas the equivalent Greek word has no such ambiguity. This, and the cult title Mamertos and Mamersa for Ares (Mars) and Athena (Minerva), are precious indicators that Lykophron was bilingual or even trilingual, in Greek, Latin, and Oscan. This bears on the poet's identity.

Performance or Recitation; Readership

Whether the *Alexandra* was a tragedy, or an epic, or a history, or something else, or (more likely) a carefree generic hybrid, it impersonates speaking individuals, so it is natural to ask about possible audiences as well as about readership. Hellenistic literary culture has traditionally been regarded as bookish, but there has been a reaction against this, partly as a result of scholarly work on *symposia*, elite ritualized drinking sessions.[61] An actual theatrical performance of the poem is unlikely: it would have been a small-scale, two-hour, very much off-Broadway sort of production, requiring a maximum of three actors: King Priam as a (strictly unnecessary) 'mute figure'; the guard; and a third actor, taking over as Kassandra at 31. But since her prophecy is a messenger-speech, the three could be collapsed into just one: the guard.

[59] A hymn to Rome by Melinno (a woman) also knows the 'speaking name'. But this is now thought to be not Hellenistic but Hadrianic (second century CE).

[60] He founded a city Aineia near the future Thessaloniki. A festival commemorating this was celebrated there in 182 BCE: Livy 40.4.9 and coins. See 1236–41n.

[61] See A. Cameron, *Callimachus and his Critics* (Princeton, Princeton University Press, 1995); *OCD* 'symposium' and 'symposium literature' (both O. Murray).

Recitation is more plausible, whether at a symposium, or in some religious context (Aristodama recited at Delphi, and see below for a historian who did the same). From epigrams we hear of *chanteuses* or *diseuses* who resemble the *Alexandra* in their Trojan War themes. The third-century BCE epigrammatist Dioskorides told of a woman called Athenion who sang of the Fall of Troy and the Wooden Horse;[62] and a woman called Aristo, who sang of the deceitful Nauplios (see *Structure*), was the subject of a similar and imitative epigram by Krinagoras (Augustan).[63] In Theokritos (*Idyll* 15.96–7), yet another woman is 'about to sing the Adonis song' (this has however no obvious Trojan War connection). Some of these female performers, like Aristodama, may have been envisaged as writing their own material, as did the male historian, *historiographos*, Aristotheos of Troizen (mid-second century BCE), who like her was honoured at Delphi.[64] He gave recitations there lasting several days (!); these included 'public readings of encomia of the Romans, the common benefactors of Greece'.

The inscribed testimonial for the historian Aristotheos is a clue to the likely composition of the audience or readership of the *Alexandra* and their political sympathies. The poem would have appealed to educated pro-Roman Greeks, perhaps citizens of S. Italian towns, who wished to know more about the new masters of the Mediterranean. It would not bother them that some of the greatest figures of Greek mythology were presented in a bad light: the same is true of many of the Classical tragedies with which they were familiar from school (n. 22). The analogy between Aristotheos and Lykophron must not be overdone: we know nothing about the manner of Aristotheos' work, but it is unlikely to have been riddling or periphrastic. The poet of the *Alexandra* has, however, far more in common with this encomiast of Roman benefactors than with whoever composed those virulently anti-Roman diatribes, the hexameter Sibylline Oracles.

Reception; a Feminist Poem?

Early Greek literary reception of the *Alexandra* is very muted. But if the composition date argued for above is right, that is not too surprising,

---

[62] *Anth. Pal.* 5.138 (*HE* 1471–4).

[63] *Anth. Pal.* 9.429; M. Ypsilanti, *The Epigrams of Crinagoras of Mytilene* (Oxford, Oxford University Press, 2018), 64–71, no. 2.

[64] *Syll.* 702; *FGrHist* 835.

because the great period of Hellenistic poetry-writing (epigrams apart) was over by the 190s BCE. Later in the second century, the Greek historian Polybius shows no awareness of Lykophron, but only a third of his *Histories* survives; their attitudes to Rome are surprisingly similar.[65] The multilingual Roman poet Ennius[66] perhaps knew the *Alexandra*, as did, more certainly, the Augustans Virgil (not only in the *Aeneid*)[67] and Ovid, especially but not only in the *Metamorphoses*. And the 'Lykophron epigram' (see *Difficulty*) may also have been of Augustan date. The *Alexandra* was certainly used by Trifiodoros (about 300 CE) in his Greek hexameter epic *The Capture of Troy*.[68] But none of these actually names poet or poem. Theon's commentary surely named both, but is lost. An inscribed Greek letter, recently discovered, implies that the emperor Hadrian himself knew the *Alexandra*: 1148n.

Actual ancient mentions of the *Alexandra* or its author by name are rare, down to Byzantine times. Ovid in a strange curse-poem (*Ibis* 529–30) has a story about the death of Lykophron, but this is the tragedian from Chalkis, not the *Alexandra*'s author (although Ovid may of course have identified the two). Early grammarians and geographical writers like Oros (see *OCD* 'Orus') drew on the *Alexandra*, as shown by the citations of 'Lykophron' in Stephanos of Byzantium's dictionary of place-names. Otherwise there are[69] only two words in the Latin epic poet Statius (first century CE);[70] a passing allusion in the *Lexiphanes* of the playful Greek writer Lucian in the second century CE (para. 25); a mention of 'the *Alexandra* of Lykophron' by the Christian Greek polymath Clement of Alexandria (about 150–216 CE) in a list of difficult and allusive literary texts;[71] and another and

---

[65] See Hornblower 2018: 141–5.

[66] The bilingual Naevius (fragmentary, about 280–200 BCE, see *OCD*) resembles in some ways the author of the *Alexandra* (see 1273–80n., citing Barchiesi), but is too early to have read him, rather than vice versa.

[67] 22n., 252–3n., 365n., 604–5n., 1242–9n., 1250–2n., 1253–72n., 1273–80n. On the Augustan poets and Lykophron, see F. Klein, *Eclats*, 561–92 (in French).

[68] Ovid: 447–9n., 597n.; Klein (previous n.). Trifiodoros: see now the fine edition, with modern Greek translation, introduction, and commentary, by Maria Ypsilanti (Stigmi, Athens, 2019); cf. also M. Tsakiris, 'Triphiodorus' *Sack of Troy* and the poetics of Cassandra', *Classical Quarterly* 72 (2022).

[69] The rest of this paragraph draws on the first page of Zybert and Hornblower 2020 (n. 12).

[70] *Silvae* 5.3.157, the earliest known description of the author of the *Alexandra* as 'black' i.e. dark: *Lycophronis atri*.

[71] *Stromateis* ('Miscellanies') 5.8, 50.3. The list includes two other learned Hellenistic poets, Euphorion and Kallimachos.

unexpected mention in a list in Artemidoros' *Interpretation of Dreams*—a Greek treatise whose date is, like that of the *Alexandra* itself, uncertain: probably late second to third centuries CE.[72]

Byzantine scholars and poets were fascinated by the *Alexandra*. We have seen that John Tzetzes wrote an entire commentary; he also imitated it in his own poetry, and was not alone in this.[73] In 1513, just sixty years after the fall of Constantinople/Byzantium to the Turks on 29 May 1453, the enterprising Venetian printing house of Aldus Manutius published the first printed edition of the *Alexandra*, nervously warning purchasers by calling it an 'obscure poem', *obscurum poema*. Lykophron shares this little 'Aldine' volume with two other Greek poetic works, Pindar's *Odes* and the verse geography of Dionysios Periegetes. All three are stuffed full of Greek mythology; this feature (especially the non-standard versions of myths) had helped to keep the *Alexandra* useful as an educational tool.

The next important event in the poem's afterlife was the exact and virtuosic translation into Latin iambics by the great J. J. Scaliger, on the facing pages of Willem Canter's edition (Basel, Johannes Oporinus, 1566). This must have opened up a whole new readership, given the status of Latin in the following centuries. Scaliger used, as far as he could, what he took to be archaic Latin words, so as to capture the recherché flavour of the original.[74] Scaliger's wonderful achievement continued to be appended to editions and commentaries right down into the nineteenth century; the last to do so was the fine work by Bachmann (1830), which led the commentary field until largely superseded by Holzinger in 1895. The reason for dropping Scaliger after about 1830 was the rise of translations into vernacular languages: Lord Royston had already published a vigorous English verse rendering in the old *Classical Journal* for March 1816 (vol. 25, 1–55), and in 1853, F. D. Dehèque turned it into French,[75] albeit with a commentary which is not worth bothering with. With Holzinger,

---

[72] 4.63.3: 'There are many recondite and out-of-the-way legends to be found in the *Alexandra* of Lycophron, the *Discourses* of Heraclides of Pontus, the *Elegies* of Parthenius, and in many other authors.' See the OWC edition, translation by M. Hammond, Introduction and notes by P. Thonemann, 2019.

[73] See C. de Stefani and E. Magnelli, 'Lycophron in Byzantine poetry (and prose)', *Eclats*, 593–620.

[74] See A. T. Grafton, *Joseph Scaliger*, vol. 1 (Oxford, Oxford University Press, 1983), 114.

[75] Paris, Durand.

and Ciaceri (1901), we enter the period covered by the list of modern editions and commentaries listed in *Select Bibliography*.

So far, so factual. How has the *Alexandra* been regarded?[76] As an *obscurum poema*, certainly;[77] but its literary merits have started to be recognized, notably in monographs by MacNelis and Sens (2016), and Pillinger (2019). Its historical importance is still under-valued, although the Roman prophecy at 1229 has always attracted speculation. A poem with so many examples of male violence, deception, and injustice against women might have been expected to catch feminist attention. But here we must distinguish between the attractions of the mythical Kassandra generally, and the far more limited influence of Lykophron's presentation of her. The pioneering modern novel is Christa Wolf's 1983 *Kassandra*: for Wolf, Achilles is 'the brute', and this recalls Kassandra's hatred.[78] But it shows fewer specific traces of Lykophron than might have been expected.[79] More recent novelists such as Pat Barker also handle male behaviour in the Trojan War from a similar outraged female and feminist viewpoint: Achilles the 'butcher'.[80] The *Alexandra* itself, although its author was probably not a woman, can be called proto-feminist. To be sure, not all its female victims receive sympathetic handling. Hostility to Helen, who caused the war which destroyed Kassandra's home city, is unsurprising; and accusations of promiscuity against Penelope, contrary to most of the tradition, are easily explained as a function of Kassandra's hatred for her husband Odysseus. But this is a good moment for feminist literary criticism to begin to engage properly with the *Alexandra*.

---

[76] There is much of interest (including material about Milton, C. J. Fox, Coleridge, and Byron) in S. West, 'The *Alexandra*'s fluctuating fortunes', *Terminus* (Krakow) 1–2 (2001), 127–40.

[77] As in Marguerite Yourcenar, *Memoirs of Hadrian* (1148n.) and Paul Auster, *Moon Palace* (London, Faber and Faber, 1989), 88.

[78] C. Wolf, translated from the 1983 German edition by J. van Heurck, *Cassandra*, London, Virago Press, 1984, 107 and frequently: 'the brute'.

[79] S. West, 'Christa Wolf's *Kassandra*: a Classical perspective', *Oxford German Studies* 20/21 (1991/2), 164–85.

[80] See *The Silence of the Girls* (London, Hamish Hamilton, 2018), 3. Feminist: see Emily Wilson's review of Barker, *The Guardian*, 22 August 2018. It is tempting to include Margaret Atwood, *The Penelopiad* (London, Canongate, 2005), a retelling of parts of Homer's *Odyssey* from Penelope's angle, but the author is reported as having reservations about calling it feminist merely because it portrays events from a woman's point of view: *National Post*, 22 October 2005, 'A weaver's tale', interview with Susanne Hiller. The same could, of course, be said about the *Alexandra* (whose author is not in a position to give helpful press interviews).

NOTE ON THE TEXT AND TRANSLATION

THIS translation is essentially reproduced from my own large-scale edition of the poem which provided a full Introduction, followed by a Greek text, facing English translation, and a detailed commentary running across each double page. Under the Greek text there was a select *apparatus criticus*, i.e. an indication of variant manuscript readings or occasional modern emendations, as far as these were discussed in the commentary. For a fuller, up-to-date apparatus, and more detailed textual discussions, the reader is referred to the French edition by Hurst and Kolde (2008; see *Select Bibliography*). The endnotes in the present edition do not go into textual problems, which are few and not serious.

The poem has come down to us essentially through the manuscript tradition, like the *Odes* of Pindar with which it shared the first printed edition, the Venetian Aldine of 1513 (see Introduction, *Reception*), but unlike Pindar's *Paians*, which survive only on a papyrus found in Egypt, and first published as recently as the early twentieth century. Papyri provide a few unimportant variant readings of the *Alexandra*.

The best manuscript of the *Alexandra* is in Venice (Biblioteca Nazionale Marciana, Marc. gr. 476), and was not collated, i.e. deciphered, copied, and edited, until the 1870s; it was therefore unknown to the anonymous scholar who prepared the Aldine edition in the same city. The collation was carried out independently in the same decade by two scholars, G. Kinkel and E. Scheer, neither of whom knew that the other had done it, and it would seem that neither was alerted to the fact by the library authorities. There are two other important manuscripts, one in Paris (Bibliothèque nationale), the other in Rome (Vatican library). All three date from the tenth or eleventh centuries. The Venetian manuscript also contains the most valuable of the set of marginal *scholia* or ancient explanatory notes; see *Select Bibliography* for modern editions of these, and of the commentary by John Tzetzes in the Byzantine period.

My translation is in plain prose: a verse rendering such as Holzinger's or Mooney's is bound to sacrifice much of the richness of detail which is such a feature of the original. Nor have I tried to imitate its recherché language. I have made a very few further small

changes for this edition. A special problem is posed by the handling
of the very many cult-epithets. I have preferred not to eliminate the
Alexandra's obscurity of naming—but also its incantatory flavour—by
the crude simplifying solution of actually rendering 'Tripper-up' at
207 as 'Dionysos', or 'Bebrykian' at 1474 as 'Trojan'. After all, if this
were done at 355–60, I would have had to write 'Athena' seven times
in six lines.

SELECT BIBLIOGRAPHY

Complete editions and commentaries, most with Greek text, facing translation, and explanatory notes

In English:

Loeb edition: pp. 302–443 of A. W. Mair and G. R. Mair, *Callimachus*, Hymns and Epigrams, *Lycophron*, *Aratus* (Cambridge MA, Harvard University Press, 1921)

Mooney, G. W., *The* Alexandra *of Lycophron* (London, G. Bell and Sons, 1921)

Hornblower, S., *Lykophron* Alexandra: *Greek Text, Translation, Commentary and Introduction* (Oxford, Oxford University Press, 2015, corrected pb. 2017); abbrev. Hornblower 2015

In other languages (a selection):

E. Scheer, *Lycophronis* Alexandra (2 vols., Berlin, Weidmann, 1881 (vol. 1, Greek text, no translation) and 1908 (for vol. 2 see below, under *Ancient Commentaries*)

Holzinger, C. von, *Lycophron's* Alexandra (Leipzig, B. G. Teubner, 1895); still the best commentary; abbrev. Holzinger

Bachmann, L. *Lycophronis* Alexandra (Leipzig, I. C. Hinrichs, 1930): still valuable (footnotes in Latin, Scaliger's Latin translation at pp. 455–504, for which see Introduction, *Reception*); abbrev. Bachmann

Ciaceri, E., *La* Alessandra *di Licofrone* (Catania, M. Giannotta, 1901, reprinted Naples, G. Macchiaroli, 1982); abbrev. Ciaceri

Fusillo, M., A. Hurst, and G. Paduano, *Licofrone* Alessandra (Edizioni Guerini e Associati, Milan, 1991)

Gigante Lanzara, V., *Licofrone* Alessandra (Milan, Biblioteca Universale Rizzoli, 2000)

Lambin, G., *L'Alexandra de Lycophron* (Rennes, Presses Universitaires de Rennes, 2005)

Hurst, A. and A. Kolde, *Lycophron*, Alexandra (Paris, Les Belles Lettres, 2008); abbrev. Hurst/Kolde

Zybert-Pruchnicka, E., *Lykofron* Aleksandra (Wrocław, Instytut Studiów Klasycznych, Śródziemnomorskich i Orientalnych Uniwerstitetu Wrocławskiego, 2018): Polish translation; notes with Greek lemmata but no full text

Horn, F., *Lykophron*, Alexandra. Griechisch–deutsch (Berlin and Boston, De Gruyter, Sammlung Tusculum, 2022)

Lexicon:

Ciani, M. G., *Lexikon zu Lycophron* (Hildesheim and New York, G. Olms, 1975); indispensable

Ancient commentaries on the Alexandra:

Sadly, none of this precious Greek material has been translated into any modern language. The *scholia* (linguistic and mythological notes), the two prose paraphrases, and Tzetzes' commentary, can all be found in vol. 2 of Scheer (see above, *Complete Editions*), but the layout of this uncompromising work makes it extraordinarily difficult to use. Tzetzes' commentary is much more simply presented by M. C. G. Müller, 3 vols., Leipzig, F. C. G. Vogel, 1811. The old Teubner edition of Lykophron by G. Kinkel (Leipzig, B. G. Teubner, 1880) prints the best set of *scholia* (in the margins of the Venice manuscript, see *Note on the Text*) in a straightforward way at the end of the volume. (The more recent Teubner edition by L. Mascialino, Leipzig, 1964, does not include the *scholia*.) For all the *scholia* and the paraphrases, but not Tzetzes' commentary, see P. A. M. Leone, *Scholia vetera et paraphrases in Lycophronis Alexandram* (Lecce, Concedo Editore, 2002).

Modern books:

West, M. L., *The Epic Cycle: A Commentary on the Lost Troy Epics* (Oxford, Oxford University Press, 2013); abbrev. West 2013

Kotlinska-Toma, A., *Hellenistic Tragedy: Texts, Translations and a Critical Survey* (London, Bloomsbury, 2015); abbrev. Kotlinska-Toma

McNelis, C. and A. Sens, *The* Alexandra *of Lycophron: A Literary Study* (Oxford, Oxford University Press, 2016); abbrev. McNelis and Sens

Hornblower, S., *Lykophron's* Alexandra, *Rome, and the Hellenistic World* (Oxford, Oxford University Press, 2018); abbrev. Hornblower 2018

Pillinger, E., *Cassandra and the Poetics of Prophecy in Greek and Latin Literature* (Cambridge, Cambridge University Press, 2019); abbrev. Pillinger

Pellettieri, A., *I composti nell'*Alessandra *di Licofrone. Studi filologici e linguistici* (De Gruyter, Berlin and Boston, 2021); abbrev. Pellettieri (on rare compound words in the poem, cf. Introduction n. 14)

Collections of essays:

Cusset, C. and E. Prioux (eds.), *Lycophron: Eclats d'Obscurité* (Saint-Étienne, Publications de l'Université de Saint-Étienne, 2009) (some chapters in English); abbrev. *Eclats*

Durbec, Y. *Essais sur l'*Alexandra *de Lycophron* (Amsterdam, Hakkert, 2011)

Hurst, A., *Sur Lycophron* (Geneva, Droz, 2012)

Hornblower, S. and G. Biffis (eds.), *The Returning Hero*: Nostoi *and Traditions of Mediterranean Settlement* (Oxford, Oxford University Press, 2018); abbrev. *Returning Hero*

Liapis, V. and A. Petrides (eds.), *Greek Tragedy after the Fifth Century: A Survey from ca. 400 BCE to ca. 400 AD* (Cambridge, Cambridge University Press, 2019), 90–124; abbrev. Liapis and Petrides

Articles, book chapters:

Fraser, P. M., 'Lycophron on Cyprus', *Report of the Department of Antiquities of Cyprus* 1979, 328–43; abbrev. Fraser 1979

West, S. 'Lycophron italicised', *Journal of Hellenic Studies* 104 (1984), 127–51; abbrev S. West

Fraser, P. M. 'Agathon and Cassandra (*IG* IX. 1² 4. 1750)', *Journal of Hellenic Studies* 123 (2003), 26–40; abbrev. Fraser 2003

Fantuzzi, M. and R. Hunter, *Tradition and Innovation in Hellenistic Poetry* (Cambridge, Cambridge University Press, 2004), 437–43

Sens, A., 'Hellenistic tragedy and Lycophron's *Alexandra*', in J. J. Clauss and M. Cuypers (eds.), *A Companion to Hellenistic Literature* (Chichester, Wiley Blackwell, 2010), 297–313

Fraser, P. M. 'Lycophron (2)' in *OCD* (*see Abbreviations*)

Sistakou, E. *The Aesthetics of Darkness. A Study of Hellenistic Romanticism in Apollonius, Lycophron and Nicander* (Leuven and Paris, Peeters, 2012), 131–90; abbrev. Sistakou

Priestley, J. *Herodotus and Hellenistic Culture* (Oxford, Oxford University Press, 2014), 179–86; abbrev. Priestley

Kolde, A., 'L'*Alexandra* en dialogue avec Pindare?', *Aitia* 8.1/2018; abbrev. Kolde 2018

Hornblower, S. 'Hellenistic tragedy and satyr-drama; Lycophron's *Alexandra*', in Liapis and Petrides, 90–124

Most of the above articles and chapters are in English, but the fundamental such study is in German:

Ziegler, K., 'Lykophron der Tragiker und die Alexandra Frage', *Real-Encyclopädie der classischen Wissenschaft* 13 (1927), columns 2316–81

Background:

Fraser, P. M., *Ptolemaic Alexandria*, 3 vols. (Oxford, Clarendon Press, 1972); abbrev. Fraser 1972

Malkin, I., *The Returns of Odysseus: Colonization and Ethnicity* (Berkeley, University of California Press, 1998)

Shipley, G., *The Greek World after Alexander, 323–30 BC* (London, Routledge, 2000)

Erskine, A., *Troy Between Greece and Rome* (Oxford, Oxford University Press, 2001); abbrev. Erskine

Lane Fox, R., *Travelling Heroes: Greeks and their Myths in the Epic Age of Homer* (London, Allen Lane, 2008); abbrev. Lane Fox

Edmunds, L., *Stealing Helen. The Myth of the Abducted Wife in Comparative Perspective* (Princeton, Princeton University Press, 2016); abbrev. Edmunds

Chaniotis, A., *Age of Conquests: the Greek World between Alexander and Hadrian* (Cambridge MA, Harvard University Press, 2018)

Other OWC volumes which include Hellenistic poets:

Apollonius of Rhodes, *Jason and the Golden Fleece* (The Argonautica*)*, translation and notes by R. Hunter, 2009

Epigrams from the Greek Anthology, translation and notes by G. Nisbet, 2020

Eratosthenes and Hyginus, *Constellation Myths*, with Aratus' *Phaenomena*, translation and notes by R. Hard, 2015, 139–67 for Aratos' poem

Theocritus, *Idylls*, translation by A. Verity, notes by R. Hunter, 2008

Fragments:

'Fragments' of ancient authors (i.e. quotations by other authors, or scraps on papyrus and elsewhere) are referred to by the numberings in the following editions:

Alkaios: D. A. Campbell, Loeb *Greek Lyric* vol. 1, *Sappho and Alcaeus* (Cambridge MA, Harvard University Press, 1990)

Aristotle: V. Rose (Leipzig, B. G. Teubner, 1886)

Ennius, *Annals*: S. Goldberg and G. Manuwald, Loeb ed., *Fragmentary Republican Latin*, vol. 1, *Ennius, Testimonia, Epic Fragments* (Cambridge MA, Harvard University Press, 2018)

Epic Cycle: M. West, Loeb ed. *Greek Epic Fragments* (Cambridge MA, Harvard University Press, 2003)

Hesiod: G. Most, Loeb *Hesiod* vol. 2 (Cambridge MA, Harvard University Press, 2007)

Historians: see *Abbreviations* for *FGrHist* and *BNJ* (Greek) and *FRHist* (Roman)

Kallimachos: R. Pfeiffer, *Callimachu*s (2 vols., Oxford, Oxford University Press, 1949–51), vol. 1

Naevius: W. Strzelecki (Leipzig, B. G. Teubner, 1964)

Pindar's *Paians*: I. Rutherford (Oxford, Oxford University Press, 2011)

Sappho (as for Alkaios, above)

Stesichoros: P. J. Finglass in M. Davies and Finglass, *Stesichorus: the Poems* (Cambridge, Cambridge University Press, 2013)

Tragic fragments: S. Radt and R. Kannicht, *Tragicorum graecorum Fragmente* (6 vols., Göttingen, Vandenhoeck and Ruprecht, 1986–2004), and for English translations of the three great tragedians, all using the same numberings as Radt and Kannicht, see the 'fragments' volumes of the Loeb eds. of Aeschylus (A. Sommerstein, 2008), Euripides (C. Collard and M. Cropp, 2 vols., 2008), and Sophocles (H. Lloyd-Jones, 1996), all Cambridge MA, Harvard University Press.

Timaios: no. 566 in both *FGrHist* and, in English translation and with English commentary by C. Champion, *BNJ*, also no. 566

ABBREVIATIONS

Anth. Pal.	*The Palatine Anthology* (collection of Greek epigrams); Loeb edition (W. Paton, *The Greek Anthology*, 5 vols., Cambridge MA, Harvard University Press, 1917) in process of revision by M. Tueller, 2014–
Austin	Austin M. M., *The Hellenistic World from Alexander to the Roman Conquest*, 2nd edition (Cambridge, Cambridge University Press, 2006), translated sourcebook)
Barrington Atlas	R. Talbert (ed.), *Barrington Atlas of the Greek and Roman World* (Princeton, Princeton University Press, 2000)
BNJ	I. Worthington (ed.), *Brill's New Jacoby*, online 2006– (English translations, with commentaries, of *FGrHist*. Not yet complete)
CAH	*Cambridge Ancient History*, 2nd edition (Cambridge, Cambridge University Press, 1982–)
Ciaceri	Ciaceri, E., *La* Alessandra *di Licofrone* (Catania, M. Giannotta, 1901, reprinted Naples, G. Macchiaroli, 1982)
Eclats	Cusset, C. and E. Prioux (eds.), *Lycophron: éclats d'obscurité* (Saint-Étienne, Publications de l'Université de Saint-Étienne, 2009) (some chapters in English); abbrev.
EGM or Fowler	R. Fowler, *Early Greek Mythography* (2 vols.,
EGM	Oxford, Oxford University Press, 2000 and 2013), vol. 1, fragments, vol. 2, discussion
Erskine	Erskine, A., *Troy Between Greece and Rome* (Oxford, Oxford University Press, 2001)
FGrHist	F. Jacoby, *Die Fragmente der griechischen Historiker* (15 vols, Leiden, Brill, 1953–8); see also *BNJ*
Fontenrose	Fontenrose J., *The Delphic Oracle* (Berkeley, University of California Press, 1978)
Fraser 1972	Fraser, P. M., *Ptolemaic Alexandria*, 3 vols. (Oxford, Clarendon Press, 1972)
Fraser 1979	Fraser, P. M., 'Lycophron on Cyprus', *Report of the Department of Antiquities of Cyprus* 1979, 328–43

FRHist	T. Cornell (ed.), *The Fragments of the Roman Historians* (3 vols., Oxford, Oxford University Press, 2013): texts and translations of the fragments in vol. 2; commentaries in vol. 3
HCP	F. W. Walbank, *Historical Commentary on Polybius* (3 vols., Oxford, Oxford University Press, 1956–79)
HE	A. S. F. Gow and D. L. Page, *Hellenistic Epigrams* (Cambridge, Cambridge University Press, 1965)
Holzinger	Holzinger, C. von, *Lycophron's* Alexandra (Leipzig, B. G. Teubner, 1895)
Hornblower 2018	Hornblower, S., *Lykophron's* Alexandra, *Rome, and the Hellenistic World* (Oxford, Oxford University Press, 2018)
Hurst/Kolde	Hurst, A. and A. Kolde, *Lycophron*, Alexandra (Paris, Les Belles Lettres, 2008)
IACP	M. H. Hansen and T. H. Nielsen (eds.), *Inventory of Archaic and Classical* Poleis (Oxford, Oxford University Press, 2004)
IG	*Inscriptiones Graecae* (Berlin, De Gruyter for the Berlin Academy, 1873–)
Kolde 2018	'L'*Alexandra* en dialogue avec Pindare?', *Aitia* 8.1/2018
Kotlinska-Toma	Kotlinska-Toma, A., *Hellenistic Tragedy: Texts, Translations and a Critical Survey* (London, Bloomsbury, 2015)
Lane Fox	Lane Fox, R., *Travelling Heroes: Greeks and their Myths in the Epic Age of Homer* (London, Allen Lane, 2008)
LGPN	P. M. Fraser, E. Matthews and others (eds.), *Lexicon of Greek Personal Names* (8 fascicles so far, Oxford, Oxford University Press, 1987–)
Liapis and Petrides	Liapis, V. and A. Petrides (eds.), *Greek Tragedy after the Fifth Century: A Survey from ca. 400 BCE to ca. 400 AD* (Cambridge, Cambridge University Press, 2019), 90–124
LSJ	Liddell, H. G. and R. Scott, *Greek-English Lexicon*, 9th edition (Oxford, Clarendon Press, 1940)
McNelis and Sens	McNelis, C. and A. Sens, *The* Alexandra *of Lycophron: A Literary Study* (Oxford, Oxford University Press, 2016)
OCD	S. Hornblower, A. Spawforth, E. Eidinow (eds.), *Oxford Classical Dictionary*, 4th edition (Oxford, Oxford University Press, 2011)

OGIS	W. Dittenberger, *Orientis graecae inscriptiones selectae* (Leipzig, Hirzel, 1903–5)
On Marvellous Things Heard	(collection of wonders: the work is attributed to Aristotle, using material from Timaios): W. S. Hett, Loeb ed., *Aristotle Minor Works* (Cambridge MA, Harvard University Press, 1936), 49–82
O/R	Osborne, R., and P. J. Rhodes, *Greek Historical Inscriptions 478–404 BC* (Oxford, Oxford University Press, 2017)
OWC	Oxford World's Classics series (Oxford, Oxford University Press)
Pellettieri	Pellettieri, A., *I composti nell' Alessandra di Licofrone. Studi filologici e linguistici* (De Gruyter, Berlin and Boston, 2021)
Pillinger	Pillinger, E., *Cassandra and the Poetics of Prophecy in Greek and Latin Literature* (Cambridge, Cambridge University Press, 2019)
Priestley	Priestley, J., *Herodotus and Hellenistic Culture* (Oxford, Oxford University Press, 2014), 179–86
Returning Hero	S. Hornblower and G. Biffis (eds.), *The Returning Hero* (Oxford, Oxford University Press, 2018)
R/O	Rhodes, P. J., and R. Osborne, *Greek Historical Inscriptions*, 404–323 BC (Oxford, Oxford University Press, 2003)
S. West	West, S., 'Lycophron italicised', *Journal of Hellenic Studies* 104 (1984), 127–51
SEG	*Supplementum epigraphicum graecum* (Leiden and Amsterdam, various publishers, 1923–)
Sherk	Sherk, R. K., *Translated Documents of Greece and Rome, vol. 4, Rome and the Greek East to the Death of Augustus* (Cambridge, Cambridge University Press, 1984)
Sistakou	Sistakou, E., *The Aesthetics of Darkness. A Study of Hellenistic Romanticism in Apollonius, Lycophron and Nicander* (Leuven and Paris, Peeters, 2012), 131–90
SVT	H. Bengtson, H. H. Schmitt, and R. M. Errington, *Die Staatsverträge des Altertums*, vols. II^2–IV (all published; Munich, 1969–2020): texts of ancient inter-state treaties; numbering continuous
Syll.	W. Dittenberger, *Sylloge inscriptionum graecarum*, 3rd edition (Leipzig, Hirzel, 1915–24)
West 2013	West, M. L., *The Epic Cycle: A Commentary on the Lost Troy Epics* (Oxford, Oxford University Press, 2013)

CHRONOLOGY

753 BCE	Rome founded (conventional date)	
733 BCE	Syracuse in Sicily founded by Korinth	
630 BCE	Kyrene founded by Thera	
595 BCE		Homer?
546–331 BCE	Persian Empire	Stesichoros
490–479 BCE	Ionians revolt from Persia Greco-Persian wars	
480 BCE	Battle of Salamis (Xerxes' invasion)	
500–446 BCE		Pindar active
479–404 BCE	Athenian Empire	Herodotus 485–420 Sophocles 496–406
458 BCE		Aeschylus' *Oresteia* (*Agamemnon, Libation-bearers, Eumenides*)
431–404 BCE	Peloponnesian War: Athens against Sparta	
415–413 BCE 415 BCE	Athens' expedition to Sicily	Euripides' *Trojan Women*
336–323 BCE	Alexander the Great reigns	Timaios
322–281 BCE	'Successor kingdoms' established	
197 BCE	Battle of Kynoskephalai	Eratosthenes

190s BCE		?Lykophron's *Alexandra*
31 BCE	Battle of Actium	Polybius
Late BCE to early CE		Strabo
14 CE	Death of Augustus	
100 CE		Plutarch
150 CE		Pausanias Lucian

MAP. The Mediterranean World of Lykophron

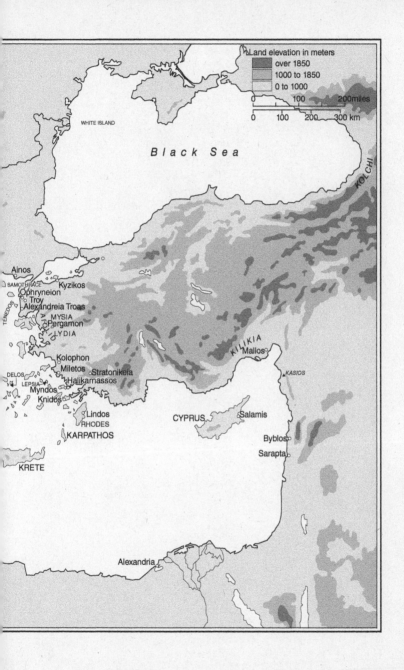

Land elevation in meters
over 1850
1000 to 1850
0 to 1000

0   100   200miles

0   100   200   300 km

WHITE ISLAND

Black   Sea

KOLCHI

Ainos

SAMOTHRACE   Kyzikos
Ophryneion
Troy
Alexandreia Troas
MYSIA
Pergamon
TENEDOS
LYDIA

Kolophon
Miletos
Stratonikeia
DELOS   Halikarnassos
LEPSIA
Myndos
Knidos
Lindos
RHODES
KARPATHOS

KILIKIA
Mallos

KASIOS

CYPRUS   Salamis

Byblos
Sarapta

KRETE

Alexandria

ALEXANDRA

THE guard addresses Priam:

'I shall tell you accurately everything you ask,*
from the very beginning. And if the telling is long,
forgive me, master. For the maiden did not calmly,
as before, let loose the varied utterance of her oracles,*
but she poured out a vast and confused cry,   5
and uttered a prophetic voice from her laurel-eating throat,*
in imitation of the speech of the cruel Sphinx.
Listen, O king, to what I retain both in my heart
and through my memory; turn it over in your shrewd brain,
and pursue and unravel the dark   10
paths of her riddles, where a clear track*
leads by a straight road through the things in darkness.
For I break through the starting rope,*
and I enter the passages of her crooked words,
and hit the starting-post like a runner with wings.   15
     The scene is set: Paris departs from Troy to Sparta
The Dawn was soaring over the tall peak of Phegion*
on the swift wings of Pegasos.
She left Tithonos in bed near Kerne—
Tithonos, your brother by a different mother.
The sailors were releasing the calm cables   20
from the hollowed rock, and loosing the starting-machines
[to take the ship] away from the land. Thetis, the maiden-killing sea,*
was struck by the oars of the many-footed, fair-eyed
stork-coloured ships, the daughters of Phalakra.
They showed their white wings past the Kalydnai islands,   25

---

  3 **maiden** Kassandra

  8 **king** Priam

16 **Phegion,** 18 **Kerne** African places

22 **Thetis** . . . the Hellespont

24 **Phalakra** Mt Ida

25 **Kalydnai islands** islets near Tenedos

their poops, and their sails, which were inflated
by the gusts of the fierce hurricane from the north.
She opened her god-possessed Bacchic mouth,
on the high hill of Ate, founded by a wandering cow,*
and then Alexandra began her speech from the beginning:*   30

The guard's report of Kassandra's speech:

First destruction of Troy by Herakles
"Woe! my wretched nurse, burnt*
once before also, by the army-bearing pine-timbered ships
of the Three-evening lion, whom the jaws*
of Triton's sharp-toothed dog devoured.
While still alive, he gnawed at its liver; and was scalded   35
by a cauldron's steam on a fireless hearth,*
and dropped the hairs of his head to the ground—
he, the killer of his own children, the devastator of my fatherland.
He struck his invulnerable second mother with a grievous*
blow to the breast with an arrow; and on the running track   40
he gripped with his hands the body of his wrestler father
by the high hill of Kronos, the place of the tomb of the
earthborn frightener of horses, Ischenos.*
He killed the fierce bitch*
who watches over the narrow creeks of the Ausonian sea   45
and who fishes above the cave—
the bull-slaughtering lioness, whose father
restored her to life by burning her with torches of vine-bark:
she no longer fears Leptynis, the infernal goddess.

29 hill of Ate Troy
30 Alexandra Kassandra
31 wretched nurse Troy
33 lion Herakles
39 second mother Hera
41 wrestler father Zeus
42 hill of Kronos Olympia
44 fierce bitch Skylla
45 narrow creeks, Ausonian straits of Messina, Italian
49 Leptynis Persephone

A corpse killed him by swordless deception,* 50
though he had defeated Hades once before.
I see you, wretched one, burning a second time,*
by Aiakid hands; by the remains of Tantalos'
son, as much as survived the flames and is housed at Letrina;
and by the arrows of Teutaros which devoured 55
the body of the cowherd.

Oinone, first wife of Paris

All that, his deeply jealous wife will bring*
to light, after sending her son to betray
his country—driven wild by her father's reproaches,
and on account of her wedding-bed and the marriage to an outsider. 60
But when she, the maker of medicines, sees the grievous
incurable wound of her husband,
inflicted by the giant-slaying arrows
of a fellow-archer, she will share his fate:
she will fling herself from the topmost towers 65
in a headlong rush, onto the newly killed corpse.
Caught by the hook of grief,
she will breathe out her life on his still palpitating body.

Lament for Troy; Dardanos' escape from the flood

I groan, I groan for you, twice and three times,*
you who see battle once again, and the plundering of houses, 70
and behold destructive fire.*
I groan for you, my fatherland, and the tomb of the diver,
the son of Atlantis' daughter, who once, in a stitched coracle,
like a four-limbed creature in a Danubian fishing-trap,
swam with one paddle, his body strapped to an inflated wine-skin. 75
Like a stormy petrel from Rhithymnos,
he left Zerynthos, the cave of the goddess to whom dogs are sacrificed,
when Saos, the mighty citadel of the Kyrbantes
was destroyed by the foaming deluge of Zeus
as it rained down on the whole earth. Towers 80

---

50 **corpse** Nessos
52 **wretched one** Troy
53-4 **Tantalos' son** Pelops, **Letrina** Olympia
72-3 **diver** Dardanos
78 **Saos** Samothrace

fell to the ground, and people began to swim,
seeing their final fate before their eyes.
Acorns and the fruit of the oak, and sweet grapes were eaten
by whales and dolphins, and by female seals
who leap lustfully on the beds of men.   85

Paris abducts Helen; the Judgement of Paris in retrospect
I see the winged firebrand*
rushing to snatch the dove, the Pephnaian bitch,
which the aquatic vulture gave birth to,
encased in a round covering of shell.
And you, white-rumped sailor, the path which leads down   90
to Acheron will receive you, no longer treading
the dung of your father's rough ox-stalls,
as previously, when you were judge of beauty for the Three.
Instead of the stables, you will cross to the Ass's jaw*
and Las. Instead of the well-foddered manger   95
and the sheepfolds and the landsman's oar,
a ship will convey you, and the sails of Phereklos,*
to the double passage-way and the flat waters of Gytheion.
There, when you have dropped the curved teeth of the pinewood ship
against the rocks, so as to resist the waves,   100
you will rest your nine-sailed fleet from its leaping.
Then you, the wolf, will snatch the young unwedded heifer,
deprived of her two daughters, those gentle doves,*
and she will fall again into the trap of a foreigner's net,
taken prisoner by the feathered snare of the fowler.   105
Just before this, on the shore, she was sacrificing sheep to the Thysai
and to the goddess Byne.

86 winged firebrand Paris
87 Pephnaian bitch Helen
90 white-rumped sailor Paris
91 Acheron the underworld
93 the Three Athena, Hera, Aphrodite
94 Ass's jaw, 95 Las, 98 Gytheion Spartan places
103 two daughters Hermione, Iphigeneia
106 Thysai acolytes of Dionysos
107 Byne Ino-Leukothea

You will hasten beyond Skandeia and the promontory of Aigilon,
a fierce hunter, exulting in your prey.
When, on Dragon's island, you have satisfied your desire,   110
in Akte, the realm of the two-formed earth-born king,
you will not see a second day of marriage,
but will have a cold embrace, the stuff of dreams,
clasping the bed with your empty arms.

Proteus the sea-god; his disapproval of Paris' abduction of Hèlen
For the grim husband of the Phlegraian wife*   115
Torone, he who hates both laughter
and tears, and is ignorant of and lacking in
both; he who once crossed from Thrace to the coastal tract
which is ploughed into furrows by the outlets of the
river Triton, not by a sea-journey,   120
but by an untrodden road, like a mole,
boring through recesses in the hollows of caves,
he made his way through submarine paths,
escaping the guest-slaying wrestling of his sons.
He sent prayers which his father heard,   125
to restore him to his fatherland, from which, as a wanderer
he went to Pallene, nurse of the Earthborn.
He, like Gouneus, executor of justice,
and arbiter of the Ichnaian daughter of the sun,
will attack you with grim reproof and deprive you of your marriage,   130
driving you away, still full of lust, from your promiscuous dove—
you, who respected neither the men who had been sent
by oracles to honour the tombs of Lykos and Chimaireus,*
nor the love of Antheus, nor the pure salt of Aigaion,
shared between guests and hosts at meals.   135
You dared criminally to transgress the justice of the gods,
kicking the table, and turning Themis upside down,

---

108 **Skandeia, Aigilon** Kythera, Antikythera

111 **Earth-born king** Erechtheus of Athens

115 **husband** Proteus

120 **Triton** the Nile

127 **Earthborn** the Giants

129 **Ichnaian daughter** Themis

134 **Aigaion** Poseidon

imitating the habits of the bear, your nurse.
To no avail you will twang the loud string of your bow,
striking from its lyre songs which bring neither food nor gifts.   140
You will return weeping to your fatherland, once burnt to ashes,
clutching in your arms the phantom
of the Pleuronian maenad, she of the five husbands.*

   *Helen's five husbands (Theseus, Paris, Menelaos, Deiphobos,
   Achilles)*

For the lame descendants of the long-lived Sea have*
ordained, with three threads of fate, that her bed-fellows   145
shall share a wedding-feast of five bridegrooms.
She will see two rapacious wolves,
winged eagles, over-sexed, keen-sighted;
and a third, sprung from roots in Plynos
and the rivers of Karia, a half-Kretan barbarian,*   150
an Epeian, not pure Argive by descent.
Ennaia—Herkynna, Erinys, Thourian, Sword-bearer—*
once sliced up the flesh of your grandfather in her jaws
and buried it in her throat,
feasting on the cartilage of his shoulder.   155
He was young twice, and when he fled from the heavy
rapacious desires of the ruler of ships,
Erechtheus sent him to the fields of Letrina,
to grind smooth the stone of Molpis
(he who sacrificed his body to Zeus the Rain-god)   160
and to kill the suitor-murderer with unholy schemes
for slaying a father-in-law, which the son of Kadmilos
devised. And as he drank the last of the cup,
and sank into the tomb of Nereus, which bears his name,

144 **lame descendants** the Fates
147 **two wolves** Theseus, Paris
149 **third** Menelaos
152 **Ennaia . . . Sword-bearer** Demeter
153 **grandfather** Pelops
157 **ruler of ships** Poseidon
158 **Erechtheus** Zeus, **Letrina** Olympia
161–2 **suitor-murderer, father-in-law** Oinomaos
162 **son of Kadmilos** Myrtilos, son of Hermes

he screamed a doom-laden curse on Pelops' whole house— 165
he who had guided the reins of fleet-footed Psylla,
and Harpinna, with hooves as swift as the Harpies.
The fourth husband she will see is brother*
of the down-swooping falcon, whom they will proclaim
as winner of the second prize among his brothers 170
in the murderous struggle. And she will make the fifth husband*
pine away on his bed,
disturbed by dreams of her phantom form.
He is the future husband of the Kytaian woman
who was madly in love with the stranger. Oinone's exile, 175
he who changed an army of six-footed ants into men,
had fathered him, to be a Pelasgian giant.
Of seven sons who were incinerated in the embers,*
he alone escaped the fiery ash.

   The Greeks sacrifice Iphigeneia; Achilles searches for her
But he shall arrive on a homeward path,* 180
drawing the fierce wasps from their crevices,
like a boy who disturbs their nest with smoke.
Savagely, they will sacrifice to the winds
the heifer, who was mother to him of the warlike name,
and gave birth to a son by the dragon of Skyros. 185
Her husband, within the Salmydesian sea,
will search for her, she who was the killer of Greeks.
For a long time he will inhabit the spray-whitened rocks
By the marshy delta of the Keltric river,
yearning for his wife, whom one day at the sacrifice the doe 190
shall save from the sword, by offering its own throat instead.
The bridegroom's wide empty running-track on the shore,
by the breakers of the sea, will be called after him.

168 **fourth husband** Deiphobos, another son of Priam

171 **fifth husband** Achilles

174 **Kytaian woman** Medea

175 **stranger** Jason, **Oinone's exile** Aigina, Peleus

180 **he** Paris

184–5 **heifer** Iphigeneia, **warlike name** Neoptolemos, son of 'dragon' Achilles

186 **husband** Achilles, **Salmydesian** the Black Sea

190 **doe** Iphigeneia

He will groan for his fate and for his vain sea-voyaging,
and for her who vanished, and is now changed in form*   195
to an old woman near sacrificial basins and lustral water,
and a cauldron, seething with flame from the depths
of hell, which the Dark Woman will blow on
as she boils the flesh of dead men in the pot, a skilled cook.
And he, lamenting, will tread the Skythian land   200
for five full periods, yearning for his marriage.

The Greeks swear oaths and set sail
Round the altar of Kronos the prophet,*
who mangled the flesh of the mother and her baby young
they will bind themselves with a second yoke of oaths*
and will take solid oars into their hands as weapons.   205
To Bacchos, as their rescuer from their previous trouble,*
they will cry Euai! and call him the Tripper-up. To him,
in the recesses of Delphinios, by the cave of the Cunning One,
the fleet-commander of a thousand city-sacking ships will begin
the secret sacrifice to the Bull-god.   210
To him, in unexpected requital for his sacrifices,
the Potent one, the Phigaleian, the Torch-god
entwines the lion's feet in tendrils, and keeps him away
from his feast, so that he cannot utterly lay waste the corn
by ravaging it with his teeth and voracious jaws.   215
For a long time now I have seen a spiral of trailing ills,
dragging across the sea, and hissing against my fatherland
terrible threats and fiery destruction.

Kassandra's regrets about the prophecies of Prylis and Aisakos
Would that Kadmos had never fathered a son*
in sea-surrounded Issa, to be a guide to our enemies: 220
the fourth descendant of miserable Atlas,
Prylis, who helped to overthrow his own kin,

206 **Bacchos,** 207 **Tripper-up** Dionysos
208 **Delphinios . . . the Cunning One** Apollo
209 **fleet-commander** Agamemnon
210 **Bull-god,** 212 **Potent one, Phigaleian, Torch-god** Dionysos
213 **lion** Telephos
219 **Kadmos, son** Hermes, Prylis
220 **Issa** Lesbos

you truthful seer! always directing towards the best.
And would that my father had not spurned
the night-wandering fears of Aisakos' oracles   225
but had done away with both of them by the same fate,
for Troy's sake, and had burnt their limbs in Lemnian fire;
in that way we would not have been overwhelmed by a sea of
      troubles.
Lo! Palaimon the baby-killer sees*
the aged Titanid wife of Okeanos   230
seething with cordage-rigged [?] shearwaters.

   Achilles kills Kyknos and his children on Tenedos; also Mnemon
And now two children are killed, together with their father,*
whose collar-bone was auspiciously struck by a solid mill-stone.
Previously, they had escaped, after the piper caused them
by his false stories to be cast adrift in a deadly chest.   235
Their stern father, murderer of his own children, believed him,
so he, whom shearwaters reared and fishermen caught in their nets,
he who was familiar with samphire and round seashells,
enclosed his two offspring in an ark,
and with them the wretch, who was not 'mindful', but failed*   240
through forgetfulness to pass on the orders of the goddess-mother;
he shall die, pierced through the breast by a sword.

   Achilles leaps ashore; Trojan territory laid waste
And now Myrina and the seaside beaches*
groan as they absorb the neighing of horses,
when the fierce wolf makes his Pelasgian leap   245
and lands his swift foot on the shore's edge.*
He causes a sparkling spring to gush forth from the sand,
and opens up long-hidden streams.
And now Ares, the dancer, sets fire to the land,
leading the song with a bloody tune on his trumpet-shell.   250
All the land lies devastated before my eyes,
and the fields bristle and glisten with spears*

229 **Palaimon** Tenedos
230 **wife of Okeanos** the sea
234 **piper** Molpos
241 **goddess-mother** Thetis
245 **fierce wolf** Achilles

as if with corn. Groans seem to fill
my ears from the topmost towers,
reaching to the windless abodes of the ether,   255
as women wail and tear their garments,
having suffered one disaster after another.

Deaths of Hektor and Achilles

One evil, O my wretched heart, one evil*
will gnaw at you above every other woe,
when the fierce black onrushing warrior—   260
an eagle sweeping the earth with his wings,
who bends the line of his tracks with a circling motion,
screaming discordant, horrendous cries—
snatches aloft your dearest brother,
the child of the Ptoan god;*   265
with beak and claws he will bloody his body,*
staining red the ground and the waters of Troy,
a ploughman cutting a level furrow.
He will take the price of the slain bull,*
suspending it in the precise balance of the scales;   270
but he will pour out an equal and compensating amount
in weight of shining Paktolian lumps
and he will enter the mixing-bowl of Bacchos, mourned*
by the nymphs, who love the waters of Bephyros
and the Leibethrian watchtower above Pimpleia.   275
He, the corpse-seller, who in fear for his future fate*
will even submit to wearing a woman's dress
on his body, handling the chattering shuttle by the loom;
and will be the last to set foot on enemy soil,*
fearing your spear, my brother, even in his sleep.   280

Hektor fires the Greek ships

O Fate, what a pillar of my house you will destroy,*
pulling away the bulwark of my wretched fatherland.
But it will not be with impunity, and not without bitter hardships,*

---

260 **warrior**, 271 **he**, 276 **corpse-seller** Achilles
264 **dearest brother**, 269 **slain bull** Hektor
265 **Ptoan god** Apollo
272 **Paktolian** Lydian
275 **Leibethria, Pimpleia** Macedonian places

that the Dorian army of looters will laugh at him,
jeering at the fate of the fallen man: 285
but at the sterns of their pine ships, running the final race
    of their lives
to the finishing tape, they will be enveloped in flames,
and will call often on Zeus of Fugitives in their prayers
to keep bitter death away from men who are being destroyed.
Then neither the trench, nor the barrier of ships 290
stationed, nor the bristling wing-shaped palisade,
nor battlements will be of any help, nor parapets,
but like bees, confused by smoke,
and gusts of thick fumes and flung firebrands,
they will jump like massed divers from the quarter-deck 295
onto the figure-heads and poops and rowing benches,
and stain the foreign soil with blood.
Many chiefs, and many who carry off with their spears
the first-spoils won by Greece, and who boast of their lineage,
will be carded by your mighty hands, 300
which drip with blood and which crave for battle.
But I shall bear no less a grief
as I mourn your burial in perpetuity.
For I shall see that pitiful, yes pitiful day,
and what will be called the uttermost woe of everything that Time, 305
as it revolves the circle of the moon, brings into being.

    Kassandra mourns her brother Troilos, killed by love-sick Achilles. . .
Woe! I groan for your milky youth,*
you whelp, dear object of your siblings' embrace,
you who will hit the savage serpent with the fiery love-charm*
of your arrows, and grip the stricken one in an inescapable noose 310
for a short and loveless moment.*
Unpenetrated by your victim,
you will bloody the altar of your father with your severed head.

    . . . and her sisters Laodike and Polyxena, and her mother Hekabe
Alas for my miserable life! I lament for you, my two nightingales,
and for your fate, wretched bitch. 315

---

309 **savage serpent**, 312 **victim** Achilles
313 **your father** Priam

One of you will be swallowed up completely in a deep cleft*
of the gaping earth which bore her,
when she sees, with groans of anguish, her approaching doom:*
there, at the grove of her ancestor, where the whore who married
secretly lies buried, her bones mixed with those   320
of her son, the heifer together with the whelp, before it gulped milk,
and before her limbs had been washed clean after childbirth.
And as for you, the grim lion-son of Iphis will lead you to a*
cruel wedding and marriage sacrifices.
Imitating the sacrificial libations of his cruel mother,   325
he will slit her throat over a deep bowl:
the dreadful murderous dragon will slaughter
the wreathed heifer with Kandaon's sword of the three owners,*
killing the first-slaughtered victim to gratify the wolves.
But you, aged prisoner on the hollow shore,*   330
stoned at the hands of the Dolonkoi
because they have been provoked by your abusive curses:
a shower of stones will cover you in its robe,
when you assume the dark shape of Maira.
    Priam's downfall; the Wooden Horse
But he, slain at the altar of Zeus-Agamemnon,*   335
will adorn its base with his white hair below it;
the wretch, who was ransomed by the veil of his sister*
and came back to find his fatherland burnt to ashes,
after losing his earlier obscure name in darkness;
at that time the fierce-crested snake,*   340
he who sold the land which bore him, shall light
the torch of doom. He will open the ghastly pregnant hiding-place,
dragging aside the wooden bars of its womb;

316 **one of you** Laodike
319 **whore,** 321 **heifer** Killa
323 **you** Polyxena, **lion-son** Neoptolemos, **Iphis** Iphigeneia
328 **Kandaon** Hephaistos
330 **aged prisoner** Hekabe (Hecuba)
331 **Dolonkoi** Thracians
337 **sister** Hesione
340 **snake** Antenor

and the crooked cousin of the Sisyphean fox
will illuminate the evil fire, as a signal   345
to those who had sailed away to narrow Leukophrys
and the double islands of Porkes the child-devourer.

    Kassandra narrates her own rape by Lokrian Ajax
And I, miserable wretch, who rejected marriage,*
here, within the stone walls of my maiden-chamber,
with no ceiling, have hidden myself in the roofless   350
cell of a gloomy prison.
I, who drove the lustful Thoraian, the Ptoian, the lord of the
    seasons,
away from my maiden bed,
as if possessed of an undying virginity
until extreme old age, in imitation of Pallas,   355
the marriage-hater, the goddess of booty and of city-gates.
At that time I shall be dragged violently to the vulture's nest,
a frenzied dove in his crooked talons,
crying out often for the help of the Ox-binder, the Seagull goddess,
the Maiden, to help and defend me from this rape.   360
And she, turning her eyes up to the wooden coffers
of the temple's ceiling, will be angry with the army,
she who fell from heaven and the throne of Zeus
to become the most precious possession of my royal ancestor.
In requital for the sin of one man, all Greece*   365
shall mourn the empty tombs of ten thousand of its children,
not placed upon the rocks which are their real coffins,*
nor containing the last ashes from their pyres,
buried in funeral urns, as is the due for mortal men,
but as pitiful names and inscriptions on cenotaphs   370
washed by the warm tears of their parents
and children, and the lamentations of their wives.

344 **Sisypheian fox** Sinon
346 **Leukophrys** Tenedos
347 **double islands** Kalydnai
352 **Thoraian . . . seasons** Apollo
355–6 **Pallas . . . city-gates,** 359–60 **Ox-binder . . . Maiden** Athena
363–4 **she who fell** Athena as the Palladion (her image)

Kassandra addresses Euboian places, where Nauplios will lure
  Greeks to their deaths

O Opheltes, and Zarex, guardian of the recesses of the cliffs,*
and you rocks by Rychas, and you, savage Nedon,
and all the caves of Dirphys and Diakria   375
and home of Phorkys!
How many groans will you hear, when the corpses
are thrown up on the shore, together with half-broken poops;
how much roaring of the inescapable flood-tide,
as the sea drags them out again with reverse-flowing eddies,   380
how many tunny-fishes, with the sutures of their skulls
split open on the frying-pan: the thunderbolt as it falls to earth
will taste them as they perish at night.
When they are drowsy with wine the viperous wrecker will
        lure them on,*
showing a lamp to guide them in the darkness,   385
applying himself to his skill without sleeping.

Lokrian Ajax the rapist is drowned, and serve him right

One, like a diving kingfisher, the wave will carry,*
as a naked sea-bream, through the narrow channel,
swept between the double rocks.
On the rocks of Gyrai, drying his wings   390
all wet from the sea, he will take a second gulp of salt-water,
flung from the cliffs by the three-forked spear,*
with which the awful avenger, the hired labourer, will wound him
and force him to share a path with whales,
a cuckoo boasting with empty insolence.   395
And his cold dolphin's corpse, thrown up on the shore,
will be dried by the sun's rays.
As putrid salt-fish, among the seaweed and moss,
he will be hidden by Nesaia's pitying sister,*
she who helped the mighty Kynaithian Disk-god.   400

384 **viperous wrecker** Nauplios
390 **Gyrai** rocks near Mykonos
392–3 **three-forked . . . labourer** Poseidon
399 **pitying sister** Thetis
400 **Disk-god** Zeus

His tomb, neighbour to the petrified quail,
will tremble as it watches the breakers of the Aegean sea.
In Hades the wretch will curse and revile
the Kastnian and Melinaian goddess.*
She will entrap him fast in the snares of desire,   405
in a love which is not love; she will spring
the Furies' bitter destructive trap.

    All Greece will mourn its dead
All Greece will be full of pain and groaning,*
everything which is hemmed in by Aratthos and the impassable
Leibethrian gates of Dotion;   410
and by the shore of Acheron
the Greeks will long lament my marriage.
For a numberless swarm of them will be entombed
in the bellies of sea-monsters, devoured by their jaws
with numberless rows of teeth. Others, destitute of kin,   415
will find tombs as strangers in strange lands.

    The long nostoi *('returns') narrative begins with Phoinix*
One will be hidden by Bisaltic Eion on the Strymon,*
near the Apsynthians and Bistones,
and neighbour to the Edonians; he, the child-rearing crab,
will never see again the Tymphrestian rock.   420
He was more hateful than any other mortal to his father,
who pierced his eyes and blinded him,*
when he shared the bastard bed of the dove.

    Kalchas, Idomeneus, and Sthenelos buried at Ionian Kolophon
Three sea-swallows will be buried in the woods of Kerkaphos.
not far from the waters of the Ales.   425
One of them, the swan of the Molossian Kypean Koitan god,*
made a mistake about the offspring of the female, the sow,
after he had drawn his rival into a contest of wits

401 **tomb** Mykonos, **quail** Delos
404 **Kastnian and Melinaian goddess** Aphrodite
419 **child** Achilles
420 **Tymphrestian rock** Thessaly
421 **father** Amyntor
424 **three sea-swallows** Kalchas, Idomeneus, Sthenelos
426 **swan** Kalchas, **Molossian Kypean Koitan god** Apollo
428 **rival** Mopsos

about figs; he shall, after his defeat,
sleep his allotted fate of sleep, as ordained by oracles.   430
Another is fourth of the descendants of Erechtheus,*
brother of Aithon in the fictitious writings.
The third is offspring of him who, with his strong two-pronged fork,*
undermined the towers of the Ektenoi.
Gongylates, the God of the Council, the Mill-god,   435
crushed his head with a purifying whip,
when the daughters of Night armed the father's brothers
with murderous desire for the death of kin.

    Mopsos and Amphilochos buried at Mallos in Kilikia
Two, by the mouths of the streams of Pyramos,*
hounds of Derainos, each killed by the other's murderous   440
blow, shall fight with their last battle-shout
at the foot of the towers of the daughter of Pamphylos.*
That tall citadel, eaten away by the sea,
Magarsos, shall stand in the middle, separating their holy tombs,
so that neither may see, even when they have gone down   445
to the seats of the dead, the other's blood-soaked tomb.

    Five Greek leaders go to Cyprus
Five, coming to Sphekeia, to Kerastia,*
and Satrachos, the land of Hylates,
shall settle near Zerynthian Morpho.

    No. 1: Teukros brother of Telamonian Ajax
The first, exiled, by his father's reproaches,*   450
from the caves of Kychreus and the waters of Bokaros—
my own cousin!—because he was the killer of his brother
foal, and a bastard shoot, and the ruin of his family.

431–2 **fourth descendant** Idomeneus, **Erechtheus** Zeus

433 **third** Kapaneus

434 **towers of Ektenoi** Thebes

435 **Gongylates . . . Mill-god** Zeus

437 **daughters of Night** Erinyes (Furies), **father's brothers** Eteokles, Polyneikes

440 **Derainos**, 448 **Hylates** Apollo

449 **Zerynthian Morpho** Aphrodite of Paphos

450 **father** Telamon

452–3 **brother foal** Telamonian Ajax

His brother had vented his warlike rage on flocks of sheep,
he whom the skin of the fierce lion   455
had made invulnerable to bronze weapons in battle.
He had only one way to Hades and the land of the dead,
a way which was hidden by the Skythian bow-case.
When the lion burned sacrifices to Komyros,*
his father, he uttered prayers which were heard,   460
as he tossed his companion's whelp in his arms.
He will never persuade their father that the Lemnian*
whirlwind of Enyo, he who was never turned to flight,
the savage bull, could have pierced his innards with the gift
from the guest-friend who was his bitterest enemy,*   465
and have leapt in a fatal fall on his sword in self-slaughter.
He will drive Trambelos' brother far from his fatherland,
     The story of Hesione, Phoinodamas, and Herakles
whom my father's sister bore,*
she who was given as the first spoils to the tower-underminer.
It was she whom once, as he stood in the assembly of the citizens,   470
the babbler father of three daughters urged should be sent
as a grim meal to the bright-eyed hound,
which made the whole earth into mud with sea-water,
when it spewed out the billows from its jaws,
and shook the whole plain with boisterous waves.   475
He sucked a scorpion, not a woodpecker, into his gullet,
and wept the heavy weight of his dire woes
to Phorkos, wanting advice in his trouble.*
     No. 2: Agapenor, one of the autochthonous Arkadians
The second, a hunter, comes to the island,*
a landsman, earth-nourished, one of the sons of the oak,   480
who took the shape of wolves after they cut Nyktimos to pieces;

459 lion Herakles, Komyros Zeus
462–4 the Lemnian . . . savage bull Telamonian Ajax
465 guest-friend . . . enemy Hektor
467 Trambelos' brother Teukros
469 tower-underminer Telamon
476 scorpion Herakles, woodpecker Hesione
479 the island Cyprus
480 earth-nourished the Arkadians

They were older than the moon, and warmed their food of
    acorn-mast
in the ashes of their fires at dead of winter.
He will dig for copper, and will wrench the clods*
from out of the pit, mining the whole shaft with his mattock.   485

    Agapenor's father Ankaios
The Oitaian tusk killed his father,*
shattering his body in the joint of his groin.
The wretched man learnt in his agony the meaning of the proverb,
that between the lip and the drinking-cup
all-inventing mortal fate rolls many surprises.   490
The same tusk, all foaming with glistening blood,
took revenge on its killer as it fell dead,
striking the ankle-tip of the dancer with unerring blow.

    No. 3: Akamas
The third is the son of the man who took the giant's weapons*
from the hollow rock. To his furtive bed   495
the Idaian heifer shall come, self-summoned,
she who will descend, still living, to Hades,
emaciated with grief, the mother of Mounitos;
whom once, when he is out hunting, a Krestonian viper
will kill, striking his heel with its fierce sting,   500
after his grandfather's mother, the prisoner, has placed
in his father's hands the child reared in darkness,
the young cub.   503

    The Dioskouroi (Kastor and Polydeukes) and Apharetidai
    (Idas and Lynkeus) fight
      On her alone the Aktaian wolves   503 (continued)
fixed the yoke of slavery,*
in requital for the abduction of the maenad.   505
Their heads were covered by the sliced ball of an eggshell,
a protection against the bloody spear.

---

482 **older than the moon** the Arkadians
494 **the man . . .** Theseus
496 **Idaian heifer** Laodike
499 **Krestonian** Thracian
501 **grandfather's mother** Aithra
505 **the maenad** Helen

Everything else in the house is guarded by the intact
    woodworm-eaten
seal, a great marvel to the local people.
This will erect a ladder to the way of the stars   510
for the half-divine Lapersian twins.
Zeus Saviour, may you never send them to my fatherland*
as helpers of the twice-snatched corncrake,
nor let them arm their winged ships,
and, leaping from the topmost poop, set their swift naked feet   515
on the Bebrykian landing-place;
nor may those others do so, who are even stronger than those
    two lions,*
unmatched in might, beloved of Ares
and divine Enyo and the goddess who was born three times,
the Yoker, Longatis, Homolois, the Forceful.   520
For nothing that those two hard-working handymen,*
Drymas and Prophantos, lord of Kromna,
had built of stone for the perjured king,
would have held out for one day against the destructive wolves,
so as to stem their heavy destructive attack;   525
even though the city had before its towers the great
    Kanastraian giant,
local-born, to bar the enemy's way,
keen to strike, with a well-aimed spear-throw,
the first man to bring destruction on the flock.
A bold gleaming falcon will be the first to feel his spear,   530
leaping forward with a swift bound,

511 **Lapersian** Spartan
513 **corncrake** Helen
516 **Bebrykian** Trojan
517 **those others** the Apharetidai
519–20 **the goddess . . . the Forceful** Athena
521–2 **two handymen** Apollo, Poseidon
523 **perjured king** Laomedon
526 **Kanastraian giant** Hektor
530 **falcon** Protesilaos

the best of the Greeks, for whom, when killed, the ready
    Dolonkian shore
has long since built a tomb,
Mazousia, the promontory of the horn-shaped peninsula.
But someone there is, someone beyond our hopes,   535
a gracious helper, the Drymnian
god, Promantheus, Aithiops, Gyrapsios;
when they receive the wandering Orthanes*
into their home, the bitter down-swooping destroyer—
they who will suffer frightful, dreaded fates,   540
and who will try, with feasts and libations
of the first pressing of wine, to propitiate unyielding Kragos—
he will cause them to quarrel violently as they converse.
At first they will rend with biting words,
roughing each other up to fury with their taunts.   545
Then those cousins will fight with spears,
seeking to defend their cousin-chicks*
from violently forced marriage and seizure
of kin, to punish what was usurped without bride-price.
The stream of Knakion shall see many missiles   550
thrown by the daring of eagles,
an incredible wonder to the people of Pharai.
One of them, after piercing with his spear of cherry-wood the
    hollow*
trunk of a black oak-tree, will kill one of the twins,
a lion who joined battle against a bull.   555
The other lion will rend open the other bullock's flank with his spear
and level him with the ground. Against him the intrepid ram
will aim a blow, butting him for the second time,
hurling a statue from one of the Amyklaian tombs.
But bronze and thunderbolts together   560

---

532 **Dolonkian** Thracian
534 **Mazousia** the Thracian Chersonese
536–7 **Drymnian . . . Gyrapsios** Zeus
538 **Orthanes** Paris
542 **Kragos** Zeus
550 **Knakion**, 552 **Pharai**, 559 **Amyklaian** Sparta

will crush the bulls, one of whom was not disparaged*
for his strength even by the Skiastan, Orchian, and Telphousian
god, who bent his bow in the fight.
These twins Hades will take, but the plateaux of Olympos*
will greet the other twins as guests for ever on alternate days,   565
brother-loving, immortal and mortal.
A god will lull all these men's spears for us,
giving us a brief remedy in our troubles.

   Anios of Delos and his miraculous daughters
But his hand will stir up a horrendous cloud of others:
not even Rhoio's son will be able to lull*   570
their fury, urging them to stay for nine years
on the island, in obedience to the oracles.
He said his three daughters would provide food beyond reproach
for all, if they stayed by the Kynthian watchtower
and roamed near the river Inopos,   575
drawing water from Egyptian Triton.*
Bold Problastos taught those girls,
creators of mill-bruised fodder,
how to make wine and oil for anointing:
the Wine-turners, the doves, the granddaughters of Zarex.   580
They will cure the ravenous wasting hunger
of the army, those foreign dogs, when some day they come
to the sleeping-place of the daughter of Sithon.
The aged maidens have long been whirring all this
with the threads of their bronze spindles.   585
   Nos. 4 and 5: Kepheus and Praxandros
Then Kepheus and Praxandros, not as leaders of*
sailor folk, but as obscure stock,
shall come as fifth and fourth to the land
of Golge's divine queen: the latter will bring a Spartan throng*

562–3 **Skiastian, Orchian, Telphousian god** Apollo
567 **a god** Zeus
574 **Kynthian watchtower** Delos
577 **Problastos** Dionysos
583 **sleeping-place . . . Sithon** Troy
584 **aged maidens** the Fates
589 **Golge's queen** Aphrodite

from Therapne, the former, coming from Olenos   590
and Dyme, will be the leader of an army from Boura.

Diomedes in Daunia (S. Italy)

Another will build Argyrippa as a Daunian heritage*
by the side of the Ausonian Phylamos,
when he sees the bitter winged fate of his companions,*
turned into birds; they will welcome a maritime   595
way of life, like fishermen,
in shape resembling keen-sighted swans.*
Catching with their beaks the spawn of fishes,
they will inhabit the island which bears the name of their leader;*
on a protruding theatre-shaped mound,   600
with firm twigs, as if building streets, they make
their compact nests, in imitation of Zethos.*
They go out together to the hunt, and at night they come back
to the valley-glade to rest, avoiding every gathering*
of barbarian men, but seeking, in the folds   605
of Greek clothes, their customary sleep;
they will eat hand-held bread and after-dinner morsels
of barley-cake, with affectionate whimpering,
as they remember in sadness their former way of life.
His wounding of the Troizenian goddess will be part-cause   610
of his distraught wanderings and his dire calamities,
when the bold and lustful bitch will be goaded
with a craving for sex. The altar of Hoplosmia will save him
from death, when he has been made ready for slaughter.
Like a Colossus he will stand in the recesses*   615
of Ausonia, and will place his legs on stones
taken from the acres where the Exchanger once built walls;
he will throw these ballast-rocks out of his ship.

590 **Therapne** Sparta
590–1 **Olenos . . . Boura** Achaian places
593 **Phylamos** River Aufidus
610 **Troizenian goddess** Aphrodite
612 **bitch** Aigialeia
613 **Hoplosmia** Hera
616 **Ausonia** Italy
617 **the acres** Troy, **the Exchanger** Poseidon

When defeated in the arbitration by his brother Alainos,
he will utter effective curses against the soil,   620
that it should never produce Deo's bountiful grain,
although Zeus should irrigate the fields with showers,
unless someone deriving from his own Aitolian stock
should dig the land, cutting the furrows with oxen.
With unmovable pillars he will secure the plain   625
and no man shall boast that he has been able
to shift them even a little. For without wings, but speedily,
they will make a return journey,
treading the shore with footless steps.
He shall be called a high god by many,   630
all those who live by Io's hollow basin—*
he who killed the dragon which harried the Phaiakians.

    Boiotians in the Balearic islands
Others, crabs clad in coats made of skin,*
will sail to the sea-washed Gymnesian rocks,
and drag out their lives without cloaks and barefoot,   635
armed with three slings of two thongs.
Their mothers will teach the art of shooting from afar
to their young unfed children.
For none of them will chew barley-bread
until with a well-aimed stone they earn their food,   640
placed as a mark above the baker's board.
They shall climb the rough headlands
which nurture Iberians, near the gates of Tartessos:*
the race of ancient Arne, lords of Temmikia,*
yearning for Graia and the crags of Leontarne,   645
and Skolos and Tegyra and the seat of Onchestos,
and Thermodon river, and the waters of Hypsarnos.

---

621 **Deo** Demeter

631–2 **Io's basin** the Ionian (east Adriatic) sea, **Phaiakians** Kerkyra (Corcyra, Corfu)

634 **Gymnesian rocks** the Balearic islands

643 **Tartessos** southern Spain

644–7 **Arne . . . Hypsarnos** Boiotian ('Temmikian') places

Lykophron's 'Odyssey'

Those who have wandered round the Gulf of Syrtis and
    the Libyan lands,*
and the narrow contraction of the Tyrrhenian straits,
and the sailor-slaughtering lookout-post of the half-beast,   650
who once died at the hands of Mekisteus,
the Pelt-wearer, the Digger, the Cattle-driver,
and the rocky places, dwellings of the harpy-legged nightingales
who feast on raw flesh—
all these wanderers Hades, who is host to all, shall take in,   655
mangled by every kind of wound;
but he will spare just one of them behind to bring news of his
    friends,*
he of the dolphin sign, the thief of the Phoenician goddess.
This man will see the cave of the one-eyed
monster, and will hand the cup of wine   660
to the cannibal, as an after-dinner drink.
And he will see the survivors of the arrows*
of Keramyntes, Peukeus, Palaimon:
those who shattered the well-rounded ships,
will thread their evil catch of fish on a rope.   665
One miserable trouble after another awaits them,
each one more ruinous than the last.
What Charybdis will not feast on his dead comrades,*
and what Erinys, half maiden half bitch?
And what sterile, Centaur-killing nightingale,   670
Aitolian or Kouretan, shall not, through its varied song,*
invite their starving flesh to waste away?

648 ... **Syrtis ... lands** the Lotus-eaters
649 **Tyrrhenian** Etruscan
650 **half-beast** Skylla
651–2 **Mekisteus ... Cattle-driver** Herakles
653 **nightingales** the Sirens
658 **he of the dolphin sign ...** Odysseus
659–61 **one-eyed monster ... cannibal** Kyklops
662 **survivors** the Laistrygonians
663 **Keramyntes ...** Herakles
669 **half bitch** Skylla
670–1 **sterile ... Kouretan** Siren

And what she-dragon shall he not see,*
turner of men into wild beasts by mixing magic herbs with barley,
a monstrous-shaped doom? The wretches,   675
grunting lamentation for their fates as pigs in the sty,
shall munch grape-stones and pressed grapes
mixed with their fodder. But him the moly-root
shall save from harm, and an epiphany of Ktaros,
the Nonakrian, the Three-headed Bright One.   680
He shall come to the dark plain of the dead,*
and seek out the aged necromancer,
he who knows the sexual intercourse both of men and of women.
Sprinkling at the pit warm blood on the dead souls,
and brandishing a protective sword, object of fear to those below,   685
he will hear the thin voices of the ghosts,
the utterances of their dimly audible mouths.
Next, the island which crushed the backs of the giants*
and the savage body of Typhon,
seething with burning lava, will receive him as solitary seafarer.   690
There the King of the Immortals installed an ugly tribe
of monkeys, in mockery of those
who stirred up war against the offspring of Kronos.

    Odysseus in Campania

Then he will pass the grave of Baios the helmsman,*
and the dwellings of the Kimmerians, and the Acherousian   695
flood, swelling with the breakers of the sea;
from there to Ossa and the ox-paths built by the Lion*
from piled-up earth, and the grove of Obrimo, the underworld
    Maiden,
and the stream of Pyriphlegethon. There the inaccessible peak
of Polydegmon stretches its head to the sky;   700

673 **she-dragon** Kirke
679–80 **Ktaros . . . Bright One** Hermes
682 **aged necromancer** Teiresias
688 **the island** Pithekoussai
691 **King of the Immortals** Zeus
697 **Lion** Herakles
698 **Obrimo, the underworld Maiden** Persephone
700 **Polydegmon** the Apennines

from its caverns all streams and springs
throughout the Ausonian land descend.
He leaves the high hill of Lethaion,
and lake Aornos encircled by a noose,*
and the river of Kokytos violently roaring in darkness,   705
tributary of black Styx, where Termieus
established a place of oaths for the immortals,
drawing a libation-stream in gold vessels,
as he set out against the Giants and Titans.
He will dedicate a gift to Daeira and her husband,   710
his helmet, fixed on top of a pillar.

    The Sirens again

And he will kill three of the daughters of the son of Tethys,*
who imitated the songs of their melodious mother.
With suicidal leap from their high lookout-place
they shall dive on wings towards the Tyrrhenian waves,   715
where the bitter thread of flax draws them.
One of them, cast up on shore, Phaleros' tower will receive,*
and the Glanis, which waters the land with its streams.
There the locals will construct a tomb for the maiden,
and will honour her with yearly libations and sacrifices of oxen,   720
Parthenope, the bird-goddess.
Leukosia, thrown onto Enipeus'*
projecting headland, will long occupy
the rock named after her, where roaring Is
and its neighbour Laris spew out their waters.   725
Ligeia will be cast on shore at Tereina,
spewing out sea-water. Sailors
will bury her on the sea shore,
next to the eddies of Okinaros.
The bull-horned Ares will wash her tomb with his streams,   730
purifying with its waters the resting-place of the bird-child.
To the first of these three sister goddesses*

---

706 **Termieus** Zeus
710 **Daeira and husband** Persephone, Hades
712 **son of Tethys** Acheloos
722 **Enipeus** Poseidon

the commander of the whole fleet of Mopsops
will institute a torch-race for sailors,
in obedience to oracles. The people of   735
Neapolis will enlarge this, they who will inhabit the rough cliffs
next to the tranquil refuge of the harbour Misenon.

Aiolos and the bag of winds; the cattle of the Sun
He encloses the winds in a bag of ox-hide,*
but is forced to wander by woes which whirl him backwards.
He will be engulfed in flame by the whip of a thunderbolt,   740
a sea-swallow, perched on the branch of a wild fig-tree.
so that the roaring waves should not gulp him down,
as they suck snorting Charybdis towards the deep.

Odysseus' tribulations at sea, his unhappy return to Ithaka
After briefly enjoying his affair with the daughter of Atlas,*
he will dare to embark on a hastily built raft   745
which will never reach port, and—wretched man!—will steer
his home-made vessel, a boat which he fixed to a central keel
with fastenings, to no avail.
From this, Amphibaios hurls him out,
like the wingless chick of a female kingfisher,   750
together with the mast and yard-arm,
towards the waves, a diver entangled in the ropes.
He will be swept sleepless into the recesses of the sea,
and will share his dwelling with the god from Thracian
Anthedon. One wind after another will whirl him like a cork   755
made of pine-bark, swooping on him with its gusts.
The veil of Byne will just manage to save him*
from the deadly back-swirl; it will enclose
his chest, and the fingers, with which he grasps the flesh-lacerating
rocks: he will be bloodied by sea-corroded   760
spikes. Then he will come to Sickle-island, hateful to Kronos*

733 **commander** Diotimos, **Mopsops** Athens
736 **Neapolis** Naples
744 **daughter of Atlas** Kalypso
749 **Amphibaios** Poseidon
754-5 **the god . . . Anthedon** sea-god Glaukos
757 **Byne** Ino/Leukothea
761 **Sickle-island** Phaiakia

because it mangled his genitals;
as a naked suppliant, inventing a miserable tale of woes,
he will yell out his fictitious lament,
fulfilling the prayers of the blinded monster.   765
Not yet, not yet! May no sleep of forgetfulness
seize Melanthos, the Driver of Horses, as he surrenders to slumber.
He will come, he will come to the harbour-refuge of Reithron*
and the heights of Neriton; and he will see his entire
house utterly overthrown from its foundations   770
by wife-stealing adulterers. And that vixen,
demurely fornicating, shall waste his household,
pouring out the wretch's wealth in feasts.
He himself, a greedy beggar, will see more troubles
than he did at the Skaian gates, and he will endure   775
the odious threats of his own slaves with a patient back,
chastised with reproaches. He will submit to
blows from fists, and thrown potsherds.
Whips will be no strangers to him, but the broad*
seal of Thoas will remain visible on his side,   780
imprinted by the switches which that mischief-maker
will permit to engrave their marks on him, without a groan,
applying voluntary weals to his body:
all this to dupe his enemies, with wounds for spies,
and wailing, so deceiving our king.   785
He whom the Temmikian hill of Bombyleia
once bore to be the greatest of our woes:
the wretch comes home safe, alone of all his crew.
Last of all, like a sea-swallow racing above the waves,
or like a shell worn away from all sides by sea-water,   790
he will find his property devoured in Pronian feasts*

767 Melanthos ... Poseidon
768-9 Reithron, Neriton Ithaka
771 vixen Penelope
775 Skaian gates Troy
785 our king Priam
786 he Odysseus, Temmikian ... Bombyleia Boiotia
791 Pronian Kephallenian

by his fearfully frenzied Lakonian wife.

Odysseus' murder, and burial in Italy; Kassandra's contemptuous
farewell to him

He will die wrinkled, after fleeing the ocean-refuge,*
an armed crow near the groves of Neriton.
A spear-point, deadly and incurable, will strike his side   795
and kill him with its barb of Sardinian fish.
The son shall be called his father's killer,
cousin of the wife of Achilles.
The Eurytanian people will crown him as a seer when he dies,*
they who live on the lofty seat of Trampya.   800
There the Tymphaian snake, king of the Aithikes,
will slay Herakles during a feast,
the descendant of Aiakos, of the seed of Perseus,
no distant kin of the Temeneioi.
Perge, the Tyrrhenian mountain in Gortynaian territory,   805
will receive him when dead and cremated,
as he breathes out his life, lamenting the fate*
of his son, and of his wife, whom her husband kills
and then follows her on the path to Hades,
his throat slit by a sister's slaughter,   810
the cousin of Glaukos and of Apsyrtos.
And he, seeing such a heap of ills,
will enter Hades for the second time, with no return,
never having beheld a peaceful day in his life.
Wretch! It would have been better for you to stay in your
      fatherland*   815
driving the oxen, and to join the lustful working donkey
to the oxen under the yoke,

792 **Lakonian wife** Penelope
794 **Neriton** Ithaka
797 **the son** . . . Telegonos
799 **Eurytanian** Aitolian
800 **Trampya** Epeiros
801 **Tymphaian snake** Polyperchon
802 **Herakles** son of Alexander the Great and Barsine
805 **Gortynaian territory** Etruscan Cortona
811 **cousin** . . . Kassiphone

goaded by a pretended device of madness,
than to endure the test of such great ills.

Menelaos' wanderings in the east

And he, the husband hunting for the abducted wife*   820
who made the evil marriage, will hear of her by rumours.
Yearning for the winged phantom which had disappeared
        into the air,
what nooks of the sea shall he not investigate?
What dry land shall he not visit and search?
He shall first see the crags of Typhon,*   825
and the old woman whose body was turned to stone,
and then the protruding headlands of the Eremboi,
which sailors hate. And he shall see the strong citadel*
of sad Myrrha, whom the branch of the tree
released from her acute birth-pains;   830
and the tomb of Gauas, whom the goddess—Schoineis,
Arenta, the Stranger—mourned as victim of the Muses,
whom the boar killed with its white tusk.
And he shall see the towers of Kepheus,*
and the place kicked by the foot of Hermes Laphrios,   835
and the twin rocks, which that foolish petrel approached
in its search for food. But instead of a female,
it snatched in its jaws the eagle with the golden father,
the liver-destroying winged-footed male.
By the blade of the reaper the hateful monster will be killed,   840
its sinews slashed to pieces.
He released, from labour-pains which produced a man and a horse
born from her throat, the weasel whose gaze turned men to stone:

820 abducted wife Helen
825 Typhon Kilikia
828-9 citadel of Myrrha Phoenician Byblos
831 Gauas Adonis
831-2 Schoineis . . . Stranger Aphrodite
835 the place . . . Ethiopia
837 a female Andromeda
838 eagle Perseus, father Zeus
843 weasel Medusa

he moulded men from the toes upwards,
turning them into statues as he wrapped them in stone,　　845
he who stole the lamp which guided the feet of the wandering trio.
Then he shall see the summer-flooded fields,*
and the river Asbystos and the beds on the ground,
as he sleeps alongside foul-smelling beasts.
All this he will endure for the sake of the Spartan bitch,　　850
the maiden who was mother of daughters and wife of three men.

　　Menelaos in the west

He shall come as a wanderer to the Iapygian people,*
and shall hang up gifts to the Skyletrian maiden,
a Tamassian mixing-bowl and a shield of ox-hide,
and his wife's eastern shoes with fur lining.　　855
He shall come to Siris and the Lakinian recesses,*
where the heifer shall prepare a garden
for Hoplosmia, well-provided with plants.
And for the local women there shall be an eternal law*
to mourn the nine-cubit one, third in descent from Aiakos　　860
and Doris, the whirlwind of fierce battle,
and never to adorn their shining limbs with gold,
nor to clothe themselves in soft dresses
dyed with purple, because a goddess gave to a goddess
a great spike of dry land to build on.　　865
And he shall come to the inhospitable wrestling-arena and*
gymnasium of the bull, whom Kolotis bore,
Alentia, the mistress of the recesses of Longouros.

846　he who stole . . . Perseus, **wandering trio** the Graiai
848　**Asbystos** the Nile
850–1　**Spartan bitch . . . wife of three men** Helen
852　**Iapygian** hinterland of Taras (Tarentum)
853　**Skyletrian maiden** Athena
856　**Lakinian** of Kroton
857　**the heifer** Thetis
858　**Hoplosmia** Hera
860　**nine-cubit one** Achilles
864　**a goddess** Thetis, **to a goddess** Hera
866　**wrestling-arena** Eryx
867　**Kolotis** Aphrodite

He shall round the place where Kronos' sickle took its plunge,
And the waters of Koncheia, and Gonousa and the Sikan fields.   870
He shall visit the temple of the savage wearer of animal hide,
which the grandson of Kretheus, after anchoring his ship,
built with his fifty fellow-sailors.
The shore still preserves the oily scrapings
of the Minyans, which waves of sea-water do not cleanse,   875
nor do long showers of rain wash them away.

Thessalians shipwrecked off Libya

For others, the sandbanks and hidden reefs*
near Taucheira make lament, as they are flung ashore
at the deserted dwelling-place of Atlas,
their wounds gaping from sharp spars of wreckage.   880
That was where Titaironeian Mopsos died*
and was buried by the crew; they raised
above the foundations of his tomb a broken oar
from the ship *Argo*—a treasure for the dead.
There the Kinypheian stream makes Ausigda fertile,*   885
as it drenches it with its waters,
and there the Kolchian woman gave to Triton, descendant
    of Nereus,
a wide mixing-bowl of beaten gold,
for having pointed out a navigable passage, which enabled Tiphys
to send the ship unscathed through the narrow reefs.   890
Then the two-formed god, the child of the sea, foretold
that Greeks would take possession of the land
when a pastoral Libyan people handed back to a Greek
a gift returned to its giver, so depriving their own country of it.
So the Asbystai, fearful of these prophecies,   895

869 the place . . . Drepanon (Trapani)
870 Koncheia . . . fields Sicilian localities
871 temple Elba, savage wearer Herakles
872 grandson of Kretheus Jason
873 fifty fellow-sailors, 875 the Minyans the Argonauts
878 Taucheira, 885 Kinypheian stream, Ausigda Libyan places
887 Kolchian woman Medea
891 two-formed god Triton
895 Asbystai Libyans

shall conceal the prize, out of sight in the depths of the earth.
There the blasts of Boreas shall fling ashore the ill-fated leader*
of the Kyphaians, together with his crew;
and also the son of Tenthredon from Palauthra,
who wields his sceptre over the Amphrysian Euryampians;   900
and the lord of the petrified wolf
which dined off the atonement, and of the Tymphrestian hills.
Some of these wretches pine for Aigoneia,
their fatherland, some for Echinos, some for Titaros,
or Iros, or Trachis, or Perrhaibian   905
Gonnos, Phalanna and the meadows of the Olossonians,
and Kastanaia; but lacerated on the rocks,
they will lament their eternally unburied state.

   Recapitulation
A god shall set in motion one calamitous fate after another,*
allotting a miserable plight instead of a homecoming.   910

   Philoktetes at Italian Kroton
The streams of Aisaros, and a little city*
in the Oinotrian country called Krimisa,
shall receive him whom the snake bit, the slayer of the firebrand:
the Trumpeter herself, with her own hands, shall direct the
      arrow-head,
twinging the Maiotian bow-spring.   915
On the banks of the Dyras he set fire to the fierce lion,*
and equipped his hands with the curved Skythian
snake, the plucked lyre with the unerring teeth.
When he has fallen, the Krathis will see his tomb*

---

897   **Boreas** north wind
897–8   **leader of the Kyphaians** Gounos
899   **son of Tenthredon** Prothoos
901   **lord of the petrified wolf** Eurypylos
902–7   **Tymphrestian . . . Kastanaia** Thessalian places
911–12   **streams of Aisaros . . . Krimisa** Kroton region
913   **whom the snake bit** Philoktetes, **firebrand** Paris
914   **Trumpeter** Athena
915   **Maiotian** Skythian
916   **Dyras** Trachis, **lion** Herakles

aslant the temple of Alaios, the god of Patara,   920
where Nauaithos belches its waters at the sea.
Ausonians from Pellene will kill him,
as he goes to the help of Lindian commanders,
whom the furious howling Thraskias shall send wandering
far from Thermydron and the hills of Karpathos,   925
to settle a foreign land as strangers.
At Makalla, the local people will build a great temple*
over his tomb, and honour him as a god forever,
with libations and sacrifices of oxen.

    Epeios, builder of the Wooden Horse, at Italian Lagaria
The Horse-builder will enter the embrace of Lagaria,*   930
he who shuddered at the spear and the fierce phalanx,
paying the penalty for his father's perjury:
that wretch dared to swear an oath about the spear-won sheep,
when Komaitho's towers were confounded by the army,
in the cause of loving marriage.   935
He brought himself to swear by Aloitis, the Kydonian, Thraso,
and by the god of Krestone,
Kandaon or Mamertos, the hoplite wolf;*
he, who had fought a hateful fist-fight inside the womb,
clashing against his brother,   940
before he had even seen the bright light of Tito,
or escaped the painful birth-pangs.
Therefore the gods made his son a coward,*
a good boxer, but afraid of the spear in battle,
and of greatest use to the army through his technical skill.   945
Near Kiris and the stream of Kylistarnos
he shall make his home, far away from his fatherland.

920 **Alaios, god of Patara** Apollo

922 **Ausonians from Pellene** Italian Greeks from Achaia

923–5 **Lindian commanders . . . Karpathos** Rhodians

932 **his father, 939 who had fought . . . Panopeus**

936 **Aloitis . . . Thraso** Athena

937–8 **god of Krestone** (Thrace) **. . . hoplite wolf** Ares

940 **his brother** Krisos

941 **Tito** Dawn

946 **Kiris, Kilistarnos** rivers near Taras (Tarentum)

And the tools, with which he constructed the image,*
piercing it with nail-holes, to bring dire destruction on my
    countrymen,
he shall dedicate in the temple of the Myndian.   950

Trojans will settle in western Sicily

Others shall settle in the territory of the Sikans,*
arriving there as wanderers, in the land where Laomedon
handed the three daughters of Phoinodamas over to sailors
(he was goaded by the calamity which provided dinner for the
    monster)
to expose them far away to be food for savage animals,   955
after travelling west to the land of the Laistrygonians,
where dwells enormous solitude.
The girls built a great temple to Zerynthia, mother of
the wrestler, as a gift to the goddess,
after they had escaped death and a solitary dwelling-place.   960
One of these the river-god Krimisos, in the likeness of a dog,
joined to himself in marriage, and to this god
who was half a beast she bore a pup, a noble son,
the settler and founder of three places.
He shall guide the bastard sprig of Anchises,   965
and bring him to the furthest extremity of the three-necked island,
after he has conveyed him by sea from Dardanian places.
Unhappy Egesta! For you, by divine ordinance*
there shall be great and eternal mourning for my fatherland,
fired by the flicker of flames.   970
Desolate, you will long mourn for the calamitous destruction
of its towers, with wailing and groaning
in perpetuity. And all your people, clad

---

950 **the Myndian** Athena
958 **temple to Zerynthia** Eryx, Aphrodite
961 **one of these** Aigeste
963 **pup** Aigestes (Acestes)
965 **bastard sprig** Elymos
966 **three-necked island** Sicily
967 **Dardanian**, 969 **my fatherland**, 972 **its towers** Troy

in black suppliant dress,
shall drag out their sad lives in squalor and filth.   975
Their uncut hair will beautify their backs,
nursing the memory of old griefs.

Greeks will settle on the bay of Italian Tarentum (Taras)
And many will settle near Siris and the Leuternian*
fields, where unlucky
Kalchas lies, a Sisyphos of the countless figs,   980
his head split by the punch of a clenched fist,
there where the Sinis flows with its swift current,
watering the abundantly fertile Chonian heritage.
Ill-fated men, they take over a city similar to Ilion,
and cause pain to the Laphrian maiden,   985
the Trumpeter, killing in the very sanctuary of the goddess
the Xouthians who formerly inhabited the place.
The statue will close its bloodless eyes
when it sees the harm done by Achaians to Ionians,
and the internecine bloodshed of fierce wolves,   990
when the priest, the whelp of the priestess, is the first*
to die, and stain the altar with his dark blood.

Greeks will settle in south Italian Bruttium, the Kroton region
Others shall gain the impassable heights of Tylesos*
and the neck-like promontory of sea-anointed Linos,
and shall arrive at the plain which is the Amazons' allotted
          portion,   995
accepting the yoke of the slave-woman,
whom, as the bondswoman of the daughter of Otrere,
the waves will bring as wanderer to a foreign land.
As the young woman breathes her last, her pierced eye
will bring death to the monkey-shaped Aitolian pest,   1000

981 punch Herakles

985–6 Laphrian maiden, Trumpeter Athena

987 Xouthians Ionians

993–4 Tylesos . . . Linos places in Bruttium (S. Italy)

996 slave-woman Klete

997 daughter of Otrere the Amazon Penthesileia

1000 Aitolian pest Thersites

cut down by the bloody spear.
Krotoniates shall one day sack the city
of the Amazon, killing the intrepid maiden
Klete, queen of the country named after her.
But before that, many shall bite the dust,   1005
felled by her hand; and not without trouble
shall the descendants of Laurete overthrow the towers.
And some shall settle in Tereina, where Okinaros wets the land*
with its streams, gushing out its pure waters;
these people will be worn out by their bitter wanderings.   1010
   The Greeks Nireus and Thoas in Libya and then Illyria
He who took the second prize for beauty,*
and that other, the boar-commander from the waters
of Lykormas, the mighty child of Gorge,
will be led first to Libyan sands, as Thracian
winds fill the taut sails,   1015
and then again the south wind will burst on them
and drive them from Libya to the Argyrinian and Keraunian
groves, sweeping the sea with violent hurricane.
There they shall see a sad wandering life,
drinking from the streams of Lakmonian Aias.   1020
Neighbour Krathis and the land of the Mylakoi will receive them
within their boundaries, to live with Polai of the Kolchians,*
whom the angry lord of Korinth and Aia, husband of Eiduia,
sent out to search for his daughter.
Hunting for the bride-carrying ship,   1025
they settle at the deep Dizeros river.
   Greeks will settle on Malta
Others, after wandering near Othronos,*
shall settle on the island of Malta,
round which lap the Sikanian waves by Pachynos,

1011 **he who took** ... Nireus
1012 **boar-commander** Thoas
1017 **Argyrinian, Keraunian,** 1020–2 **Lakmonian** ... **Polai** Illyria
1023 **angry lord** ... Aietes
1024 **his daughter** Medea
1026–7 **Dizeros, Othronos** Illyria
1029 **Sikanian, Pachynos** Sicily

marking the hilly headland which will afterwards   1030
bear the name of the Sisypheian son;*
and the famous sanctuary of the maiden Longatis,
where the Heloros pours out its cold waters.

   The Euboian Greek Elephenor in Illyria and Epeiros
The wolf, the killer of his grandfather, shall dwell at Othronos,*
yearning for the distant ancestral streams of Koskynthos.   1035
Standing on a rock by the sea,
he will shout to his citizens the orders for sailing.
For because he is a murderer, for him to set foot on the dry land
of his ancestors before he has been in exile for a great period
will be forbidden by Telphousia who supports justice,*   1040
the bitch who lives round the streams of Ladon.
From there, fleeing from a terrible battle
with the creeping serpent-like enemies, he shall sail to the city
of Amantia. Going near to the land of the Atintanians,
he settles on a rock at Praktis,   1045
enjoying the waters of Chaonian Polyanthes.

   Podaleirios' incubatory cult in Italian Daunia
Of two brothers, one, near the Ausonian*
tomb of Kalchas, the cenotaph,
shall endure foreign dust upon his bones.
To all who sleep on ramskins on his tomb,   1050
he shall utter truthful prophecies;
and he shall be called a curer of sickness by the Daunians,
when they bathe in the streams of Althainos,
and pray to the son of Epios to come as gracious
helper to the citizens and the flocks.   1055

1031 **Sisypheian son** Odysseus
1032 **maiden Longatis** Sicilian Athena
1033 **Heloros** Sicily
1035 **Koskynthos** Euboia
1040 **Telphousia** a Fury
1041 **Ladon** Arkadia
1044–6 **Amantia . . . Polyanthes** places in Epeiros
1047 **two brothers** Podaleirios and Machaon
1054 **son of Epios** Asklepios

Diomedes and Daunia (again)

One day a mournful and hateful dawn*
will appear for the envoys of the Aitolians,
when they come to the territory of the Salangoi and the seats
of the Angaisoi, asking for the acres of their king,
a hereditary treasure of plough-land.   1060
Savage men shall bury them alive in a black grave
in the recesses of a hollow pit.
With no obsequies, the Daunians will erect over their corpses
a tomb with a roof of piled-up stones,
so giving them the land which they asked to have,   1065
the land of the son of the fearless brain-eating boar.*

Phokians will settle in south Italian Bruttium

The sailors of the descendants of Naubolos*
shall come to Temessa, where the harsh horn of cape Hipponion
hangs down towards Tethys
of Lampete. Instead of the boundaries of Krisa   1070
they shall, on the other side of the sea, plough the Krotoniate
furrow with a dragged blade coupled to the oxen.
They will yearn for their fatherland Lilaia and the plain
of Anemoreia, Amphissa, and famous Abai.

Setaia's story

Unhappy Setaia, a miserable fate awaits you*   1075
on the rocks, where you will die a pitiful death,
in chains of bronze pinioning
your outstretched arms, because you set fire to the ships of
        your masters.
Near the Krathis you will lament your body, thrown out
to hang in mid-air for the bloody vultures.   1080
That crag which looks out over the sea will bear your name
and be called after your fate.

Other Greeks will settle in Italian Lucania

Others will sail out near the Pelasgian streams of Membles*
and the Kerneatid island;

1058–9 **Salangoi, Angaisoi** Italian (Daunian) places

1066 **son of the boar** Diomedes, son of Tydeus

1070 **Krisa** Delphi

1073–4 **Lilaia . . . Abai** Phokian places

they will settle beyond the Tyrrhenian strait,   1085
in the Leukanian plains by the swirling waters of Lametos.

Recapitulation

So griefs and various disasters shall grip them,*
as they mourn their destiny of no return,
the requital for my ill-wedded violation.

Nauplios' revenge on the Greeks who do return

Not even those who joyfully arrive home at last*   1090
will light votive flames of sacrifice,
paying thanks to Kerdylas, the Larynthian.
With such tricks the home-wrecking hedgehog
will deceive the embittered house-bound hens
of the cockerels. But his hostile ship-destroying   1095
beacons will not put an end to his grief
for his murdered son, whom a newly dug grave
will one day hide in the territory of Methymna.

Klytaimestra will murder Agamemnon. . .

One in his bath will seek a difficult way of escape*
from the noose round his neck;   1100
entangled in a net,
he will search with blind hands among the tasselled stitches.
He will leap towards the hot roof of the bath-chamber
and sprinkle the tripod and basin with his brains,
struck through the middle of his skull by the sharp axe.   1105
His sad ghost will flutter towards Tainaron,
as it sees the baleful house-keeping of the lioness.

. . . and Kassandra herself; Orestes' revenge

And I shall lie on the ground close by the bathtub,*
shattered by a Chalybian blade,
when, just as a pine-trunk or the bole of an oak-tree   1110

1092 **Kerdylas, the Larynthian** Zeus
1093 **hedgehog** Nauplios
1097 **his son** Palamedes
1098 **Methymna** Lesbos
1106 **Tainaron** the underworld
1107 **the lioness** Klytaimestra
1109 **Chalybian** a Black Sea people

is split by a woodcutting workman on the mountains,
she splits my broad neck-muscles and my back,
tearing my cold corpse all over with bloody wounds.
The thirst-viper will trample on my neck
and sate her passion full of wild fury;   1115
as if I were an adulteress, not a spear-won prize,
the jealous woman takes her revenge pitilessly.
And I, crying out to my lord and husband, who does not hear me,
will hurry on his tracks, floating aloft on wings.
But the whelp who seeks out the bloody fate of his father   1120
shall as murderer bathe his sword in the innards of the viper,
healing with ill the ill pollution of kin-killing.*

    Cult of Agamemnon at Sparta, and of Kassandra in Italian Daunia
But my husband, lord of the slave girl,*
shall be called Zeus by wily Spartans,
and receive the greatest honours from the sons of Oibalos.   1125
Nor shall my own cult be at all obscure among men,
or wither away in forgetful darkness.
The best of the Daunians shall build a temple for me
by the banks of Salpe, they who dwell in the city of Dardanos,
and live next to the waters of the marsh.   1130
And maidens, when they wish to escape the yoke
of marriage, refusing husbands
who glory in their Hektor-like haircuts
but have some stain of body or family disgrace,
shall clutch my statue in their arms,   1135
gaining a powerful defence against marriage.
They will dress like the Erinyes and dye their faces
with the juice of magic plants.
Among these rod-bearing women
I shall be called an immortal god for ever.   1140
    The tribute of the Lokrian Maidens, sent to Troy (Ilion)
But I shall cause grief to many women in the future,*

1114 **thirst-viper** Klytaimestra
1120 **the whelp** Orestes
1125 **sons of Oibalos** Spartans
1137 **Erinyes** the Eumenides or Furies

bereft of their maiden daughters. They will long bewail the
  commander,
the breaker of sexual law, the thief of the Kyprian goddess;*
they shall send their girls to a hostile place,
deprived of wedlock.   1145
O Larymna, Spercheios, Boagrios,
Kynos, Skarpheia, and Phalorias,
and the citadel of Naryx, and the streets of Lokrian*
Thronion, and the valleys of Pyronai,
and all the Hodoidokian house of Oileus!   1150
All of you, because of his impious sexual intercourse with me,
will pay requital to Gygaia, the Agriskan goddess,
for a thousand-year period, nurturing until old age
the unmarried maidens, chosen by the arbitrament of the lot.
Foreigners in a foreign land, their sad grave, without obsequies,   1155
shall be washed away by the sandy breakers;
then shall Hephaistos burn their limbs with logs
from barren trees, and shall sprinkle into the sea
the ashes of her who perished by leaping from Traron's peaks.
Others, like women about to die, shall arrive by night   1160
at the fields of the daughter of Sithon,
peering round for secret out-of-the-way paths,
until they are able to run into the house of Ampheira,
and kneel in prayer as supplicants to Stheneia.
They shall sweep and decorate the goddess's sacred ground   1165
with pure water, escaping the hateful anger
of the citizens. For every man of Ilion
will be watching out for the maidens, holding a stone in his hands,
or a black sword, or a hefty
bull-killing axe, or a Phalakraian club,   1170

1142–3 commander . . . thief Lokrian (or 'Oilean') Ajax
1143 **Kyprian goddess** Aphrodite
1146–50 **Larymna . . . Oileus** Lokrian places
1152 **Gygaia, the Agriskan goddess** Athena
1157 **Hephaistos** fire
1159–61 **Traron . . . Sithon** places in the Troy region
1163–4 **Ampheira, Stheneia** Athena
1170 **Phalakraian** Trojan

keen to satisfy his hand which thirsts for blood.
The people shall, by an inscribed law, honour the slayer*
of that degraded race, and grant him immunity.

Hekabe's fate

O mother, wretched mother! Your fame, too*
will not be unknown. The daughter of Perses,   1175
Brimo, the Three-formed, will make you her follower,
so that you will terrify mortals with your nightly howls,
all those who do not pay torch-bearing reverence to the statues
of the queen of Strymon, the Zerynthian,
placating the Pheraian goddess with sacrifices.   1180
Pachynos, the peninsular promontory,
will hold your majestic cenotaph,
built by your master's hands as a result of dreams,*
after paying funerary rites to you by the streams of Heloros.
He will sprinkle libations by its banks to you, the miserable one;   1185
he will be fearful of the anger of the three-headed goddess.
Because he threw the first stone at you,
he will begin the black sacrifice to Hades.

Hektor's cult at Boiotian Thebes

As for you, my brother, my heart's most beloved,*
pillar of the house and of our entire fatherland,   1190
it will not be in vain that you will make red the altar-base
with the blood of bulls, giving many first-offerings of sacrifice
to the king of the throne of Ophion.*
No, he will bring you to his birthplace,
the city which is celebrated above all others by the Greeks.   1195
There his mother, the experienced wrestler,
she who threw the previous queen down to Tartaros,

1175–6 daughter of Perses, three-formed, 1179–80 queen of Strymon ...
    Pheraian goddess Hekate

1181 Pachynos, 1184 Heloros Sicily

1183 your master, 1185 he Odysseus

1186 three-headed goddess Hekate

1193 the king ... Zeus

1194 his birthplace Thebes

1196 his mother Rhea

1197 previous queen Eurynome, Tartaros the underworld

ended the pains of his secret birth.
So she averted the impious child-eating banquet
of her spouse, who was therefore not able to satisfy his belly   1200
with food. Instead, he gulped down a stone,
wrapped in limb-binding swaddling-clothes.
The savage Centaur became the tomb of his own offspring.
As a great hero, you will dwell on the Islands of the Blest,*
a helper against the arrows of plague,   1205
when the Sown People of Ogygos, obedient to the*
oracles of the Doctor-god, the Lepsian, the Terminthian,
lift you out of his grave at Ophryneion and bring you
to the tower of Kalydnos and the Aonian land
to be a Saviour, when they are hard pressed by a hoplite army   1210
ravaging the land and the temples of Teneros.
The Ektenian chiefs will celebrate your great fame
with libations, making it equal to the immortal gods.

    The troubles of Idomeneus, king of Krete
My wretched calamity will penetrate to Knossos and the*
dwellings of Gortyn, and the whole house of their army-leaders   1215
shall be overthrown. For in no peaceful way will the fisherman
row and steer his two-oared boat.
He will agitate Leukos, guardian of the kingdom,
inflaming his hatred with lying tricks.
He will not spare his children, nor his wedded   1220
wife Meda, in his wild anger,
nor his daughter Kleisithera, whose father will give her
in bitter marriage to the snake whom he reared.
He will kill them all with impure hands
tortured and mutilated in the Onkaian pit.   1225

1200 **her spouse,** 1203 **savage Centaur** Kronos
1206 **Sown People of Ogygos** Thebans
1207 **Doctor-god . . . Terminthian** Apollo
1208 **Ophryneion** Troy
1209–12 **tower of Kalydnos . . . Ektenian chiefs** Thebes, Boiotians
1216 **the fisherman** Nauplios
1222–3 **father** Idomeneus, **snake** Leukos

Rome's greatness foretold.

The glory of the race of my grandfathers*
will be greatly increased by their descendants.
With their spears, they will win the victory-wreath and the
    first-spoils,
taking sceptre and kingship over land and sea.
Nor, my miserable fatherland,   1230
will you hide your renown, withered away in darkness.
My kinsman will leave behind him such twin*
lion-whelps—a race of outstanding strength—
he who is the offspring of the Kastnian and the Choiras,
best in counsel, and far from contemptible in battle.   1235

Aineias' wanderings

He will first go to Rhaikelos and settle there,*
by the tall peak of Kissos and the horn-wearing Laphystian
women. From Almopia, Tyrrhenia will receive
the man who wanders to and fro,
and the river Lingeus which gushes out its stream of warm waters;   1240
and Pisa, and the sheep-rich groves of Agylla.
An enemy will join him with a friendly army,*
compelling him with oaths and prayers of supplication,
a dwarf, who had explored every nook of
sea and land. With him the two sons   1245
of the king of the Mysians, whose spear the Home-keeper,
the Wine-god, will bend, after tying together his limbs with tendrils,
Tarchon and Tyrrhenos, fierce wolves,
born from the blood of Herakles.

1232 **my kinsman** Aineias

1232–3 **twin lion-whelps** Romulus and Remus

1234 **Kastian and Choiras** Aphrodite

1236–8 **Rhaikelos . . . Almopia** Macedonian places

1238 **Tyrrhenia** Etruria

1239 **man who wanders** Aineias

1240 **Lingeus** river Arno or Serchio

1241 **Agylla** Caere

1242 **an enemy, 1244 a dwarf** Odysseus

1245 **the two sons** Tarchon and Tyrrhenos

1246 **king of the Mysians** Telephos

1246–7 **Home-keeper, Wine-god** Dionysos

There he will find a food-laden table,*
which will be eaten later by his companions;
this will remind him of old oracles.
He will found a place in the regions of the Aborigines,*
beyond the settlements of the Latins and Daunians:
thirty towers, numbered after the offspring   1255
of the dark sow, which he will have brought by ship
from the peaks of Ida and the Dardanian regions,
the nurse of that same number of piglets, all from one litter.
In one of those cities he will dedicate an image of her
and her suckling brood, crafting it in bronze.   1260
He will build a temple to the Myndian and Pallenian goddess,
where he will house the statues of his ancestral gods,
to which, abandoning his wife and his children
and all his wealthy store of treasure,
he will give preference, and to his aged father,   1265
after wrapping them in clothing. At that time the warlike hounds,
distributing all the spoils of his fatherland by lot,
will give to him alone the choice, so as to take and carry off
from his house whatever gift he pleases.
For this he will be judged most pious even by his enemies,   1270
and he will found a new fatherland, which will win much
     martial praise,
and be prosperous in future generations:
a tower and upland groves near Kirke,*
and great Aietes, famous harbour of the *Argo*,
and the lake of Phorke, the Marsionic waters,   1275
and the Titonian river, where a cavern plunges beneath the earth
into the invisible depths,
and the hill of Zosterios, the gloomy dwelling-place

1257 **Ida** . . . Troy

1259 **one of those cities** Lavinium

1261 **Myndian and Pallenian goddess** Athena/Minerva

1265 **aged father** Anchises

1266 **warlike hounds** the Greeks at Troy

1271 **new fatherland** Rome

1273–6 **Kirke** . . . **Titonian river** places in Latium

1278 **Zosterios** Apollo

of the maiden Sibyl,
roofed over by a hollow cave.   1280

   Recapitulation
Such are the woes, hard to bear, which they will suffer,*
they who will destroy my fatherland.

   Asia against Europe
What has the wretched mother of Prometheus
in common with the nurse of Sarpedon?
The Hellespont and the Symplegades,   1285
and Salmydesos, separate them, and the inhospitable sea,
neighbour to Skythia, with its hard ice;
the Tanais river divides them, slicing its way
with pure streams through the lake which is dear to the
      Maiotian people,
who lament the chilblains on their feet.   1290

   Abduction of Io by Phoenicians
First of all, perish the Karnitan sailor-dogs!*
They abducted the ox-eyed bull-maiden, the virgin,
from Lerna, merchant-wolves that they were,
to lead her off as a ruinous wife for the Memphian lord:
they lifted up a torch of enmity for the two continents.   1295

   Abduction of Europa by Kretans
For next, the Kouretes, the boars of Ida, seeking reprisals*
for the abduction committed by a grave act of wanton violence,
dragged off a Saraptian girl
as prisoner, in a ship with a bull-shaped ensign,
to the Diktaian palace,   1300

1283 **mother of Prometheus** Asia
1284 **nurse of Sarpedon** Europe
1286 **Salmydesos** Black (Euxine) Sea
1288 **Tanais** river Don
1289 **Maiotian lake** Sea of Azov
1291 **Karnitan** Phoenician
1293 **Lerna** Argos
1294 **Memphian** Egyptian
1296 **Kouretes, boars of Ida** Kretans
1298 **Saraptian** Phoenician

to be a bride for Asteros the Kretan commander.
Nor were they satisfied with taking like for like,
but they sent a plundering army with Teukros,
and Skamandros, his Rhaukian father,
to found a Bebrykian settlement   1305
and fight against mice. From their offspring
Dardanos fathered my ancestors,
after marrying Arisba, the noble-born Kretan.

   Abduction of Medea by Jason and the Argonauts
Second, they sent out the Atrakian wolves*
under their one-sandalled *tagos*, to steal the fleece,   1310
which was protected by the watchfulness of the dragon-guard.
He came to Libystikan Kytaia,
and put the four-nostrilled serpent to sleep with drugs.
He it was who held the curved plough of the fire-breathing
bulls; and his body was chopped up in a cauldron.   1315
Fearfully he grabbed the fleece of the ram;
but he snatched up the self-invited crow,
the brother-killer and child-murderer,
and put her as ballast onto the talking jay,*
which uttered a human cry from the Chaonian   1320
ship-timbers, and itself knew the route.

   Theseus and Herakles abduct Antiope; the Amazons retaliate
Next, he who extracted from under the rock*
his father's shoes and dagger-belt and sword—
the son of Phemios, whose sad grave
below the roaring precipices, the site of his unburied fall,   1325
will long be watched over by Skyros, the place too steep
      even for goats—

1304–5 **Skamandros . . . Bebrykian** Troy, Trojan
1309 **Atrakian** Thessalian
1312 **Kytaia** Kolchis
1317 **crow** Medea
1319 **talking jay** the ship *Argo*
1320 **Chaonian** from Dodona
1323 **his father** Aigeus
1324 **Phemios** Poseidon

he came with the beast, the initiate, who was suckled*
by the plump breast of his enemy Tropaia.
He, the thief of the war-belt, stirred up a double quarrel:
he took away the baldric, and he stole Orthosia   1330
from Themiskyra, she who subdued with the bow.
Her sisters, the virgins of Nepounis,
left Eris, Lagmos, and Telamos,
and the river Thermodon, and the Aktaian mountain,
seeking implacable vengeance and pillage.   1335
They drove their Skythian horses across the dark Danube,
uttering their threatening war-cries
against the Graikoi and the descendants of Erechtheus;
they devastated all Akte with the spear,
and set fire to the land of Mopsops.   1340

   Ilos devastates Thrace; Herakles sacks Troy
Then my ancestor, after devastating the level lands of Thrace,*
and the territory of the Eordoi and the plain of the Galadraioi,
fixed his boundaries at the waters of the Peneios,
placing a firm yoke on their necks, securing it with fetters;
he was young, strong, and the outstanding man of all his line.   1345
Then Europe, in reprisal for this, sent the herdsman
as helper, leading his six ships, and clad in the animal's hide.
He overthrew our high citadel with his mattocks;
Gorgas, author of all his troubles, relented
and deified him in the dwelling-place of the gods.   1350

   *The Lydians Tarchon and Tyrrhenos make conquests in
   central Italy*
Next the falcons, leaving Tmolos*

1327 **the beast** Herakles
1328 **Tropaia** Hera
1330 **Orthosia** an Amazon
1332 **Nepounis** Artemis
1333-4 **Eris . . . Aktaian mountain** Skythian places
1338-40 **Graikoi . . . Mopsops** Athens and Attica
1342 **Eordoi . . . Galadraioi** Macedonians
1346 **the herdsman** Herakles
1349 **Gorgas** Hera

and Kimpsos and the gold-producing streams of Paktolos,
and the waters of the lake, where the wife of Typhon
sleeps in the grim recess of her cave,
came bursting in on Ausonian Agylla.   1355
They joined in the dreadful wrestling of the spear-fight,
with Ligustinians and those who took their roots
from the blood of Sithonian giants.
They captured Pisa, and subjected all the
spear-won territory which stands as neighbour to the Umbrians   1360
and the craggy hills of the Salpians.*

Trojan Paris rekindles conflict (by stealing Helen)
Last, the firebrand wakens the old quarrel,*
setting light with his flame to the previously sleeping fire,
when he saw the Pelasgians with their foreign urns
drawing water from the streams of Rhyndakos.   1365
Then Europe, in furious revenge,
shall exact threefold, fourfold damage as requital,
devastating the shore of the land over the sea.

*Four Greek acts of aggression against Asia: (1) Agamemnon
and the Trojan War*
The first to come will be the Zeus who has the same name*
as Zeus Lapersios, who will descend like a thunderbolt   1370
and burn all the dwellings of the enemy.
I will die with him, and then, tossed around among the dead,
I will hear everything that I am now about to narrate.

*(2) Agamemnon's son Orestes attacks and colonizes the Aiolid
(NW Asia Minor)*
The second will be the son of the man who was killed*
in the nets, like a dumb fish.   1375
He will incinerate a foreign land, coming with a polyglot army
in accordance with the oracles of the Doctor-god.

(3) Neileos of Athens, son of Kodros, founds Ionian Miletos by force
The third, son of the woodcutting king*

1357 **Ligustinians** Ligurians
1364 **Pelasgians** the Argonauts
1369–70 **Zeus . . . Lapersios** Agamemnon
1377 **Doctor-god** Apollo

who deceived the Branchesian maiden
into handing him a piece of earth mixed with water—   1380
the gift which he desired,
so as to put the seal of his ring on a tablet—
he will establish his mountainous monarchy over Phtheiroi,
after slaughtering the army of the Karians, the first mercenaries.
At that time his lewd daughter, snarling mockery   1385
at her own genitals, will revile marriage,
saying she will have a wedding in the brothels of the barbarians.

(4) Greeks settle in Dorian (SW) Asia Minor

The fourth are the descendants of Dymas,*
Lakmonians and Kytinaians, 'kodrians' all,
who will occupy Thigros and Mount Satnion,   1390
and the tip of the peninsula of him
whom Kyrita altogether hated:
parent of the cunning vixen
who took every shape, and by her daily wages
eased the mighty hunger of her father   1395
Aithon, who tilled foreign lands with his ploughshare.

Midas invades Thrace and Macedonia

After that the Phrygian, in revenge for fraternal blood,*
shall in reprisal sack the land which had nursed
the lord of the dead, who pronounces incorruptible judgements
over the dead, inexorably.   1400
One day he will slice off at the roots the ears of the donkey
and will adorn his own ear-lobes,
so instilling fear into the blood-sucking feasters.

1379 **Branchesian** Milesian
1383 **Phtheiroi** Mt Latmos
1388–9 **descendants of Dymas…'kodrians all'** Dorians
1390 **Thigros and Mount Satnion** Karian places
1391 **peninsula** Knidos region, **him** Erysichthon
1392 **Kyrita** Demeter
1393 **cunning vixen** Mestra
1395–6 **her father** Erysichthon
1399 **lord of the dead** Minos

All the land of Phlegra will be enslaved by him,
and the ridge of Thrambous and the coastal   1405
rock of Titon, and the fields of the Sithonians,
and the ploughed land of Pallene, which ox-horned
Brychon fertilizes, the Giants' helper.
    Transition
Many woes, dealt by each side in turn, will be taken as
    first-offerings*
by Kandaios or Mamertos, or whatever one should call him,   1410
the one who gorges on bloody battles.
    *Asia sends Xerxes to invade Greece and sack Athens; he
    returns in failure*
But the mother of Epimetheus will not yield.*
In reprisal for everything, she will send a single giant
of the seed of Perseus, who will walk on foot
over the sea, and will sail over the land,   1415
breaking the dry land with oars. And the temple of Laphria,*
who is also Mamersa, burnt down in flames,
together with the wooden bulwarks of the walls,
will blame the seer for the damage,
because he, the servant of Plouton, falsely uttered prophecy. 1420
Everything will be eaten by that savage army,
shedding its double coating of bark:
both the fruit-bearing oak and the wild mountain-growing tree.
The waters of every torrent will be dried up,
as the troops quench their black thirst with gaping mouths.   1425
They will raise clouds of whizzing arrows from afar
over their heads; and like Kimmerian gloom,
the shadow will hide the sun, and dim its brightness.
Like a Lokrian rose, he will bloom for a brief moment;*
and then, burning everything like dry corn,   1430
he will taste of flight as he sails back home,
dreading the wooden wall of oak, peering at it from near at hand,
as a girl dreads the dusky twilight,
terrified by a sword of bronze.

1404–7 **Phlegra . . . Pallene** places in Chalkidike (N. Greece)

1410–11 **Kandaios or Mamertos . . . battles** Ares

1416–17 **Laphria . . . Mamersa** Athena

1420 **Plouton** Hades

Kassandra's final prophecy: the Roman kinsman-wrestler
will end the conflict

Many struggles, and much slaughter in the interval,*   1435
shall loosen the wrestling-hold of those who compete for hegemony,
both on the eddying waves of the Aegean
and on the ox-turned ridges of the land,
until a fierce lion put to sleep the grave conflict—
one born from Aiakos and from Dardanos,   1440
both a Thesprotian and a Chalastraian.
He will overturn and lay low the house of his brothers,
and force the trembling Argive leaders
to fawn on the wolf-commander of Galadra,
and hand over the sceptre of the ancient kingship.   1445
With him, after six generations, my kinsman,
a unique wrestler, after joining in a spear-fight,
shall come to an agreement of reconciliation about sea and land,*
and be celebrated as the greatest among his friends,
taking the first offerings of the spear-won spoils.   1450

Kassandra's farewell

But why, wretch that I am, do I cry at such length to the
    unhearing rocks,*
and the dumb waves, and the frightful woods,
twanging my mouth's empty noise?
The Lepsian robbed me of my credibility,
smearing with untrue libels my utterances   1455
and the true prophetic skill of my oracles,
because he was deprived of my bed which he so desired.
But he will make it all true: after they have learnt through suffering,
at a time when there is no remedy to help my fatherland,
men will praise the inspired swallow."   1460

The guard's final report to Priam

That is what she said; then off she went on foot,*
back into her prison. In her heart
she moaned the last song of the Siren,

1439 **fierce lion** Alexander the Great
1446–7 **with him** Philip V of Macedon? **my kinsman** Titus Quinctius Flamininus?
1454 **Lepsian** Apollo

as a Mimallon of Klaros, or the interpreter of Melankraira,
daughter of Neso, or the Phikian monster,   1465
warbling her twisted and difficult utterances.
O king, I have come to report to you the crooked
utterances of the prophetic maiden,
because you posted me as guard of her stone cell,
and ordered me to tell and repeat every word truthfully,   1470
as a returning messenger.
But may the god bring her prophecies to a happier
outcome—the god who protects your throne—
and keep safe this ancient Bebrykian heritage!'*

1464–5 **Mimallon . . . Neso** Sibyls
1465 **Phikian monster** Sphinx
1474 **Bebrykian** Trojan

SYNOPSIS OF THE *ALEXANDRA*

1302–8	Kretan settlement on the site of Troy
1309–21	Jason and the Argonauts take Medea away from Kolchis
1322–40	Theseus and Herakles abduct Antiope; the Amazons retaliate by invading Attica
1341–50	Ilos devastates Thrace and Macedon, and Herakles sacks Troy
1351–61	Lydian conquests in central Italy
1362–5	Paris rekindles the flame of conflict
1366–8	Four acts of Greek aggression introduced
1369–73	(1) The Trojan War
1374–96	Aggressive Greek settlements in Asia Minor
1374–7	(2) Orestes colonizes the Aiolid (NW Asia Minor)
1378–87	(3) The Athenian Neileos son of Kodros founds Miletos
1388–96	(4) Greek settlement of Dorian Asia Minor
1397–1408	Midas of Phrygia invades Thrace and Macedonia
1409–11	Struggles between Europe and Asia from Midas to Xerxes
1412–34	Xerxes' invasion of Greece; its humiliating failure
1435–1450	Kassandra's final prophecy: the victorious kinsman-wrestler who will bring about reconciliation between the two sides and bring an end to the conflict
1451–60	Kassandra's farewell
1461–74	Epilogue: the guard's final report to King Priam

EXPLANATORY NOTES

1-30 The prologue plunges in with little explanation: the reader/hearer is expected to guess much, or wait for explanatory hints provided later—often much later—in the poem. The identity of the 'master' or 'king/lord' (3, 8) as Priam of Troy is revealed only at 19, and then indirectly (Tithonos is Priam's half-brother: their father was Laomedon). The 'maiden' of 3 is named at 30—but by her Spartan name, Alexandra, not her Homeric and usual name, Kassandra. Even when she foretells Priam's violent death at 335, she will not describe him as her father; and the guard uses two different Greek nouns to Priam for 'maiden' (3, 1468): neither need mean 'daughter'. At 1469 we will learn that she had been placed in a stone cell, and at 1462 that she goes back into the 'prison' from which, evidently, she emerged to deliver her long speech, though the prologue does not say so. Nor is the imprisonment ever explained: presumably her prophecies were considered too discouraging for general consumption. The guard opens with a promise to inform the king 'accurately' (1), but the Greek adverb is rare: it puts us on notice that this speaker's language will be as recondite as Kassandra's own; and since 'I will tell you everything' echoes both Aeschylus (*Prometheus* 609) and a Hellenistic tragedy about the Lydian king Gyges (*TrGF* 2 no. 664 line 13), he operates in a sophisticated literary tradition no less than does Kassandra. On the first word *lexō*, 'I shall speak', see 30n. But his warning that her speech will (unlike her unspecified earlier calm utterances, 3) be a 'confused cry' (5) is indirection: she speaks allusively yet—like Kassandra in Aeschylus' *Agamemnon*—not in barbarian ravings but good idiomatic Greek; and her mythical erudition is phenomenal. The guard's opening speech is in distinct halves of fifteen lines each; his final speech (1461-74) will at fourteen lines be almost exactly as long of one of these halves: it resembles 1-15, but not 16-30, in being in the first not third person singular. There are numerous verbal correspondences between the guard's opening and closing speeches. On the prologue, see McNelis and Sens, 47-66, and the detailed commentary on 1-30 (no tr.) by Sens alone in D. Sider (ed.), *Hellenistic Poetry, A Selection* (Ann Arbor, University of Michigan Press, 2017), 372-82; Pillinger, 114-20.

4 'Varied utterance' hints programmatically at Kassandra as Siren: 671-2n., 1463.

6-7 'Laurel' hints at Apollo, the god who gave Kassandra prophetic powers, but at 28 her prophecies will be associated with the frenzy of Dionysos/Bacchos. Both gods were thought to dwell at the oracular sanctuary of Delphi by a time-share arrangement. The word for 'cruel' literally means 'dark', and can also mean 'obscure'. It is a favourite of Lykophron, the 'dark poet' of riddles. See Sistakou, 131-90. The Sphinx, who will recur at 1465 as the 'Phikian monster', told a riddle, solved by Oidipous.

11 'Paths' is another ambiguous word, because it can also mean 'songs'.

13–15 For the 'running' or 'racing' metaphor in the poem, see McNelis and Sens, 51–3: it recurs, less obviously and elaborately, in the guard's final speech, see 1471n.

16–18 The personified Dawn, Eos, owned the magic winged horse Pegasos (17). She was married to Tithonos; see *OCD* 'Tithonus'. Priam and Tithonos were both sons of Laomedon, by Leukippe and Rhoio respectively: cf. 1–30n.

22 The sea-nymph Thetis, mother of Achilles, is 'the sea' by metonymy, as at Virgil *Eclogue* 4.32, *temptare Thetin ratibus* 'to venture on the sea with boats' (copied from Lykophron?) 'Maiden-killing' because Helle (see *OCD*) was drowned in the Helles-pont i.e. 'sea of Helle' when she fell off the ram carrying the Golden Fleece sought by the Argonauts, cf. 1309–21n.

29 *Atē* (two syllables, both long), 'Doom city', is Troy. Foundation myths often featured helpful animals or birds which guided settlers, like the sow which guided Aineias (Latin Aeneas) to Alba Longa, 1256–8. Cf. M. Leigh, 'Sophocles at Patavium', *Journal of Hellenic Studies* 118 (1998), 82–100.

30 'Alexandra' was Kassandra's name at Sparta according to literary sources (Pausanias 3.19.6) and inscriptions (*Syll.* 932, and potsherds from Amyklai near Sparta attesting her cult with Agamemnon, see 1124n.). But the name literally means 'she who wards off men': suitable for her virginity, 354. Finally, there may be a play on the poem's first word *lexō*, 'I shall speak'. In Greek, '*a-*' prefixes can express negation, but also intensification. Since she is not voiceless in the poem, we might prefer 'the [pre-eminent] speaker' i.e. 'prophetess'.

Such subtleties do not, however, fully explain why Lykophron uses a Spartan cult designation when the regular 'Kassandra' would have fitted the metre perfectly well. A satisfying explanation can be found in an omission later in the poem, where Kassandra mentions only Agamemnon's cult at Sparta, not her own, which she confines to Italian Daunia (mod. Puglia, SE Italy; cf. *Barrington Atlas* map 45 B–C 1–2, 'Daunii'): 1124, 1140. But 'Alexandra' in the present passage is a broad early hint at her Spartan cult, so not too much should be made of the later silence.

31 Kassandra begins with a lament for her 'nurse' (Troy), which turns out to be double, both retrospective and predictive: we expect her to lament Troy's sack by the Greeks under Agamemnon, an event which for her lies in the future; and so she does (cf. 52 for the second burning, prepared for here by 'before'). But she immediately harks back to an event which for her lies in the past: the first destruction of Troy, or rather its predecessor city Ilion, by Herakles (see also 1346–50): King Laomedon had refused to give him the mares he had promised (Homer, *Iliad* 5.640–2 and perhaps Kallimachos frag. 698). See also 33n.

Laments for cities were a favourite subject for epigrams, a genre with which Lykophron was surely familiar. One of the most famous such laments is for the Roman sack of Korinth in 146 BCE carried out by the Roman general Mummius: Antipater of Sidon, *Anth. Pal.* 9.151.

33 Zeus lengthened one night into three to make Alkmene pregnant with the super-strong Herakles, who went on to kill his own children when mad, **38**. The sea-monster was sent by Poseidon to punish King Laomedon for his failure to pay him and Apollo for building Troy's walls; cf. 'hired labourer' at **393**; cf. **521–2**. When Virgil wrote of Roman 'expiation of the perjury of Laomedon's Troy' (*Georgics* 1.502), he meant this, and perhaps also the king's dishonest treatment of Herakles, see **31**n. An oracle told Laomedon to give his daughter Hesione (**468–78**n.) to the monster as a sacrifice, but Herakles rescued her. She is not named or directly alluded to here, but will feature several times later, so she is the first of the poem's many innocent female victims of men. Kassandra here identifies Herakles with a lion, a common style of denomination in the poem. The habit owes a debt to epic, but there is a difference: in epic, lions and other creatures occur in similes, whereas Lykophron uses them metaphorically (with exceptions, cf. **115**n. on the humble mole at **121**. See McNelis and Sens, 26–38). There is a further influence: animal and bird metaphors were a traditional feature of oracular discourse (e.g. Herodotus 5.56), so it is appropriate that they should be favoured by the prophetic Kassandra. Lykophron's varied bestiary is an attractive feature of the poem.

36 The word for cauldron may also mean 'stomach'; if so, Lykophron perhaps borrowed it from the earlier Hellenistic poet Kerkidas: cf.: C. De Stefani, *Studi su Fenice di Colofone* (Hildesheim, G. Olms, 2018), 142 and n. 10.

39 Herakles wounded Hera, who had suckled him ('second mother'): *Iliad* 5.392–4. Cf. **1328**.

43 Ischenos is 'horse-frightener' Taraxippos, a malign hero who perhaps featured in race-track curses: J. G. Howie, *Exemplum and Myth* (Prenton, Francis Cairns Publications, 2012), 206–13. Heroes (in the technical religious sense; see *OCD* 'hero-cult') were often place-specific—here Olympia—but this one has definite attributes also.

44–8 'Ausonia' and related words are common, metrically handy, terms for 'Italy'. The western angle, so important in the poem, here makes an early if casual appearance. Skylla and her opposite number Charybdis (**668–9**n.) were believed to live on rocks straddling the straits of Messina between Italy and Sicily: Thucydides 4.24.5. Skylla's father was Phorkys, who restored her to life by burning her flesh, so she no longer feared the goddess of the underworld Persephone ('Leptynis', **49**).

50 This refers riddlingly to the death of Herakles, to whose wife Deianeira the dying centaur Nessos gave a love-philtre for him which was really poison, hence 'swordless deception'.

52–6 Kassandra lists three requirements for the second and main fall of Troy: (i) an Aiakid family member (i.e. descended from Aiakos), either Epeios who built the Wooden Horse full of hidden Greek warriors by which Troy was captured (**930–50**n.), or, less likely, Achilles' son Neoptolemos, great-grandson of Aiakos (**184**; Achilles himself will die before the fall of Troy); (ii) Pelops' bones; (iii) Herakles' bow, which he gives to the Greek

Philoktetes, who (913) uses it to shoot and kill Paris ('herdsman' because he was a shepherd on Mt Ida when he judged the beauty of the three goddesses, 91–3). For Pelops and his father Tantalos (53), see 152–67n.

57–68 The sense of 57 is that Oinone, by contributing to Paris' death because she initially refused to use her medical knowledge to heal him from the arrow-wound, and then relented too late, will 'bring to light' i.e. fulfil prophecy (iii) at 52–6n. After this she will kill herself in remorse. She is (like Hesione) another of the many injured women in the poem, so Kassandra withholds explicit negative judgement, and her unspecific language plays down Oinone's role as part-author of Troy's downfall. The background is that in rage at her rejection in favour of Helen, Oinone had sent Korythos, her son by Paris, to spy for the Greeks. Her angry father (59) was Kebren. The story was known to the fifth-century BCE prose mythographer Hellanikos, *EGM* 1 frag. 29; but Oinone enters the ancient poetic mainstream only after Lykophron. Parthenios, *Sufferings in Love* 4 and 34, gives the full story; cf. also Ovid, *Heroides* 5—in which Kassandra is given a short but very Lykophronic speech—and *Anth. Pal.* 2.215–21, part of a late epigram. Tennyson's melancholy poem *Oenone* ends with her resolving to go 'down into Troy' (from Mt Ida) and 'talk with the wild Cassandra'.

69–85 The story of 'diver' Dardanos, son of Elektra (not the famous daughter of Agamemnon and Klytaimestra, Orestes' sister) and early king-founder of Troy, is attached to the lament by a tenuous thread: he was buried there. He fled Samothrace in a desperate solitary sea-voyage, when the island suffered a cataclysmic deluge like the floods of Noah or Deukalion. The story may reflect dim memories of emigration to the mainland. Lines 84–6 are an impossibility, modelled on exaggerated rhetoric like the start of the speech at Herodotus 5.92: 'fishes will change places with men! (if you do this)'.

Why the bird of the simile at 76 should be Kretan ('Rhithymnos') is unexplained.

71 A terrifying line: the tiny monosyllabic Greek word for fire is followed by two huge five-syllable words, enacting the rapid, all-consuming spread of the conflagration which devoured Troy. For the importance of the fire theme in the poem, usually about Troy, see esp. 249, 340–7n. (two occurrences), 970, 1340 (Attica), and cf. 86–9n.; cf. Pillinger, 122–3.

86–9 Fire again, 71n. Hekabe dreamed she gave birth to a firebrand, which was interpreted as her and Priam's disastrous son Paris (cf. 219–28n., 913 with 911–29n., 1362–8n.). The dream was not in Homer, nor in what survives of the *Kypria*, part of the post-Homeric Epic Cycle of poems (Introduction, *Sources*), although Holzinger thought it might have featured there. The dream is first attested for certain in Euripides, *Trojan Women* 922, then in mythographers later than Lykophron. Pindar (*Paian* 8A Rutherford) made Hekabe dream of fire, but not of a firebrand specifically.

The egg-shell of 89 means that Helen of Sparta (Messenian Pephnos was in Spartan territory) was born from an egg, either as daughter of

Leda, raped by Zeus in the form of a swan (the usual version, cf. **504–68n.** for her brothers the Dioskouroi); or else (the *Kypria*) as daughter of Nemesis, metamorphosed into a goose ('aquatic vulture'). Lykophron's language ('gave birth') suits the second and rarer version better: the poem often prefers non-standard versions of myths, cf. **103n.**

94–143 Sequence and itinerary are complicated by the poet's need to hold in his hand several threads of myth, which are neither made explicit nor easily reconciled: Paris went from Troy to Sparta (**94–7**), abducted Helen (see Edmunds), and had sex with her on an island ('Dragon's island') near Attica or 'Akte' (**110–11**); he took a phantom of her to Troy (**141–2**; this goes back to the sixth-century poet Stesichoros); she was whisked away to Egypt by Proteus (next section). At **108**, Skandeia is on Kythera (an island off Sparta), but Aigilon (Antikythera) is between Kythera and Krete, which reads like a trace of an out-of-sequence journey to Egypt.

97 Phereklos built the ships on which Paris brought Helen to Troy: *Iliad* 5.59–63.

103 Helen's daughters are (i) Hermione by Menelaos and (ii) Iphigeneia by Theseus (usually said to be the daughter of Agamemnon and Klytaimestra). The variant denies Klytaimestra an understandable revenge motive for killing her husband, who on the standard version sacrificed Iphigeneia to obtain favourable winds for the Greek fleet, cf. **183**).

115–43 The Proteus excursus is motivated by his removal of Helen to Egypt and safety, out of disapproval of Paris' abduction and abuse of Trojan hospitality, **132–8**, cf. **847–51n.** This role for Proteus derives from a favourite author of Lykophron, Herodotus (2.112–16), for whom Proteus is king of Egypt. Lykophron combines this Proteus with a mythical Old Man of the Sea, son of Poseidon (this paternity was a riddle, *Anth. Pal.* 11.347.4, to which Lykophron thus provides the answer). A native of Egypt, Proteus went to Thrace and married Torone (eponym of a city on the central Chalkidike peninsula Sithone, inaccurately called Pallene at **127**: *Barrington Atlas* map 57 B2). Their sons killed travellers until themselves killed by Herakles. Proteus could neither rejoice at nor regret this just retribution (**116–18**). Poseidon allowed him to return to Egypt under the sea, 'like a mole' (**121**); the humble simile is a departure from epic: McNelis and Sens, 29. But (as they admit) not all epic animal-similes are grandiose. Stubborn fighter Ajax is compared to a donkey which, despite beatings by boys with sticks, will not leave a field until he has eaten his fill: *Iliad* 11.558–62. Gouneus (**128**) was a famously just Arab king, but the name also suggests Gonnoi in Thessaly (cf. **897–908n.** for a Thessalian Gouneus); 'Ichnaian' (**129**) was a Thessalian and Macedonian epithet for Themis.

133–5 This explains how Trojan Paris met Spartan Helen. Her husband Menelaos led a peace-time deputation to Troy in obedience to an oracle (**133**) which told the Spartans to cure a famine by honouring two ancient tombs there; this is the first of many oracular responses in the poem, and the oracular appeal is of a familiar type in Greek myth and real life also. Paris was Menelaos' host, and when Paris accidentally killed a fellow-Trojan, Antheus son of Antenor, Menelaos helped Paris by taking him back to Sparta. So Paris was guilty not only of wife-stealing but of ungrateful abuse of hospitality: he had eaten Menelaos' salt, **134** (the name Aigaion for the sea-god Poseidon implies 'salty'). A bear had nursed him, **138**.

143 Helen's descent is through her mother Leda from Pleuron, eponym of an Aitolian city.

150 Menelaos (husband no. 3) is half-Kretan because his maternal grandfather was Katreus king of Krete, son of Minos. Homer hints at Menelaos' Kretan connection at *Iliad* 3.232: he regularly entertained Idomeneus of Krete: A. Bowie, *Homer*, Iliad *III* (Cambridge, Cambridge University Press, 2019), 138. Menelaos is 'Karian' and 'barbarian' because Minos ruled over non-Greek Karia, Herodotus 1.171. For historical Karian-Kretan links, cf. e.g. R/O no. 55.

152–67 Of the epithets for Demeter at **152**, Erinys—usually a name for the Eumenides or Furies—was specifically Arkadian (Pausanias 8.25.4); cf. **1040–1n.** The Furies upheld justice (**404–7n.**), and Demeter was Thesmophoros, 'upholder of right'.

The Pelops excursus is prompted as follows. Menelaos was son of Atreus, and grandson of Hippodameia of Elis or Pisa ('Epeian', **151**, 'stone of Molpis', **159**) and Pelops. 'Grind smooth' means the chariots flatten the race-track of Elis (i.e. Olympia), but Molpis is obscure. Pelops' father Tantalos (**53**) killed his son and served him up to the gods, for obscure reasons (it was probably for this crime that he was punished eternally by being 'tantalized' in the underworld with out-of-reach food). Only Demeter, grieving for her daughter Persephone, absentmindedly ate Pelops' shoulder (**155**). Hermes revived him ('young twice', **156**), substituting an ivory prosthesis. Pelops won Hippodameia in a chariot-race against her father Oinomaos at Pisa, near Olympia ('Letrina', **158**, cf. **54**. Pelops' link with the area was part of the aetiology of the Olympic contest: Pindar, *Olympian* 1, cf. Kolde 2018). His charioteer Myrtilos' trickery prevailed over the speed of Oinomaos' horses, named at **166–7**. (Kassandra does not mind naming *animals*, cf. **347n.**, Porkes.) Pelops' father-in-law Oinomaos had decapitated all previous unsuccessful suitors but was now himself killed (**161–2**). Instead of rewarding Myrtilos, Pelops threw him into the sea ('Nereus' tomb'), which acquired the name 'Myrtoan': **164**. Myrtilos screamed a dying curse on Pelops' family (**165**). It took effect in Atreus' generation, notably with Klytaimestra's murder of his other son Agamemnon (**1099**), together with Kassandra. So the Pelops excursus does more than provide background information about Menelaos' genealogy: it foreshadows a key, climactic episode of the poem. For Menelaos himself see **820–76**.

168–70 That Deiphobos (husband no. 4), second only to Hektor as Trojan warrior (**170**), was married by Priam to Helen after Paris' death (**913**), goes back to the *Little Iliad* (part of the Epic Cycle, see Introduction, *Sources*). Virgil makes Helen betray Deiphobos to Menelaos at the fall of Troy (*Aeneid* 6.493–534). In the *Iliad* proper (22.227), Athena impersonates Deiphobos to lure Hektor to his doom. The 'falcon' brother is more likely to be Hektor than Paris. For such bird and animal metaphors for people see 33n.

171–7 Helen's fifth husband is Achilles; he later married Medea, who had previously loved Jason (175–6). Achilles' father Peleus had killed his own brother Phokos, so—like many homicides in Greek myth and history—he went into exile. His home was the island of Aigina (175), here, as at Herodotus 8.46, called by its old name Oinone (confusingly, so soon after the narrative about a different Oinone, Paris' wife). The ant-army assumes knowledge of Hesiod (frag. 145): Achilles' grandfather Aiakos was lonely, so he turned the ants of Aigina into 'men and deep-girdled women' and populated the island with them. This belongs to a category of foundation myths which entail metamorphosis into animals or birds; cf. the wasps at Cyprus (447) or Diomedes' birds (594–5); Aristophanes' *Birds* is a variant of this sort of colonial myth. See R. Buxton, *Forms of Astonishment: Greek Myths of Metamorphosis* (Oxford, Oxford University Press, 2009), 68–9. There are twenty-eight metamorphoses in the poem (full list at Hornblower 2015: 161–3). Their functions vary, but they all magically reverse reality. One key theme of Kassandra's speech is that of defeated Troy's glorious re-emergence as Rome (see Introduction, *Themes*), and this itself is a kind of—non-magical—metamorphosis; for something like this idea cf., for Ovid, A. Feldherr, in P. Hardie (ed.), *Cambridge Companion to Ovid* (Cambridge, Cambridge University Press, 2002), 168.

As often, Kassandra inverts Homer's presentation of Achilles: here he mopes after women, not only Helen but Iphigeneia: next section. In Homer he is a loner, emotionally self-sufficient except for his—not necessarily homo-erotic—love for Patroklos. The juxtaposition and contrast with Deiphobos, presented as a mighty warrior, is pointed: McNelis and Sens, 104.

178–9 Achilles' mother Thetis tried to make all her sons immortal by incinerating them; only Achilles escaped. The 'Achilles' heel' story (she dipped the baby in the Styx with the same intention, but held him by the heel) is first attested late, but may have been in the Epic Cycle: West 2013, 149–50. True heroes must not be invulnerable.

180–201 The grammatical subject changes without warning from Achilles to Paris. The Greeks, angry at Helen's abduction, are wasps (a typical metaphor, see on 33), whereas Paris is likened to a boy disturbing the wasps with smoke (a simile). The image recalls *Iliad* 16.257–65, Greeks compared to wasps irritated by children, but that was an elaborate simile throughout. Lykophron plays with the epic model, as often.

Probably only after his death (below), Achilles is located on the 'White Island' in the Black Sea (188–9), also called Euxine and here (186) Salmydesian. This tradition goes back to the *Aithiopis*, part of the Epic

Cycle, cf. Introduction, *Sources*. The 'Keltric river' (**189**) seems to be the
Danube, and 'Achilles' running-track' (**192-3**) is a historically attested
site. The religious truth behind this is the epigraphically well-attested cult
of Achilles in the Black Sea region: G. Hedreen, 'The Cult of Achilles in
the Black Sea', *Hesperia* 60 (1991), 313-33 and J. S. Burgess, *The Death
and Afterlife of Achilles* (Baltimore, Johns Hopkins University Press,
2009), 126-31; interesting votive disk at p. 130. He searches there for
Iphigeneia (seemingly sacrificed at Aulis by Agamemnon, **183**, but see
below), by whom at some point he fathered Neoptolemos, literally 'young
warrior', i.e. possessor of a 'warlike name', **184**. This adopts a minority
version: Neoptolemos' mother was usually Deidameia, a princess whom
Achilles met in his youth on Skyros: **185**, cf. **276-8n**. Lykophron here
elaborates hints in his sources that Iphigeneia was lured to Aulis by
a promise of marriage to Achilles. But Neoptolemos was an adult when
Troy fell (cf. **323-9n**.), and Iphigeneia's sacrifice or averted sacrifice
(below) happened just before the ten-year war began. So Achilles' sexual
relations with Iphigeneia must precede the events at Aulis by some years.
Some modern critics accept this, and conjecture that Achilles searched for
her in the Black Sea region on his way to Troy and the war. (Lykophron,
self-correcting the implication of **183**, now follows the tradition which
made the goddess Artemis rescue her from sacrifice and replace her with
a deer and take her to the Black Sea, **190-1**, cf. 'vanished' at **195**). The
main trouble with this timetable is that other literary traditions about
Achilles in the Black Sea placed him there only in an afterlife, and identified the White Island with the Islands of the Blest, home of the happy
virtuous shades (cf. **1204** for Hektor, where these islands are oddly placed
at inland Thebes!); for these other traditions see T. Gantz, *Early Greek
Myth* (Baltimore, Johns Hopkins University Press, 1993), 135. But
Kassandra is not offering a coherent biography, and strict chronology
should not be expected of her. She needs Iphigeneia as another example of
Achilles' unmanly yearning for unattainable women, so she amalgamates
two separate myths, both of which located Achilles and Iphigeneia roughly
in the Black Sea region: cf. **195-9n**.

195-9 Iphigeneia, rescued by Artemis (see **180-201n**.), was taken to Tauris
(Black Sea region) where she killed Greek visitors: Herodotus 4.103;
Euripides *Iphigeneia in Tauris*.

202-3 Kronos is a puzzle; we expect his son Zeus (*Iliad* 2.324), who sent a por-
tent of a serpent which killed a sparrow and its eight chicks, so Troy's siege
would take nine years.

204 'Second' oaths because they had sworn to Helen's mortal father Tyndareus
that they would avenge her abduction.

206-15 There was an earlier expedition by the Greeks against Troy. They were
pursued by Telephos, king of Mysia in the Troy region, but Dionysos
tripped him up on a vine (**213**) in return for pious sacrifices by Agamemnon:
211 (Kassandra suppresses Achilles' martial contribution to the rout of

Telephos: cf. **171–7n.**). The myth was recounted in the *Kypria* (Introduction, *Sources*), in the mostly lost *Telephos* of Euripides, and on the Great Altar at Mysian Pergamon. (But this does not mean that Lykophron wrote for one of the Attalid kings of Pergamon, or under any other royal patronage.) Dionysos' epithet 'Tripper-up' is a genuine cult title, attested epigraphically at Delphi (*SEG* 19.399): a rare example of a myth giving rise to a divine epithet. (Dionysos co-existed with Apollo at Delphi for part of the year, cf. **6–7n.** and **208**). See also **1242–9n.** The plethora of cult titles for the same god at **206–12** is typical of the poem. (F. Horn, 'Zu den Kulttiteln in Lykophrons *Alexandra*', *Hermes* 149 (2021), 166–76, sees the accumulations of different regional cult-epithets as an intended aid to the reader's understanding.) First-letter alphabetization has been detected in some of these clusters (e.g. the Greek words at **212**), which might indicate use of a mythological handbook: see McNelis and Sens, 38–46. But they acknowledge that any such principle is not implemented mechanically or consistently, and does not diminish the artistry with which particular epithets are chosen and arranged. Nor does it reduce the religious importance of the poem's reflection of cultic realities: this reflection goes well beyond choice of epithets.

219–28 Kassandra's prophetic mind's eye sees the Greeks sailing east against Troy; this will soon lead to a reworking of some of the action of the *Iliad*. Prylis and Aisakos are, unusually, named without equivocation, as minor characters sometimes are: the poet feels no urge to increase their obscurity. The first, son of Hermes, predicted that Troy would fall by means of the Wooden Horse; the second was a son of Priam who interpreted Hekabe's 'firebrand' dream as being about Paris (see **86–9n.**). The opening 'would that . . .' recalls e.g. the opening of Euripides' *Medea*, 'would that the Argo had never winged its way . . .'.

229 'Palaimon' here denotes tiny Tenedos, the island closest to Troy. A Palaimon received child-sacrifice there: Kallimachos frags. 91–2; hence 'baby-killer'. For his complicated story see *OCD* under 'Melicertes', his earlier name. There may be a connection with Phoenician Melqart because Phoenicians sacrificed children (but to Baal Hammon, Greek Kronos: J. Quinn, *In Search of the Phoenicians* (Princeton, Princeton University Press, 2018), 91–112).

232–9 Achilles' killing of Kyknos was listed by Pindar (*Isthmian* 5.39) among his exploits. It took place on Tenedos, which is the frail link with Palaimon/ Tenedos at **229**, and therefore with Achilles' progress towards Troy. Kyknos, king of Kolonai in the Troy region (Diodorus 5.83), was persuaded by a false accuser (Molpos, the 'piper', **234–5**) that his son Ten(n)es had raped his stepmother, from whom the accusation originated: a common type of wicked lustful stepmother pattern. So Kyknos cast him and his sister adrift with murderous intent (that is all that is meant by 'murderer' at **236**). The children were washed ashore on the island which became known as Tenedos after the boy's name, and Kyknos pursued them in remorse. So this is a foundation myth, one of many in the poem. Much later (1374–7), Kassandra will give an alternative foundation myth: Agamemnon's son Orestes settled the Aiolid (see 243–57n. for this region), including Lesbos—and presumably also nearby Tenedos, as explicitly in Pindar, *Nemean* 11. Many places, notably Boiotian Thebes, had more than one foundation myth, but more conventional authors tended to choose between them.

240–2 This is more than usually difficult, because it presupposes a variant paternity for Tennes as Apollo's son. Mnemon, 'Mr Mindful', was under orders from Achilles' mother Thetis (241) to *remind* Achilles not to kill any son of Apollo, or he himself would die soon after. But he forgot to warn him not to kill Tennes, so Achilles killed him too, 'the wretch'. There may once have been a version in which Thetis warned Achilles not to kill Hektor, who also had a variant or double father, Apollo as well as Priam (265): West 2013, 112. Cf. 307–13n.: Hektor's brother Troilos as son of Apollo.

243–57 The leap of Achilles ('Pelasgian' means from Thessaly) was famous, though not Homeric: his descendant Alexander the Great imitated it (Diodorus 17.17. The family of his mother Olympias of Epirus claimed descent from Achilles' son Neoptolemos). 'Myrina' here stands for Troy, by carefree geography. She was a compulsively city-founding Amazon who gave her name to Myrina in the Aiolid, an area some way south of Troy; for this foundation myth, see A. Ellis-Evans, *The Kingdom of Priam* (Oxford, Oxford University Press, 2019), 231 and 261 n. 35. This allusion neatly prepares for the role of the Amazons in the east–west conflicts at the end of the poem: 1332–40. At 249, the war-god Ares is, unusually for a god, named without equivocation (as also, sometimes, is Zeus).

246 The text of 'edge' is uncertain: on another reading, it might mean that Achilles was the 'last' to leap ashore, i.e. he was a coward. That is certainly the force of 279.

252–3 The striking simile was copied by Virgil, *Georgics* 2.142; perhaps Ennius (*Annals* 384) was the intermediary.

258–80 Kassandra here reprises Homer's *Iliad* (e.g. 266–8 allude to Achilles' dragging of Hektor's corpse), but with significant changes of order and nuance, as in her more fully developed '*Odyssey*', 648–819. Most conspicuously, her Achilles is a mercenary draft-dodger and coward; and see 266–7n. See however 856–65n. for a different nuance.

265 The Ptoan god is Apollo, named from his important Boiotian sanctuary the Ptoion (see *OCD*). See 240–2n. for the myth which made him son of Apollo as well as of Priam (she calls him 'brother' at 280 and 1189).

266–7 In Homer (*Iliad* 22.335–6, 354), Achilles threatens polluting maltreatment of Hektor's corpse, but the gods prevent it. Kassandra makes it happen for real (McNelis and Sens, 120), and ignores Achilles' reconciliation with Priam in *Iliad* 24. (Similarly, Kassandra erases the happy ending of Homer's *Odyssey*: 768–78n.) Her Achilles is not Homer's ultimately humane hero but the 'beast' or 'butcher' of modern feminist readings of the Troy myth: Christa Wolf's *Kassandra* (1983), or Pat Barker's *Silence of the Girls* (2018). For details see Introduction, *Reception; a Feminist Poem?*.

269–72 The verbs here are hard to disentangle, because they refer to the aftermaths of two separate deaths, those of Hektor and then Achilles himself, with an unflagged transition at **271**. At **269–70** (cf. 'corpse-seller' at **276**) Achilles sells *Hektor*'s body for a carefully weighed sum in gold (the river Paktolos in Lydia, **272**, was famously gold-bearing, Herodotus 5.101, cf. **1352**); this up-ends Homer, for whom Achilles cared nothing for ransom money, only for his wounded honour. At **271–2**, it is implied that the Trojans will sell *Achilles*' body after his killing by Paris.

273–5 Kassandra reverts to Homer. At *Odyssey* 24.73–5 (cf. 23.91–2), Agamemnon tells Achilles in the underworld that his mother Thetis, and Dionysos ('Bacchos', **273**), gave a splendid jar to hold his remains and those of Patroklos. The 'nymphs' (**274**) are the Muses of Helicon ('Bephyros') who are said to mourn Achilles at *Odyssey* 24.60.

276–8 A non-Homeric tradition (the mythographer Apollodoros, 3.13.8) made Thetis try to avert her young son's death at Troy by hiding him on the island of Skyros in female disguise; the transvestism was perhaps originally a myth of initiation by which temporary change of dress is a signifier for a new stage of life. Kassandra, as part of her blackening of Achilles, makes him, not his mother, responsible: M. Fantuzzi, *Achilles in Love* (Oxford, Oxford University Press, 2012), 38–42.

279 See **246**n.

281–306 Just as Kassandra writes down Achilles, so she writes up Hektor, dwelling patriotically on his successes in life. This entails a breathtaking illogicality: **283–95**n.

283–95 Although Hektor's corpse will be prodded with spears and jeered at by the Greeks ('Dorians'), as at *Iliad* 22.371–5, this will not go unpunished (**283**) because Hektor will set fire to their ships, *Iliad* 15.718–46. But this inverts Homer illogically: what Hektor did in life cannot be retribution for what he suffered in death.

307–13 Troilos hardly features in Homer: he is merely one of Priam's many sons, a mature 'fighter from the chariot' (*Iliad* 24.257). In Sophocles (frags. 618–35), Achilles surprised him when he was exercising horses; for this theme in art see R. R. R. Smith and C. H. Hallett, 'Troilos and Achilles, a Monumental Statue Group from Aphrodisias', *Journal of Roman Studies* 105 (2015), 124–82, discussing a then recently discovered marble statue group from W. Turkey. But Kassandra follows the *Kypria* (**86–9**n.), in which Achilles killed an extremely youthful Troilos in a temple of Apollo, his father: **313** (like Hektor and Tennes, **240–2**n., Troilos had double paternity).

The point of the paradoxical **309–12** is that Achilles is both killer and victim. He is subdued by love for Troilos; this may go back to the sixth-century poet Ibykos (Fantuzzi (**276–8**n.) 14–15. For this homoerotic version, see also J. Davidson, *The Greeks and Greek Love* (London, Weidenfeld

and Nicolson, 2007), 283–4. The sacrilegious killing in a temple anticipates Troilos' sister Kassandra's own violation under the statue of Athena
(**359**): Achilles is no better than Ajax. See also **335–6**n. (Priam).

Shakespeare's sources for the main plot of *Troilus and Cressida* were
medieval, not ancient.

309 The word for 'love-charm' (here only in the poem) is *iynx* or wryneck,
a bird tied to a wheel: *OCD* 'iynx'. Pindar (*Pythian* 4.214) used it of the
spell that made Jason fall disastrously in love with Medea, so the connotations are sinister, as in the magical refrain in Theocritus 2: 'iynx, draw that
man to my house', cf. the 'witch' epigram *Anth. Pal.* 5.205.

311–12 Achilles is further diminished by a hint of sexual impotence (Troilos is
'unpenetrated'): McNelis and Sens, 125.

316–22 That Laodike escaped violation and slavery—the usual fate of women
when a city was captured—by leaping into a cleft in the earth (cf. **497**) is
a rare variant myth. But it recurs, with close echo of Kassandra's language,
in an anonymous epigram, *Anth. Pal.* 7.564. A Hellenistic queen, wife of
the second-century BCE Macedonian king Perseus, was a famous historical Laodike; it has been suggested that Lykophron has her in mind.

The whore/heifer and her whelp at **319** and **321** are Killa (with whom
Priam had sex, though she was his relative by marriage) and her son.

318 The word for 'approaching' (lit. 'close-footed') was thought until recently
to be an invention of Lykophron (see Introduction, *Difficulty*, for the hun-
dreds of such '*hapax*' or 'once only' words in the poem). But it is now
attested at line 47 of a long inscribed Greek poem from Hellenistic Karia
by a poet called Hyssaldomos, which is similar in other ways to the
Alexandra: C. Marek and E. Zingg, *Asia Minor Studien* 90 (2018), 32. Our
knowledge of ancient Greek is not complete, and Lykophron's diction
may be less innovative than we think (or had Hyssaldomos read the
Alexandra?). Cf. Pellettieri, 137–9.

323–9 The passage certainly begins with the sacrifice of Priam's daughter
Polyxena by Neoptolemos (son of Iphis=Iphigeneia), a main theme of
Euripides' *Hekabe*, and cf. his *Trojan Women* 622–3: Achilles' ghost
demanded this, perhaps from frustrated sexual desire (a scholiast says he
was in love with her). But some details of **326–9** suggest Agamemnon's
sacrifice of Iphigeneia at Boiotian Aulis: U. von Wilamowitz, *Kleine
Schriften* 6 (Berlin, Akademie-Verlag, 1972), 200–1. A double allusion is
possible, the poet's idea being to set up a parallel between the two virgin
sacrifices.

328 Kandaon (or Kandaios) will be the war-god Ares at **938** and **1410**, but is
probably here Hephaistos, who gave the sword to Peleus, from whom it
passed to Achilles then Neoptolemos, its 'three owners'. (Kassandra
sometimes calls different gods by the same allusive designation, so
'Maiden' is Athena at **360**, but Persephone at **698**.) Or the expression
might mean, redundantly, 'sword of war'. If the sacrificer is Agamemnon,
the two other owners are his father Atreus and grandfather Pelops.

330–4 Maira (**334**) was a mythical hound: Apollod. 3.14.7. This refers to Hekabe's divinely ordained metamorphosis into a dog, such as attended the sinister (and similarly named) Karian goddess Hekate; see Euripides, *Hecuba*. Hekabe blinded the Thracian king Polymestor in revenge for his murder of her son Polydoros, hence the gods' punishment (the human stoning for her curses is not attested before Lykophron; here the Thracian Dolonkoi are alone responsible, **332**, but later in the poem, it is initiated by Odysseus; see **1174–88**n. for the slight inconsistency). Greek men found excessive revenges specially shocking when *women* inflicted them, and naturally attributed the same attitude to their gods: Herodotus 4.205. The Hekabe-Hekate theme will be developed at **1174–88**, but more positively, as a prophecy of Hekabe's future fame, *kleos*, and heroine cult in Sicily.

335–6 The poet displays dramatic consistency and tact: the guard (we have probably forgotten about him by now) has just reported to Priam that Kassandra addressed her absent sisters and mother in the second person (**314, 330**), but he now makes her speak of her father in the third person. It would be inartistic to have her recount to the listening Priam his own life-history, even through an intermediary. (There is a modern Greek saying: 'Hey, granddad, let me show you your own vineyards.') The Greek for 'Zeus-Agamemnon' is just 'Agamemnon', the king of the Greeks equated with the king of the gods; for the converse equation see 'Zeus' at **1369–70**, and cf. **1123–40**n. Priam's slaughter in Zeus' temple (by Neoptolemos, though Lykophron does not say so) is sacrilege on a par with the violence against Troilos and Kassandra: **307–13**n. The surprising 'adorn' (**336**) inverts *Iliad* 22.73–6 (Priam on the ugly deaths of the old): McNelis and Sens, 185–6.

337–9 Priam's name is here fancifully connected with the Greek root 'ransom', but more probably = Luwian 'supreme in force'. In youth he was called Podarkes ('swift-footed', applied to Achilles in the *Iliad*) but was then *ransomed* by his sister Hesione.

340–7 A neat slice of narrative, including the trick of the talismanic Wooden Horse full of troops, by which Troy was taken, the 'ghastly pregnant hiding-place'; the story is elaborated in Virgil, *Aeneid* 2; cf. C. Faraone, *Talismans and Trojan Horses* (New York, Oxford University Press, 1992), 92–100. Priam's brother-in-law Antenor, 'the snake' (**340**), was regarded as a traitor to Troy; this is developed out of *Iliad* 7.347–53, where he urged that Helen be returned. Here he seems to have opened up the Wooden Horse, perhaps lighting a torch to show the Greeks the way out of it (?). The 'Sisypheian [i.e. cunning] fox' is Odysseus (cf. **1031**); his cousin is Sinon, here represented as having sent fire-signals to the Greeks to return from 'Leucophrys' (Tenedos) and the Kalydnai islets (cf. **25**). For the fire-theme (here doubled, torch and fire-signals) see **71**n.: here, as often, it refers to the destruction of Troy. Line **347** evokes the killing of Apollo's priest Laokoon and his sons—depicted on the cover of this book—by two named serpents Porkes and Chariboia, which swam from Tenedos, hence 'child-devourer'. (Laokoon had famously warned against receiving the

Horse: 'I fear Greeks even when they bring gifts': *Aen.* 2.49.) For
Kassandra's naming of animals, cf. **152–67**n. West 2013, 231–2 speculates
that behind this naming is a human metamorphosis. For more on the
Horse, see **930–50**: the 'horse-builder' Epeios in Italy.

348–72 For Greek text and detailed commentary (with tr.), see N. Hopkinson,
A Hellenistic Anthology, 2nd edition (Cambridge, Cambridge University
Press (2020), 69 and 272–6, poem XXV. Kassandra's account of her
assault by Lokrian Ajax is, from the 'autobiographical' point of view, one
of the poem's two climaxes; the other is her murder by Klytaimestra,
1108–22. The present section also functions as a bridge between Troy's
fall and the long narrative sequence of *nostoi*, 'returns' (from Troy); for
this theme see the contributions to *Returning Hero*.

Ajax is already a disagreeable figure in *Iliad* 23.473–81, 773–84, the
funeral games for Patroklos: perhaps the germ of this story. The *Sack of
Troy* (part of the Epic Cycle) described the rape, and said that the Greeks
would have stoned Ajax for it, but he fled to Athena's altar as a suppliant
(presumably the one from which he had dragged Kassandra) and so
escaped death: for a translation of the relevant item see West 2003, 147.
See also **365**n. for Alkaios' important testimony.

Ajax's assault of Kassandra was sexual violation, but was it actual pene-
trative rape? The sources hesitate (Euripides' *Trojan Women* has it both
ways, 169, 324). The scene was a favourite in art, where nakedness usually
meant rape. But in some depictions she is clothed, in others naked (offering a good opportunity to paint the female nude). Lykophron describes
her appealing for help to Athena, in whose temple the assault took place:
see **307–13**n. and **335–6**n. for the sacrilege. But Athena averted her eyes.
In art, she often clutches the goddess's statue, a detail taken from Arktinos
(Epic Cycle). Athena receives six names or epithets in these lines—seven
if we print 'marriage-hater' in capitals—a record in the poem (see **206–15**n.
and Introduction, *Difficulty*), and a token of her importance in this crucial
episode. They are not randomly chosen (e.g. 'goddess of city-gates'
reproachfully implies a protective role).

'Who rejected marriage' (**348**) is a pre-echo of **1132**, Kassandra's premarital cult at Daunia (**30**n.). It does not mean 'who refused Ajax'
(although *gamos*, 'marriage', can mean sexual intercourse, **412**) but
refers—as lines **352–3** make clear—to her earlier refusal to have sex with
Apollo (cf. **1451–60**n.).

365 A crucial line, as seen by Virgil, who virtually translated it, *Aeneid* 1.41.
Already in Homer Athena laid a 'painful return, *nostos*, on the Greeks',
Odyssey 1.327; and she hated Ajax, 4.502. And Ajax's watery death at
Poseidon's hands was already narrated by Proteus at *Odyssey* 4.499–511.
See **348–72**n. for the treatment in the epic *Sack of Troy*; and Ajax's failed
nostos and death by drowning was narrated in the epic *Nostoi* (for the
scanty surviving evidence see West 2003, 155 and 2013, 260–3). But the
long-lived idea that the woes of homecoming Greeks were in reprisal for
one man's fault, namely Kassandra's violation by Ajax and his sacrilege

against Athena, was first clearly expressed by the Archaic lyric poet Alkaios (about 600 BCE, see *OCD* 'Alcaeus'): see R. Tarrant, *Seneca*, Agamemnon (Cambridge, Cambridge University Press, 1976), 19–20. Alkaios made the connexion between Ajax's crime and the fate of the other Greeks: if they had punished Ajax they would have avoided the storm at sea. See frag. 298, including an important new papyrus fragment published in 1967, the 'Cologne papyrus'. The idea is developed in the exchange between Athena and Poseidon which begins Euripides' *Trojan Women*: 65–97 (stressing Ajax's impiety rather than the rape), cf. 431–44, Kassandra foretells sufferings for Odysseus, reprising the *Odyssey* in a nutshell. This could have influenced the architecture of Lykophron's poem in a general way.

367 These 'rocks' prepare us for Ajax's rocky fate, **389**: McNelis and Sens, 81.

373–83 Ajax's companions were drowned with him, hence the pathetic list of Euboian places. The poet is not merely showing off arcane topographical knowledge. Cf. A. Parry, *The Language of Achilles and Other Papers* (Oxford, Oxford University Press, 1989), 81, on the short place-list at Virgil *Aeneid* 7.759–60: 'the real pathos is for the places that mourn him (i.e. Umbro)'. For a change, these Euboian places are not taken from the relevant list in the Homeric *Catalogue* (*Iliad* 2.536–9).

384–5 Nauplios the 'viper' was father of Palamedes who outsmarted Odysseus, when he feigned insanity to avoid the Trojan War: **815–19n.**, cf. Achilles, **276–8n.** Odysseus took a variously reported but always horrible revenge; Nauplios' counter-revenge was twofold: (1) he wrecked the ships of drunken returning Greeks by luring them onto the rocks with false lights and (2) he made their wives unfaithful, **1090–8**, cf. **1216**. Palamedes was treated by Sophocles, Euripides, and Lykophron's third-century tragedian namesake. Nauplios, 'shell-fish', is an attested personal name, as is Palamedes: P. M. Fraser, 'Palamedes at Baglan', *Afghan Studies* 3–4 (1982), 77–8.

387–407 Twenty lines are devoted to Ajax's death by drowning; this section obviously looks back to Kassandra's rape, but can also be seen as the first of the poem's many failed *nostoi*, 'returns' (**348–72n.**), although **408–16** serves as formal introduction to the main *nostoi* narrative. For the early sources for the drowning (Homer, the Epic Cycle, Alkaios) see **365n.** For Gyrai in particular (**390**), cf. *Odyssey* 4.500.

These lines (on which see McNelis and Sens, 31 and Pillinger, 131) mix metaphor and simile (**180–201n.**), and play with many animal and bird species (cf. **33n.**), ranging from the kingfisher (a 'sacred bird' for the Archaic poet Alkman, frag. 26) to the cuckoo. The opening, **387–8**, ingeniously compares Ajax to both the kingfisher and its prey. Even the portly quail gets a mention (**401**): it signifies Delos, because Asteria turned herself into a quail to escape Zeus the sex-pest, and became Ortygia, 'Quail Island': I. Rutherford, *Pindar's Paeans* (Oxford, Oxford University Press, 2001), 252 n. 35. It may also be relevant that Delos is a staging post for migrating quails: P. Thonemann in M. Hammond (tr.) *Artemidorus: The Interpretation of Dreams* (OWC, Oxford, Oxford University Press, 2019), 277.

One influence here is the many Hellenistic epigrams lamenting deaths at sea; in particular, the stranded dolphin of **396** recalls the creature commemorated by the female epigrammatist Anyte: *HE* lines 708–13.

392–3 Poseidon is designated metonymically, by his trademark trident (cf. *Iliad* 12.27). His role here is puzzling, but clearer in the *Odyssey* (cf. **365**n.): he saved Ajax initially, but changed his mind when Ajax boasted that he had escaped death despite the gods, angry Athena above all. Kassandra is not so much abbreviating (her account is actually longer) as subtly equating Ajax with the hated Odysseus, persecuted by Poseidon for blinding the god's son the Kyklops. 'Hired labourer': see **33**n.

399–400 For Thetis' help to Zeus, see *Iliad* 1.398–406.

404–7 Aphrodite's epithet 'Kastnian' derives from Mt Kastnion in Pamphylia, and is attested in Kallimachos (frag. 200a) and a Pamphylian inscription, *SEG* 17.641. Ajax is punished in Hades by the Furies (Erinyes, cf. **152–67**n.) for the rape; Kassandra seems to imply that Aphrodite tempted him in the first place, but in Greek thinking that would not lessen his guilt.

408–16 The preamble to the main *nostoi* sequence picks up the 'all Greece' motif of **365**, but whereas **373–83** listed and addressed purely Euboian sites of drownings, the present list covers much of north mainland Greece: Macedon, Thessaly, Thesprotia. Acheron was in NW Greece, but there was another in Italy, and it was an underworld river: **695**. At **415** the poetic word for 'numberless' is rare, but has now turned up on an unusual and learned inscribed Greek poem from Afghanistan, *SEG* 54.1568, 14; cf. R. Hunter, *Greek Epitaphic Poetry. A Selection* (Cambridge, Cambridge University Press, 2022), 130.

417–23 Phoinix was a Thessalian, from Tymphrestos (**420**, cf. **902**). He raised Achilles ('child-rearing', **419**), cf. *Iliad* 9.485 (Homer knows the alternative tradition in which his teacher was the centaur Cheiron, e.g. 11.832, but downplays this as too monstrous: J. Griffin, *Homer* Iliad *IX* (Oxford, Oxford University Press, 1995), 96). Phoinix was therefore a suitable choice as one of the three-man delegation which tried (*Iliad* 9) to persuade Achilles to return to the fighting. Eion and the other named places are in what was later the Amphipolis region of Thrace. They open a roughly clockwise circuit of *nostoi* (east Mediterranean–Libya–Italy and the west): McNelis and Sens, 83–4. A convincing thematic connection between these early *nostoi* is harder to find. In the Epic *Nostoi*, Thetis tells Neoptolemos to bury Phoinix, and gives him travel advice. It has been suggested that this quasi-prophetic glance at the future offers a thematic link with the prescience possessed by the seers of the next section; but Kassandra does not mention or hint at Thetis' role on this occasion. It is better to start with the one detail Kassandra allows us, the blinding, a physical defect for a moral fault (**422**n.). Kalchas is an imperfect seer who fails the test against Mopsos (**427**); Idomeneus (**431–2**) was one of Nauplios' victims (**1214–25**); Sthenelos' father was punished by Zeus for impiety (**433–8**n.); Teukros failed to prevent the suicide of his brother

Telamonian Ajax (**450**); Diomedes was punished for wounding Aphrodite (**610**); and so on. So imperfection and failure are the key.

422 Phoinix was punished by (temporary) blinding by his father Amyntor for having had sex with his, Amyntor's, concubine Klytia or Phthia, the 'dove' of **423**. In Homer, Phoinix himself narrates this (*Iliad* 9.447–80), but without the blinding, which was perhaps an invention of Euripides (frag. 816, cf. Aristophanes *Acharnians* 421), later picked up by Menander (*Samia* 498–500) and a late epigram (*Anth. Pal.* 3.3). Lykophron may have got it direct from Euripides. Blinding was an appropriate punishment for illicit sex: G. Devereux, 'The self-blinding of Oidipous in Sophokles', *Journal of Hellenic Studies* 93 (1973), 36–49, esp. 43–4 on Phoinix.

426–9 Kalchas is the Greek seer ('swan of Apollo', god of prophecy, **426**), prominent in *Iliad* 1. He lost a competition in skill against his Anatolian rival Mopsos (see *OCD* 'Mopsus'); the Anatolian prophetess Kassandra is happy to report a Greek failure, if this Mopsos is not the like-named seer of the Greek Argonauts: **881**. Kalchas challenged Mopsos to guess the number of figs on a tree. Mopsos got it right and asked Kalchas the number of a sow's unborn piglets; Kalchas got it wrong and died. The myth is narrated by Hesiod in frag. 214, cited by Strabo (14.1.27), who shows that the contest was also told the other way round. It probably featured in the epic *Nostoi*. The clash hints at inter-city struggles for control of the nearby oracular site of Klaros. It may also reflect guessing games played in Archaic Greek villages in the slack winter months. The spectacular contest between Elijah and Baal's prophets at I Kings 18 had similarly fatal consequence for the losers, but did not entail a riddle. It was a competition between rival gods as to who could set fire to a sacrificial animal.

431–2 The second 'sea-swallow' (**424**) buried at Kolophon is Kretan Idomeneus, on whom see further **1214–25**. He was descended from Zeus ('Erechtheus') via Minos. Odysseus, back on Ithaka, told Penelope he was Aithon, Idomeneus' brother: *Odyssey* 19.178–84; 'fictitious' could be the lie—or it could be the *Odyssey*.

433–8 At *Iliad* 2.563–4 (the *Catalogue of Ships*), Sthenelos is Argive leader alongside his chief Diomedes, for whose *nostos* see **592–632**. But Kassandra's interest is in Sthenelos' father Kapaneus, one of the Seven Against Thebes, who scaled the Theban walls in defiance of Zeus, so was blasted by his thunderbolt ('whip'): Euripides, *Phoenician Women* 1181. **437** is a riddle: Eteokles and Polyneikes were sons but also brothers of the incestuous Oidipous. Sthenelos appeared at *Iliad* 9.48, not long before Phoinix at 9.168; this proximity may have triggered an association in Lykophron's mind.

439–46 Another struggle between seers, though this aspect is not to the fore, and they fight with blows not puzzles. They are rival founders (of Mallos on the river Pyramos, later 'Antioch on the Pyramos'): settlements abroad often entailed tensions, even bloodshed, between clans: **1374–7n.** On Mopsos see **426–9n.**; Amphilochos was an Argive, to whom Alexander the

Great (a sort of Argive, cf. Herodotus 5.22) sacrificed at Mallos (Arrian, *Anabasis* 2.5.9), perhaps deciding in his favour against Mopsos: Lane Fox, 237. In 1908, the publication of a papyrus containing Pindar *Paian* 2 confirmed that 'Derainos' (440) was an epithet of Apollo.

442 Magarsos (444) was, despite the usually masculine ending '-os', daughter of Pamphylos, eponym of Pamphylia in S. Asia Minor; Magarsos was the eponym of Mallos' port.

447-591 Nearly 150 lines about Cyprus—10 per cent of the poem—may seem out of scale, but the Five Settlers are a peg on which hang excursuses with little or no Cypriot connection (most conspicuously 503-68, Dioskouroi and Apharetidai): it is surprising that Kassandra specifies no city founded by the Five, though readers might be expected to know that Teukros of Greek Salamis founded Cypriot Salamis (the myth was familiar to Horace, *Odes* 1.7.27-9). Lykophron's immediate prompt may have been the appearance in the later third century BCE of some Cyprus-related prose and poetic writings by the multi-tasking author Eratosthenes; see 484n. and Introduction, *Authorship and Date* for the bearing of this on composition date. Another possible source is the royal historian Androkles of Amathous, who called his kingdom Kerastia, 'place of horns' (*FGrHist* 751 frag. 1, cf. 447-9n.): he was a naval ally of Alexander (Arrian, *Anabasis* 2.22.2), and called himself king: *SEG* 30.1571, metrical dedication.

447-9 The horned men of Kerastia/Cyprus (447-591n.) sacrificed strangers, until they themselves were turned into bulls by Aphrodite: Ovid. *Met.* 10.225-37. Behind this myth are perhaps the Cypriot bull-masks revealed by archaeology: F. Graf in P. Hardie (ed.), *Cambridge Companion to Ovid* (Cambridge, Cambridge University Press, 2002), 118, cf. V. Karageorghis, *Cyprus* (London, Thames and Hudson, 1982), 141-3 with fig. 109. 'Sphekeia' is 'place of wasps'; for such foundation myths see 171-7n.: ants. Hylates is Apollo 'grove god', an epithet attested in Greek and syllabic Cypriot inscriptions at Kourion: for the syllabic texts, see *IG* 15.1 (2020). Satrachos was a river on Cyprus.

450-69 Teukros was exiled from Greek Salamis (concealed in river-names Kychreus and Bokaros, 451) by his father Telamon because he failed to prevent the suicide (466) of his brother Ajax ('Telamonian', to distinguish him from the Lokrian). Only in this sense was he Ajax's 'killer' (452). Ajax, angry at losing to Odysseus the contest for the armour of Achilles, went mad and killed sheep (454) thinking they were men: for this and the suicide, see Sophocles' *Ajax*. The lion at 455 is a real lion, the Nemean lion killed by Herakles, who is—teasingly—the metaphorical 'lion' of 459. Herakles prayed that the lion-skin would make baby Ajax invulnerable, a non-Homeric magical tale, cf. Aeschylus frag. 83, Pindar *Isthmian* 6.47, cf. Kolde 2018. (On invulnerability see 178-9n.). Teukros was Kassandra's cousin (452) through Hesione. On brother Trambelos (467), see 468-78n.

459 The ancient commentators knew that Komyros was a cult title of Zeus at Karian Halikarnassos; many inscriptions found at the sanctuary of

Panamara in the years around 1900 show that it was indeed Karian, and that there was a Komyria festival: M. Ç. Sahin, *Inschriften von Stratonikeia* (3 vols., Bonn, Habelt, 1981–90). This is a satisfying example of epigraphic confirmation of the historical reality of one of Lykophron's more obscure cult-epithets.

462–3 Lemnian is 'fierce' because Lemnos was linked to the fire-god Hephaistos; Enyo is the war-god Ares, as also at **519**. So all this denotes the great warrior Ajax.

465 Hektor (the 'enemy') gave Ajax his sword: *Iliad* 7.303–5, Sophocles, *Ajax* 661–2.

468–78 Hesione is Laomedon's daughter, Priam's sister, Kassandra's aunt, and mother of Teukros and Trambelos by Telamon, the 'tower-underminer' (**469**, referring to an auxiliary role in Troy's capture by Herakles, **31n.**, who gave him Hesione as spoils). Her sacrifice (**33n.**) was urged by 'babbler' Phoinodamas (**471**), whose own daughters were then banished by Laomedon to punish the father: yet more male aggression against guiltless women. The girls' western adventures will be recounted at **951–67**. On 'woodpecker' Hesione's rescue from the sea-monster ('hound', **472**) by 'scorpion' Herakles (**476**), see again **33n.** The rescue anticipates Andromeda's, **837–9**.

478 'Phorkos' who comforts the monster is obscure: perhaps the sea-god Nereus.

479–85 Agapenor (founder of Paphos in S. Cyprus, Pausanias 8.5.2) was from Arkadia. Its inhabitants claimed to be autochthonous (**480**, 'earth-nourished'); 'older than the moon', **482** and frequently; 'acorn-eaters', again **482** (cf. Herodotus 1.66, an oracle); and 'sons of the oak' (**480**), a hint at Arkadia's eponym Arkas, who rescued an oak-dwelling nymph. Such autochthony myths conferred prestige: T. Scheer, '"They that held Arkadia" . . .' in L. Foxhall and others (eds.), *Intentional History* (Stuttgart, F. Steiner Verlag, 2010), 275–98. Cf. **1206n.** For the literary primitivism of this passage, see T. Rosenmeyer, *The Green Cabinet* (Berkeley, University of California Press, 1969), 234. The Arkado-Cypriot dialect confirms a primeval link between the regions (cf. S. Colvin, *A Brief History of Ancient Greek* (Oxford, Blackwell, 2014), 99–100). Nyktimos, son of Lykaion, was killed and served up by his brothers to Zeus, who turned them into wolves as punishment: **481**. Arkadian temporary lycanthropy on Mt Lykaion is an example of an extreme mythical counterpart of a civic initiatory ritual (cf. **1141–73n.**, the Lokrian Maidens): R. Buxton, *Myths and Tragedies in their Ancient Greek Contexts* (Oxford, Oxford University Press, 2013), 33–51. In the fourth century BCE, Plato (*Republic* 565) used the Arkadian lycanthropy myth to illustrate tyranny; this has historical resonances: E. Eidinow, 'Consuming narratives: the politics of cannibalism on Mt Lykaion', *Classica et Medievalia* 67 (2019), 63–89.

484 Eratosthenes knew of copper-mining on Cyprus, a recherché detail (Strabo 14.6.5). So he is probably Lykophron's source.

486–93 Kassandra conflates two men called Ankaios: (a) father of Agapenor: an Argonaut, killed by the Kalydonian boar in a hunt which brought together many early heroes, Apollodoros 1.8.2, *OCD* 'Meleager (1)'; (b) another Argonaut, king of Samos, to whom a 'many a slip 'twixt cup and lip' story (**489**) was usually attached. Kalydon was in Aitolia, as was (roughly) Mt Oita (**486**): *Barrington Atlas* map 55 B4, C3.

494–585 Settler (2), Theseus' son Akamas has the longest excursus of the five. Theseus lifted the rock under which his father Aigeus king of Athens hid his sandals as recognition tokens (**494–5**, cf. Kallimachos frag. 235, Plutarch, *Theseus* 3; the identification will be closely repeated at **1322–3**). Akamas was associated with overseas settlement in the Troy region (Erskine, 107–8) and the Chersonese, a role probably invented under fifth-century BCE Athenian imperialism. Lykophron is the first to take him to Cyprus, where in one tradition he founded Soloi: Strabo 14.6.3. The epic *Sack of Troy* (Introduction, *Sources*) told how he and his brother Demophon rescued their grandmother Aithra who had been taken to Troy as prisoner (**501–2**). While there, Akamas fathered Mounitos by Priam's daughter Laodike; her fatal leap is reprised at **497**: see **316–22**n.

504–68 Kassandra ingeniously uses Aithra, Akamas' grandmother and Theseus' mother, as an opportunity to tell of Helen's brothers the Dioskouroi (Kastor and Polydeukes, Latin Castor and Pollux, twins who became the constellation Gemini, cf. 'stars' at **510**). Their fight against the Apharetidai Idas and Lynkeus was treated in the *Kypria* (frag. 16, West 2003, 95–7), and by Stesichoros (probably), Pindar (*Nemean* 10, cf. Kolde 2018), and Theocritus 22; the first three were certainly available to Lykophron, the fourth probably, depending on Lykophron's date. The Dioskouroi were mythical Spartans ('Lapersian', **511**), the Apharetidai were Messenians, so the fight between the pairs of brothers is a signifier for the age-old enmity between these neighbouring communities, down to Hellenistic times: Pausanias 4.28, Polybius 5.92. See map. The myth is connected to the Trojan War at **512–16** and **567–8**. 'Twice' (**513**) anticipates the war.

Helen the 'maenad' (**505**, cf. **513**) was abducted to Athens as a young girl by Theseus: cf. **850–1**; her brothers the Dioskouroi rescued her and took Aithra with them as well, in revenge. Their eggshell helmets (**506**) allude to their birth from Leda by Zeus as a swan (cf. **86–9**n. for their sister Helen). They are 'half-divine' (**511**) for reasons given at **564–8**, see n. there.

512–16 At **567–8** this prayer to Zeus is treated as answered: by the mutual destruction of the four Greek brothers, Troy ('Bebrykia', **516**, cf. **1474**) will be spared their participation in the war (conveyed by the vivid counterfactual image of the Dioskouroi actually landing at Troy). This rewrites Homer, for whom the crucial absentee was Achilles: McNelis and Sens, 224.

517–37 Kassandra turns to the Apharetidai, here treated as the stronger pair; this follows Homer (*Iliad* 9.560–1 on Idas) but departs from Theocritus (22.212–13) and Pindar (*Nemean* 10.72): McNelis and Sens, 223 n. 8. Counterfactual or 'if . . . not' presentation (**512–16**n.) continues at **521–9**:

Zeus ('gracious helper', **535–7**, with four sonorous epithets as focusing device) arranged that Troy (**521–3**) did not fall *as soon as it would have done if* it had been attacked by the Apharetidai; even Hektor's might (**526–7**) *would not have* availed. But **530–4** (Hektor killed the 'falcon' Protesilaos) 'really' happened.

Why Athena was 'born three times' (**519**) has been variously explained, nor is the translation quite certain.

521–2 On Troy's walls, built by Apollo and Poseidon, and Laomedon's perjury, cf. **33**n.

530–4 Protesilaos was the first Greek to be killed at Troy, and was buried at Mazousia on the tip of the Thracian Chersonese: *Barrington Atlas* map 51 G4, marking it 'Mas(t)ousia'.

538 Kassandra now reverts to the Dioskouroi, who gave hospitality to Paris ('Orthanes') at Sparta. This detail—causally important if the fight broke out at a banquet held by Menelaos on this occasion—was in the *Kypria* (West 2003, 69).

547 The 'cousin-chicks' are daughters of Leukippos, cousins of both sets of brothers: *OCD* 'Leucippides'. Anthropological fieldwork in modern Greece confirms that alcohol-fuelled brawls between touchy kinsmen tend to break out at feasts, especially but not only at weddings: J. K. Campbell, *Honour, Family and Patronage: A Study of Institutions and Moral Values in a Greek Mountain Community* (Oxford, Clarendon Press, 1964), 97.

553–63 Kassandra narrates the fight with gusto, drawing heavily (but with variations) on Pindar; probably also Theocritus, among fully surviving sources (**504–68**n.).

561–2 Idas once fought Apollo for Marpessa's hand: *Iliad* 9.558–60. Like Kassandra, she rejected Apollo. 'Telphousian' here means Boiotian, not Arkadian as at **1040**.

564–8 The Apharetidai went down to Hades, but the Dioskouroi were immortal on alternate days, as a result of a display of brotherly love by Polydeukes (Pindar *Nemean* 10.55–90, cf. *Pythian* 11.62–4), who declined the option of full immortality for himself alone. They are therefore 'half-divine' (**511**), as at *Odyssey* 11.303–4 (but both dead at *Iliad* 3.243, not necessarily by the same poet). The arrangements for the alternation are not entirely clear and the sources vary slightly; the *Odyssey* passage is particularly confused. Line **566** beautifully rewrites Homer in a different metre. On the 'brief remedy' at **568** see next n.

570–85 Anios of Delos, king and prophet, was son of Apollo and Rhoio ('pomegranate'). Zarex (**580**) was Rhoio's second 'husband', so he was really *step*-grandfather to the miraculous girls. Anios told the Greeks they would capture Troy only in the tenth year, and urged them to stay on Delos (**572**). They refused, but he nevertheless fed the hungry Greek army later: endless wine, corn, and olives were provided by his magical daughters. The connection of thought is that the mutual destruction of the mighty pairs of

Greek twins gave a 'brief remedy' (568) by postponing the fall of Troy, which would have happened sooner with their participation; now Kassandra imagines, counterfactually, another cause of postponement. In Virgil (*Aeneid* 3.80–2), Anios is a friend of Troy and Aeneas' father Anchises, but this is not inconsistent: he delayed the Greek onslaught. He received hero-cult as 'founder' of Delos (*OCD* 'Anius'), and an inscription attests friendship and closeness, i.e. kinship, between Delos and Troy's daughter city Rome: Sherk no. 10. So the Rome-Troy theme, so important towards the end of the poem, is already hinted at here.

576 Hellenistic Delos was famously full of Egyptian cults.

586–91 The fifth and fourth settlers of Cyprus (the natural word-order is reversed for metrical reasons) are—unusually—named, as Kassandra sometimes does with minor figures. 'Not as leaders of sailor folk' is the most explicit literary reference in the poem. It means 'not in Homer *Iliad* 2, *Catalogue of Ships*'. This, in the language of narratology, is 'presentation by negation', a concealed address to the reader: it implies 'not, as you might expect . . .'. Kepheus, leader of people from the Achaian places at 591–2 (see map for Dyme), is deeply obscure. But Spartan Praxandros founded Lapethos on Cyprus (Strabo 14.6.3). Personal names in Prax- are extremely rare in the Greek world generally but common in, precisely, Cyprus, including one called in Cypriot syllabic script *pa-ra-ka-sa-to-ro* = Praxa(n)dro.

589 Aphrodite's usual Cypriot ethnic (designator of origin) was 'of Paphos', but poets (Theocritus 15.100, Catullus 64.96) sometimes call her 'queen of Golgoi', in the east of the island: see *Barrington Atlas* map 72 B3 and D2 for the two places.

592–632 An attractive, poignant section, eloquent on colonial homesickness: 609 (cf. 645, with 644–7n.). Diomedes son of Tydeus led the Peloponnesian Argives in the Trojan War—cf. 433–8n. on his fellow officer Sthenelos—and was an energetic stand-in for Achilles when he stayed aloof from the fighting: *Iliad* 5, in which Diomedes wounded 'Troizenian' Aphrodite (610). Diomedes was also Aitolian (NW Greek) by descent; this will be important (see 615–29n.). He helped Odysseus steal the Trojan Athena's cult-image, the Palladion (658). He returned safe to Argos, but left again on learning that his wife Aigialeia had been unfaithful in his absence (612). This was Aphrodite's revenge for her own wounding, but it is also a mythical expression of age-old fears, felt by men away on military service, of female infidelity back home. Diomedes' S. Italian operations, in Lykophron's presentation, illustrate historical tensions between local populations and Greek settlers: I. Malkin, *Returns of Odysseus* (Berkeley, University of California Press, 1998), 238–42. Important archaeological finds and Greek inscriptions, the results of excavations in the mid 1990s (just too late for Malkin), reveal that he had cult on a mid-Adriatic island as early as the fifth century BCE: 599n. His cult is a western counterpart to the Black Sea (eastern) cult of Achilles: 180–201n. Kassandra may hint at a further parallel, with Odysseus, by reversing the usual image of Penelope as faithful wife (McNelis and Sens, 160–2), although this motif comes later in the poem: 771–3, Penelope as 'fornicating vixen'.

592–3 Argyrippa features as Latin Arpi in Livy's history of the Hannibalic War. The site (see map) is north of mod. Foggia in Puglia. 'Phylamos' probably denotes the river Aufidus, mod. Ofanto, scene of Rome's defeat by Hannibal at Cannae, 216 BCE. But Arpi was really on mod. Aquilo. 'Ausonian' = 'Italian' (cf. 616, and see 44–8n.). Diomedes' is the first western *nostos*.

594–5 The metamorphosis of Diomedes' companions into birds marks this section as a familiar type of foundation myth: 171–9n.

597 This line was imitated by Ovid, *Metamorphoses* 14.509: E. J. Kenney, in A. D. Melville (tr.), OWC *Ovid* Metamorphoses (1986), 437; cf. F. Klein, *Eclats*, 576–7.

599 For a long time the 'island(s) of Diomedes' here referred to were believed to be the Tremiti islands, a little archipelago off the coast of Italy near mod. Peschici, and a favourite destination for holiday ferry-boats. This was not wrong: at any rate that was the identification made in antiquity. Strabo (6.3.9) says that in the sea nearby (i.e. to Argyrippa) there are two islands which are called 'of Diomedes', one inhabited, one deserted. (Strabo follows this with the metamorphosis of Diomedes' companions into birds. Other literary sources, Latin and Greek, knew the 'birds' story, and all of them, Lykophron included, probably drew on Timaios.) But in 1995, excavations on the tiny island of Palagruza, just inside Croatian waters (see map), revealed a sanctuary to Diomedes. The evidence is potsherds inscribed with part of his name in Greek: *SEG* 48.692bis–694. The island is on a much-used sea-lane, and the dedications will have been made by anxious sailors. So there were several Adriatic islands of Diomedes (cf. 688–93n. on Pithekoussai). He received mainland cult too: 'called a high god by many', 630, where 'called' does not convey a doubt. Cf. Pindar *Nemean* 10.7: Athena deified him.

602 Zethos and Amphion were the legendary human (not avian) builders of Boiotian Thebes; Boiotians are the subject of the next section (633–47), so this is a tiny 'trailer'.

604–5 The birds avoid non-Greek i.e. indigenous Italian contacts; this introduces a hostile-settler theme absent from Virgil's otherwise similar account, which is indebted to the *Alexandra* (*Aeneid* 11.273–4).

615–29 Diomedes has brought ballast-stones to Italy ('Ausonia', 616), from Troy, whose walls were built by Poseidon (617, cf. 33n.). These stones are presumably the same as the magic pillars of 625–9. Daunos, eponymous king of Daunia (30n.), promised Diomedes some land, of which he was deprived by an arbiter called Alainos, Daunos' wicked half-brother. Diomedes utters a curse of infertility on the land until someone of Aitolian (i.e. his own) stock shall till it: 619–24, cf. 1056–66n. This might refer to an influential local Apulian family in the Hannibalic War, the Dasii, who claimed descent from Diomedes: Appian, *Hannibalike* 31.130; but see Pellettieri, 11 for doubts. The magical moving pillars (625–9) could be related to the mysterious relief sculptures, the 'Daunian stelai', now in the Manfredonia museum (illustrations at Hornblower 2015, fig. 5).

The story will be resumed at 1056–66, 'Diomedes and Daunia (again)'.

631–2 Homer's Phaiakia was identified with Kerkyra as early as Thucydides (1.25.4; 3.70.4). En route from Argos to Italy, Diomedes stopped on Kerkyra, an 'Ionian' island, and killed the dragon which had guarded the Golden Fleece: cf. 22n. This may be code for historical captures of strategically important Kerkyra in Hellenistic times, by Kleonymos of Sparta or Agathokles, 303 or 299 BCE: Diodorus 20.104; 21.2.

633–47 This is one of the hardest episodes of the poem to make historical sense of, because there is no other good evidence for Boiotian settlement of the Balearic islands (mainly Majorca, Minorca, Ibiza; for 'Gymnesian', cf. below), nor is such a presence likely: Boiotians were not noted overseas adventurers in any geographical direction, after the early Aiolian migration to the NE Aegean. The Greek colonizers of the Balearics were normally held to be Rhodians: Strabo 14.2.10. Kassandra teasingly delays the settlers' identity until the end: some readers or hearers may have expected Rhodians. A definite fragment of Timaios (no. 66), and a probably Timaian part of Diodorus (5.17–18, close to Lykophron on the harsh training of the children), indicate that he was Lykophron's source. *On Marvellous Things Heard* 100 says that Boiotians from Thespiai (the mythical fifty 'Thespiadai') went to Sardinia; this too may be Timaian. It has been speculated that this may lie behind these Balearic Boiotians, but see Hornblower 2018, 34 n. 164.

From the literary point of view, the section's subject-matter is at first sight remote from the poem's usual concerns. But, just as Zethos at 602 (the Theban analogy) anticipated the present section, so in a small way the Boiotian theme anticipates the next section, Lykophron's '*Odyssey*' (648–819): at 786 Kassandra alludes to the eccentric tradition which made Odysseus a Boiotian ('Temmikian'). Again, the Homeric *Catalogue of Ships* (in *Iliad* 2) is here as elsewhere a point of reference for Lykophron (see e.g. 433–8n., 586–91n., 1141–73nn.). Half of the Boiotian places about to be listed are taken from the *Catalogue*, which had in this way given Boiotia—as a literary entity at least—a distinguished nautical pedigree. In the structure of the poem's structure, the Balearic settlement functions as the most westerly *nostos*.

Finally, the settlers are depicted as slingers (Balearic islanders often feature in Livy as slingers, *funditores*, in Hannibal's army: see Livy 22.4.3 with J. Briscoe and S. Hornblower, *Livy Book XXII* (Cambridge, Cambridge University Press, 2020), 164, although these are presumably not Boiotian or Rhodian Greek immigrants but indigenous or Punic people). Hellenistic Boiotians were slingers—but so were the Rhodians, in whom Lykophron elsewhere takes an interest (923–6). The coincidence—two sets of Greek slingers, both linked with the Balearics by different authorities—is intriguing. Discovery of a full text of Timaios might throw light. Slingers were light-armed skirmishers, hence 'Gymnesian' (**634**), from the root for 'naked'.

643 Fabulously wealthy Tartessos (biblical Tarshish) in S. Spain ('Iberia'), on the Guadalquivir, was known to Stesichoros (frag. 9) and Herodotus (1.163; 4.152).

644–7 Of these eight places, Arne, Graia, Skolos, and Onchestos are in the *Catalogue*: *Iliad* 2.497–506. Onchestos is a topical item: it was Poseidon's 'seat', but his sanctuary was also the political 'seat' of the Boiotian Federation—in the Hellenistic period only.

Homesick colonial 'yearning' (**645**), Greek *pothos* (and the related verb), is an important theme in the poem; see **897–908**n., **1034–46**n., **1067–74**n., and cf. **609** for the thought without the word. For such 'place attachment' in Greek literature, see N. Lowe in *Returning Hero*, ch. 8. Greeks at Italian Poseidonia (Latin Paestum) met once a year at a festival to weep and remember their old customs and then go on their way: Aristoxenos of Taras (Tarentum), cited at Athenaeus 632. Cf. also Diodorus 18.7.1, Greek settlers stranded in Baktria returning home after Alexander's death, out of *pothos* for their Greek way of life.

648–819 Lykophron's '*Odyssey*', the longest, most eventful, and most sustainedly intertextual of the *nostoi* narratives, straddles the exact centre of the poem at **737**, the climax of the important Naples section. But to separate it off as a structural unit may obscure its close organic connections with the Menelaos episode which follows it (**820–76**) and which is almost exactly one-third of its length: certain phrases are shared (e.g. the same non-obvious compound verb 'he will see', **662, 825**), and certain themes. Lykophron tracks *Odyssey* 9–12 (and in the closing stages parts of the Epic Cycle)—but only up to a point, and with conscious divergences and reworking. Some examples: (1) Kassandra does not follow Homer's order of events or distribution of attention scrupulously, e.g. the Kikones (*Odyssey* 9.39–61) are omitted; and the Lotus-eaters are despatched in one line. By contrast, the Sirens are developed fully and with unHomeric thematic repetition: **653–4, 670–2, 712–37**. This is partly because they are an analogue for Kassandra herself (**671–2**n., cf. **4**n., **1463**), partly because the best-known, Parthenope, stands for the great naval city and Roman ally, Naples: at **1229–30** Kassandra will predict Roman rule over land *and sea*. (2) In the best and central sub-section (**681–737**, cf. **805**) the location of Odysseus' experiences is explicitly and unHomerically the Greek west (Italy). (3) Kassandra is (cf. **592–632**n.) made to reverse the usual characterization of Penelope as faithful waiting wife; this is part of the 'unhappy Greek *nostoi* as punishment for Ajax' mytheme: **365–6**. (4) The characterization of Penelope's husband is also and less surprisingly damning, here as elsewhere in the poem. Kassandra plays down Odysseus' achievements—as she did those of Achilles—and his fighting prowess and skill: no macho suitor-slaying here. Tragedy had often shown Odysseus

in a worse light than did Homer, but this negativity has Homeric precedent: Achilles denounced his duplicity at *Iliad* 9.312–13. In any case,
Trojan Kassandra will qualify her hatred at **1242–5**: the Greek 'dwarf'
Odysseus is the enemy of her kinsman Aineias, but in Italy becomes
a friend and ally, a 'frenemy'.

Kassandra surrenders the subject of this *nostos* slowly and with gradually increasing precision. The plural first word 'Those' is artful misdirection: Kassandra has no real interest in Odysseus' crew-mates. He himself
is not only never named at all (this is usual for famous individuals), but not
even designated periphrastically until ten lines into the narrative (**658**).
Only an alert, well-read reader or listener would pick up the implication of
the opening allusion to the Lotus-eaters concealed in **648**: their Libyan
location was in Herodotus (4.177) and, maybe not long before Lykophron's
time, in Eratosthenes (cited by Pliny, *Natural History* 5.41). The half-
beast at the 'Tyrrhenian' straits of Messina (Skylla, **649–50**), and the car-
nivorous nightingales (the Sirens, **653–4**) are more easily guessable.
Educated Hellenistic Greeks would need to be half-asleep or badly forgetful of their schooldays not to spot that the one-eyed cannibal (**659–61**) is
the Kyklops of *Odyssey* 9; but by then they have been introduced to
Odysseus himself, see above. Of these monsters, Skylla was prepared for
early and explicitly at **44** (see **44–8**n.), as was her killing by Herakles; and
the Sirens even earlier, at **4**, although inexplicitly, see **671–2**n.

For an edition of this section with German introduction and commentary, see G. Schade, *Lykophrons 'Odyssee'*, Alexandra *648–819* (Berlin and
New York, De Gruyter, 1999).

657–8 Odysseus makes his appearance gradually: his crew went to Hades, he
was the only survivor. A dolphin saved his baby son Telemachos by
Penelope from drowning, so he adopted it as his shield-sign. 'Thief . . .'
means he stole the Palladion (**592–632**n.).

662–5 The Laistrygonians (named only at **956**) were outsize cannibals who
drove Odysseus' ship away by throwing rocks: *Od.* 10.80–132. Herakles
(**663**) had killed some of them (but that is not in Homer). They were sup-
posed to live in east Sicily (Thucydides 6.2.1, Theopompos *FGrHist* 115
frag. 225, specifying Leontinoi), but Kassandra does not imply that here.
She postpones Aiolos and the bag of winds to **738–9** (in Homer this episode separated the Laistrygonians from the Kyklops), so juxtaposing two
sets of cannibals: 'one . . . trouble after another' (**666**).

668–9 The whirlpool Charybdis (*Odyssey* 12.235) faced Skylla across the
Messina straits, **44–8**n. The 'Erinyes' are the Furies (**152–67**n., **404–7**n.),
here used in a general horrific sense.

671–2 That the Sirens killed the Centaurs is a poorly attested tradition. The
Sirens are 'Aitolian or Kouretan' because they are fathered by the NW
Greek river Acheloos, who mated with a muse, either Terpsichore or
Melpomene. In a hymn to Demetrius the Besieger (Austin no. 43), the
generally hated Hellenistic Aitolians are compared to another predatory

mythical creature, the Sphinx. 'Varied utterance' at 4, of Kasssandra, anticipated 'varied song' here, of the Sirens; at 1463 the equation of those females will at last be made explicit. The Sirens killed by starvation: their song made their entranced victims forget to eat.

673–80 Kirke, the seductive goddess who turned Odysseus' men into pigs and back again (*Od.* 10.153–574), offers a prime opportunity for Lykophron to display his interest in, and to experiment with the vocabulary of, metamorphosis. It has been thought (K. Stratton, *Naming the Witch* (New York, Columbia University Press, 2007), 43) that Homer's Kirke exerts divine powers rather than operating as a Hellenistic witch (as in Lykophron's version), but this distinction is too sharp.

The protective drug *moly* provided by Hermes (678) is as mysterious here as in Homer. Kirke continues the Italian theme because she was supposedly mother of Latinus, 'the Latin man', by Odysseus, according to some lines ascribed to Hesiod (*Theogony* 1011–13). But again (cf. 662–5n.) Lykophron does not specify this.

681–7 Homer devoted all of *Odyssey* 11 to Odysseus' underworld visit, in addition to Kirke's preparatory instructions late in Book 10; Kassandra reduces this to just seven lines, suppressing all individual ghosts. The most relevant Homeric passages for her are Agamemnon's account (11.421–3) of his own murder by Klytaimestra, with Kassandra herself as fellow-victim; she reserves this for full treatment at 1108–22. The seer Teiresias, early in Book 11, tells Odysseus that to make ghosts speak they need blood, which he must generate by animal sacrifice (684; lines 686–7 inconsistently imply mere inarticulate squeaking). Teiresias is the archetypal seer for Greek tragedy—as in Sophocles' *Oidipous the King*, where he is blind—and for Pindar: *Nemean* 1.60. His divinely enforced sex-change, a kind of metamorphosis, is first found not in Homer but in Hesiod: frag. 211. Years later he was changed back, and his report of his unusual experiences was used to fuel male anxieties that women enjoy sex more than men do.

'Necromancer' is, surprisingly, a *hapax* word (318n.), Pellettieri no. 50: behind Odysseus' 'underworld' visit may lie an older story of his consultation of an 'oracle of the dead', as at Italian Avernus/Aornos.

688–93 Homer is dropped for a few lines. Odysseus' western destination is now near-explicit. After the battle between gods ('offspring of Kronos', 693) and Giants, won by the gods thanks to Herakles, the losers were buried in Sicily under Mt Etna: the monstrous Typhon, here treated as a Giant, lay beneath Sicily and under the sea to Italian Campania: Pindar *Pythian* 1.17–20. Herakles also defeated the Kerkopes, pests who were changed (691) to ugly monkeys and installed by Zeus on another volcanic island, Pithekoussai, 'Monkey island', mod. Ischia, off Italian Campania. This was the site of a pioneering and archaeologically important settlement of Greeks from Euboia: Livy 8.22 (they established a bridgehead on the island, then moved to the mainland) and cf. Lane Fox, ch. 9, 'Monkey islands'. The *Alexandra* is a prime document for early colonization traditions; hence Kassandra's

coverage of and interest in this place. If the Tremiti islands (599n.) were
excavated properly, they might turn out to be an Adriatic counterpart to
Campanian Pithekoussai on the west ('Tyrrhenian') coast of Italy: another
offshore insular bridgehead preceding Greek occupation of the mainland.

694–711 Here, in Campania, Kassandra flags sites as Italian with little equivocation: 'Ausonian' ('Italian') at 702 is a giveaway, cf. 44–8n., 592–3n.
Baios, who gave his name to the spa town of Baiae on the bay of Naples,
would be familiar to S. Italians, whether Greek or Latin speakers or both.
He was Odysseus' helmsman (Strabo 5.4.6, a non-Homeric detail).
A Trojan helmsman, Aineias' friend Palinurus, was drowned near here
and, like Baios, was immortalized in a place name, Cape Palinuro. (Cf.
Virgil *Aen.* 5.827–71 and 6.333–83 for this aetiology, but Kassandra
ignores him.) For another such helmsman, Misenos, see 737 and n. Several
of the Italian places in these lines feature in the history of Rome's war
against Hannibal (218–202 BCE), a recent and traumatic episode, if
Lykophron wrote in the 190s. In the poem's structure, the underworld
links this section to 681–7: several names do double duty as real Campanian
sites and underworld locations. Even the shadowy Kimmerians (695, elsewhere attested as a northern—*Odyssey* 11.14–19—or an eastern people)
were located in Campania by Ephoros (*FGrHist* 70 frag. 134), near a cult-
place of Hades. Kassandra here contrives to name all the traditional rivers
of the underworld: Acheron (mod. Foce del Fusaro), (Pyri) Phlegethon,
Lethaion i.e. Lethe ('forgetfulness'), Kokytos (the Lucrine lake), Styx,
Aornos (704n.).

697–700 Ossa (697) was a famous mountain in NE Greece, but an Italian one
was known to the learned Metrodoros of Skepsis, *FGrHist* 184 frag. 17.
Herakles was in this neighbourhood when he stole Geryon's cattle, subject
of a poem by Stesichoros, hence 'ox-paths' (also at 697). Polydegmon
(700) must be the Apennines, but the name ('all-receiver') was a cult-epithet
of Hades. His consort Persephone (abducted by him at Sicilian Enna)
appears in disguise at 698 and 710: Odysseus' helmet dedication to her is
not otherwise attested. (At 710 the subject changes without warning from
Zeus to Odysseus.)

704 'Aornos' in Greek means 'place of no birds'; in its Latin form, the historical lake Avernus was circular (hence 'noose') because it was a volcanic
crater. It was sometimes identified with the Styx (Silius Italicus 12.120–1).
Hannibal sacrificed there: Livy 24.13.6.

712–37 In this, the main Sirens passage (cf. 671–2n.), Kassandra treats the
three fatally seductive bird-maidens in sequence, Parthenope, Leucosia,
and Ligeia, then returns at 732 to concentrate on the first, Parthenope,
and her cult at Naples, cf. 721. Homer knew of only two (*Odyssey* 12.52),
and does not name or locate them except to put them on an island (12.167);
but other authorities, not only Lykophron, had three, which suited Italian
local pride better: all could now be associated with definite rival places.
The actual word 'Siren' is not used until 1463, and see 1461–74n. there for

Kassandra herself as Siren. She takes for granted the Homeric Odysseus' defeat of the singing Sirens: he had himself tied to his ship's mast and made his crew row past them, wax in ears; but she is the first to imply the Sirens' suicide after this failure (only in this sense does Odysseus 'kill' them, **712**). 'Tyrrhenian waves' (**715**) are the sea opposite Etruria (Tuscany).

717–18 Phaleros, Athenian hero and Argonaut, was the eponym of Phaleron harbour near Athens, and refounder of Naples in myth; he prefigures the Athenian material at **732–5**. See M. Fragoulaki, *Kinship in Thucydides: Intercommunal Ties and Historical Narrative* (Oxford, Oxford University Press, 2013), 314, cf. 259. Glanis is the Campanian river Clanius, and Virgil *Georgics* 2.225 echoes **718**.

722–31 The name Leukosia survives as mod. Punta Licosa. Poseidon ('Enipeus') hints at Paestum's Greek name Poseidonia. Ligeia ('sweet-sounding') dwelt further south than her sisters, at Tereina (**726**): Thucydides 6.104.2. The Is and Laris are unidentified rivers. So is the Okinaros, **729**, cf. **1008**. 'Ares' (**730**) may be a separate river, or perhaps means the Okinaros was strong like the war-god. Either way, river-gods were often depicted as horned and bull-like.

732–7 Kassandra resumes the 'Parthenope and Naples' theme; for **737** as the exact centre of the poem see **648–819n.** Naples's importance in the poem is signalled by the unusual use of the name without riddling periphrasis or synonym. The inaugurator of the cultic torch-race for Parthenope is an Athenian naval commander (Mopsops was a mythical king of Athens, not to be confused with the seer Mopsos of **426–30**; cf. **1340**). He is Diotimos son of Strombichos, a fully historical figure from the time of the fifth-century Athenian empire, and a 'western expert': Thucydides 1.45.2, O/R no. 148 (expenses of expedition to Kerkyra), Timaios frag. 98 (quoted by an ancient commentator on Lykophron); all these name him. His Naples visit in the 440s or 430s was a western probe ahead of Athens' expedition against Sicily in 415–13, and even a sort of refoundation: 'Neapolis' means 'new city' (for a tradition about earlier Rhodian settlement, see **919–26n.**). 'Neapolitai' is the regular ethnic (**589n.**) of the city, whose importance in the poem is thus flagged by the avoidance of the usual riddling periphrasis or obscure synonym.

Another, later, historical figure may also be in Kassandra's mind, depending on the poem's date: Hannibal, who tried to take Naples after Cannae (**592–3n.**) when he urgently needed a good harbour (Livy 23.1.5); but the Neapolitans stayed true to their Roman alliance. The unHomeric Misenos (**737**) was either Odysseus' helmsman (Strabo 1.2.18) or Aeneias' trumpeter (Stesichoros frag. 105; Virgil, *Aeneid* 6.162–78).

738–43 For Kassandra's postponement of Aiolos (*Odyssey* 10.1–76), see **662–5n.** He hospitably gives Odyssey a bag of winds. But his crew opens it, the ship is forced back, Aiolos realizes Odysseus is hateful to a god (Poseidon, angry father of Odysseus' victim the Kyklops), and curses him. Volcanic islands north of Sicily still bear Aiolos' name, the 'Isole Eolie'; cf. Thucydides 3.88. At **740**, Kassandra reverts to Homer's order, condensing *Odyssey* 12.261–425: the crew eat the Sun-god's cattle, so Zeus smashes the ship with a thunderbolt. Odysseus, now alone (cf. **788**), again escapes Charybdis (**668–9n.**).

744–61 Odysseus' stay with Kalypso was recounted fully in *Odyssey* 5 (authorial) and again in his narrative to his Phaiakian hosts: 9.29–30, 12.447–9. 'Briefly enjoying' an affair subverts Homer's miserable seven years at 5.151–8: McNelis and Sens, 140. Kassandra's description of Odysseus' building of a raft is vocabulary-rich, but typically contrives to avoid Homer's actual word for 'raft'. Poseidon (**749**) throws him off it.

757 Byne is the goddess Ino-Leukothea, as at **107**. She saves Odysseus from drowning by giving him her 'immortal veil', *Odyssey* 5.333–51, a mysterious episode.

761–7 Odysseus reaches 'Sickle-island', Homer's Phaiakia, located at (convincingly sickle-shaped) Kerkyra: **631–2n.** (Zeus castrated his father Kronos with a sickle). Here he recounts his wanderings, dismissed with a sneer by Kassandra (who has just narrated them herself!) as fictions. Before bringing him home to Ithaka, she prays that his tormentor Poseidon ('Melanthos', **767**) will not rest.

768–78 For a detailed commentary (no tr.) on these lines, which open the narrative of Odysseus' return to Ithaka, see Sens in Sider 2017 (see **1–30n.**), 382–5.

For the hostile, unHomeric presentation of both Odysseus and Penelope see **648–819n.**, examples 3 and 4. The 'fornicating Penelope' motif assimilates Odysseus to all the other Greek heroes whose wives were made unfaithful as part of the revenge taken by Nauplios father of Palamedes (**1090–8**). 'Wife-stealing adulterers' at **771** is Homeric, but a misdirection: Kassandra makes Penelope have willing sex with all the suitors, who are never punished, and she does not mention Penelope's happy reunion with Odysseus. She exaggerates the pains of the initially disguised Odysseus: the flung potsherd at **778** is an unHomeric humiliation, a chamber-pot, taken over from Aeschylus (frag. 180).

There were few better-known, better-loved stories than Homer's tale of Odysseus' ultimately successful return and armed recovery of wife and kingdom. Until far on in Kassandra's narrative (as late as the self-contradictory **788**, he is a 'wretch' but 'safe'), the traditional version floats as a possibility. But Kassandra envisages a different parallel world. This is 'future reflexive' treatment: A. Barchiesi, *Speaking Volumes* (London, Duckworth, 2001), 106. Given her reliable second sight, which precludes ironic collusion between author and reader against an ignorant character, this was a bold move, not reduced by hints of Penelope's infidelity in earlier writers such as Douris of Samos in the fourth century, *FGrHist* 76 frag. 21.

779–86 Odysseus' temporary acceptance of blows and abuse on Ithaka prompts a flashback to an episode in the Troy siege: he entered as a spy, covered in wounds, so as to carry conviction: *Odyssey* 4.242–64, cf. Zopyros at Herodotus 3.153–8. The role of the Aitolian Thoas is taken from the Epic Cycle (*Little Iliad* frag. 8): West 2013, 196. For Thoas see further **1013–16**. Odysseus is Boiotian (**786**) because he was born there in one tradition: Istros, *FGrHist* 334 frag 58. This has no clear negative point, except that Boiotians were reputedly slow-witted. See also **633–47n.** for this detail.

791–2 Pronnoi was on Kephallenia, part of Odysseus' island kingdom: *Iliad* 2.631. The ethnic 'Lakonian' for Penelope (alluding to her Spartan father Ikarios) assimilates her to depraved Helen.

793–8 For the rest of her negatively revised '*Odyssey*', Kassandra abandons Homer's happy ending in favour of a horrific narrative thread from the *Telegony*, part of the Epic Cycle: Odysseus' son by Kirke, Telegonos, kills him with the barb of a sting-ray. See West 2003, 169 and 17, also 2013, 300–3 and 307–15. Kirke was sister of Aietes, father of Medea, Achilles' wife (as at **174**), and Telegonos' cousin.

799–806 Aristotle (frag. 508) knew of Odysseus' oracular sanctuary in Eurytania, part of Aitolia in NW Greece and inland from Ithaka; Trampya (in Epeiros) and the nearby Macedonian canton Tymphaia (or Stymphaia) are much further north, so Kassandra's Balkan geography ('they who live . . .') is very approximate. But that is nothing to the geographical jump by which Odysseus is cremated in 'Gortynaia' (the Etruscan hilltop town Cortona) in Italy: **805**. Presumably Telegonos took his body there from Ithaka. Tymphaia is an excuse to bring in the only named historical individual in the poem, Herakles, Alexander the Great's son by Barsine (a few such persons are mentioned but unnamed, such as Diotimos, Xerxes, and ?Flamininus). The young prince Herakles was treacherously assassinated at dinner in 309 BCE by Polyperchon of Tymphaia: Diodorus 20.20 and 28, from the history of Alexander's Successors by Hieronymos of Kardia, a source for Lykophron elsewhere. Lines **803–4** assert the mythical genealogical claims of Alexander the Great and his son Herakles. They were descended from Aiakos because Alexander's mother Olympias of Epeiros was descended from Achilles' son Neoptolemos, and Achilles' father Peleus was son of Aiakos (**171–7n.**). They were 'of the seed of Perseus' because Temenos (**804**), ancestor of the Macedonian kings (Herodotus 8.137), was descended from Perseus via the mythical Herakles. Cf. **1448–50n.** The name Perseus prepares for his full but unnamed treatment at **834–46**.

807–14 The identifications here are unusually challenging. Telemachos (**657–8n.**) killed Kirke, and was in turn killed by Kassiphone, his (half-) sister, daughter of Kirke and Odysseus. The three 'cousins' at **810–11** are all descendants of the Sun-god.

This is Odysseus' second (**813**) and permanent entry to Hades; for the first visit see **681–7**.

815–19 By deliberate symmetry with the closural lines on Achilles, **276–8**, Odysseus' *nostos* ends with a flashback to before the Trojan War, when both of them tried to dodge the draft: cowards, not heroes. Odysseus feigned insanity by ploughing with donkeys yoked to oxen. Palamedes (see **384–5n.**) called his bluff by placing baby Telemachos in his path and Odysseus braked. The tale is variously told (West 2013: 102–3); Sophocles wrote a lost *Mad Odysseus*. Lykophron's version is also found in the late mythographer Hyginus: *Fabulae* 95.

820–76 For Menelaos see **150n.** and **152–67n.** The narrative of his travels is a pocket edition of Odysseus': almost a third as long (57:172 lines; 57 x 3 = 171). There are linguistic and thematic parallels: both men strive to regain their wives (for Helen as phantom, **822**, cf. **94–143n.**), and in each case the western element gathers in prominence: for Menelaos in the west see **852–76.** But he is a Spartan king, who operates in the Iapygian vicinity of Sparta's daughter-city Taras (**852**), so it has been ingeniously argued that there is a special historical dimension to his western visits: starting with Dorieus, half-brother of Kleomenes I (Herodotus 5.42–8, Sicily), Spartan royal adventurers had tried their luck in the Greek west, or responded to appeals from Taras. An unlucky later example is Archidamos III in 338 BCE, Diodorus 16.62–3 and 88. But there is a risk of special pleading: Odysseus too went west, and was not a Spartan.

825–8 This Typhon is Kilikian, unlike the western one at **689**, but there may (as also at Pindar *Pythian* 1.16) be deliberate geographical ambiguity, in view of **852–76**, the west. After the detection of her affair with Ares (*Odyssey* 8), Aphrodite first fled to her native Cyprus, then hid on Mt Kasios (a sacred site on the Syrian mainland: Lane Fox 255–72). A nosy, spiteful old woman revealed the adulterer's hiding-place—a realistic village touch—and was, not so realistically, punished with petrification. The Eremboi of **827** are as mysterious here as they were in the *Odyssey* (4.84).

828–33 This metamorphosis story is a roundabout way of saying 'Menelaos went to Phoenicia': Byblos is 'citadel of Myrrha', mother of Adonis by incestuous sex with her father. The beautiful youth, Aphrodite's favourite, was killed by a boar (cf. Bion *Adonis* 7) sent by Artemis as revenge for Aphrodite's killing of Hippolytos; Myrrha was changed into a myrrh-tree. Like Kassandra, Myrrha is a pitiable victim of divine wrath: her unnatural lust is Aphrodite's punishment of her mother for boasting of Myrrha's beauty. There is a western aspect too: Adonis is depicted on painted reliefs, *pinakes*, from Italian Lokroi.

834–46 Kassandra condenses the Perseus myths, alluding to them in this order: (1) his rescue, from a sea-monster (cf. **33–4**, Hesione), of Andromeda daughter of Kepheus king of Ethiopia, **837–41**; (2) his birth by Zeus' impregnation of Danae in a gold shower, **838**; (3) kindly nymphs who gave him magical accessories: winged sandals (**839**), a cap of invisibility, and a pouch to hide Medusa's death-dealing head; (4) his decapitation of the Gorgon Medusa, **842–5**; (5) the tactic by which he forced the three Graiai, hags with one tooth and eye between them, to tell him the way to the nymphs. His tactic was to confiscate their eye ('he stole [their] lamp', **846**) and tooth. Kassandra's telling of the myths mixes up their logical order, which is (2) (5), (3), (4), (1). For Perseus as initiatory hero see M. H. Jameson, *Cults and Rites in Ancient Greece* (Cambridge, Cambridge University Press, 2014), 22–40, also warily discussing theories of Gorgons as embodying dangerous female sexuality. From Medusa's neck were born 'a man (Chrysaor) and a horse' (the winged Pegasos), 842–3; weasels were thought to give birth in this bizarre way. Andromeda, like Myrrha, was vicariously punished for the boasts of her mother.

Hermes (835), guarding thirsty Io in Ethiopia, produced a spring by kicking a rock.

847–51 Menelaos seeks Helen in Egypt: he wants to interrogate 'Old Man of the Sea' Proteus about her, cf. 115–43n. For the stratagem at 849, cf. *Odyssey* 4.435–53. It is not quite absurd. In his television series *Life of Birds*, David Attenborough covered himself with stinking seaweed on a New Zealand beach to get close to kiwis, who are short-sighted·but have a strong sense of smell. The compound word here translated 'mother of daughters' (851) may refer to Hermione and Iphigeneia (103n.), but may also mean 'girl [penetrated] like a boy' i.e. Helen was buggered by Theseus in her adolescence (cf. 504–68n.): L. Holford-Strevens, *Classical Quarterly* 50 (2000), 606–10; cf. Edmunds, 119. The 'three men' (851) are Menelaos, Paris, and Deiphobos; Theseus and Achilles are here ignored (contrast 143–71).

852–55 The western half of Menelaos' travels has (like that of Odysseus) no model in Homer or the Epic Cycle; it may derive from the western poet Stesichoros. Iapygians, Peuketians, and Messapians were indigenous peoples in the hinterland of, and often in conflict with, Sparta's colony Taras (820–76n.). The Athena sanctuary (853) where Menelaos made his dedications may be the 'citadel of Minerva' where Aineias first made landfall: Virgil *Aeneid* 3.531. 'Tamassian' bowl (854) refers to Italian Temessa, Latin Tempsa (1068); or possibly to Tamassos on Cyprus: if so, it could have been a gift to Menelaos from Kinyras, king of Cyprus, cf. Helen's *eastern* shoes, a sad memento. The ox-hide shield might be spoils taken from Iapygians (Athena's epithet 'Skyletrian' suggests 'spoils'), and the bowl, too, but only if Italian not Cypriot. The objects were perhaps displayed in Athena's temple (West 2013: 272): a hint at autopsy by the possibly S. Italian Lykophron. On the word for 'people' (*stratos*) at 852, see 1242–9n.: it usually means 'army'.

856–65 For Italian Siris see 978–92n. Lakinian Hera/Juno had a famous sanctuary at the edge of the territory of Kroton (919–26n.): for such delimiting Hera temples see F. de Polignac, *Cults, Territory, and the Origins of the Greek City-State* (Chicago, Chicago University Press, 1995), esp. 103 for Kroton. These attractive lines, an aetiology for Kroton's possession of the area, tell of a deal between two goddesses, Achilles' mother Thetis (the 'heifer' of 857) and Hera ('Hoplosmia', 858). In return for Thetis' gift of a 'spike of dry land to build on' (865), Hera guarantees that local women will eternally mourn Achilles: 860–1, where the heroic diction is at odds with the poem's earlier hostile presentation: 258–80n. For the austere dress-code, cf. R. Parker, *Miasma* (Oxford, Oxford University Press,

1983), 83 n. 36, with epigraphic parallels. Achilles (**861–2**) was grandson of Doris through Thetis (Hesiod, *Theogony* 241 and 244), and of Aiakos through Peleus (**171–7n.**).

866–76 Menelaos crosses to W. Sicily (historically an area of Phoenician settlement; the fertile east coast was Greek); then north to Elba. The 'bull' is Eryx, son of Aphrodite =Venus, whom the Greek hero Herakles defeated at wrestling (Diodorus 4.23), a hint at early Greek efforts to gain a foothold in the region: Herodotus 5.43. Eryx is one of three Elymian (indigenous Sicilian) cities: **964**. See further **951–77n.**

The bizarre aetiological myth (**871–6**) of the 'Minyan' Argonauts (cf. **22n.**, **877–910n.**) on Elba, whose post-exercise scrapings congealed into pebbles, is in Apollonios of Rhodes (4.654–8). It goes back to Timaios, frag. 85: the island's harbour was supposedly named for the ship Argo. Here too Herakles features, this time for his temple, built by Jason.

877–910 After the 228 lines of the great central diptych of the poem, devoted to the famous Odysseus and Menelaos, attention switches to lesser-known heroes, Thessalians who arrive in Libya (for their identity see **897–908n.**); these will in turn provide the transition to a higher-profile Thessalian, Philoktetes: **911–29**. If the previous narrative was a rewritten *Odyssey* (with western additions), its successor is an *Argonautika*, indebted to Herodotus, Pindar, Apollonios, and no doubt other, lost, treatments. The Elba episode (**871–6**) has prepared for this theme, as has 'Minyans' (i.e. Argonauts, **875**), a name with Thessalian connotations. Taucheira was a Ptolemaic Arsinoe; the other name lives on as mod. Tocra, an important excavated coastal site in Cyrenaica: *OCD* 'Pentapolis'. For Atlas in N. Africa (**879**), cf. *OCD* 'Atlas mountains'.

881–4 This Mopsos (not the same as the seer at **426–30**) was one of the two seers on the ship Argo; the other was Idmon. Both died on the voyage: Apollonios 4.1502–36 (Mopsos), 1.139–41, 2.815–50 (Idmon), and both received burial mounds, but in Apollonios it was Idmon's which had a maritime wooden marker like that at **883**. Mopsos is 'Titaresios' at Apollonios 1.65–6, cf. **881**; for Thessalian Titaros see **904**. The two poets use ethnics which fit their respective metres. The Argonautic theme may (McNelis and Sens, 87) point a contrast between the Argo's safe return (**890**) and the shipwrecked Greeks of the next mythical generation. But not all the details can be pressed: ancient readers of Apollonios might have recalled that both of the Argonautic seers met horrible deaths: Idmon gored by a wild boar, Mopsos killed by a snake-bite.

885–96 The sea-god Triton's prophecy to the Argonauts is a classic charter myth, variously told: Herodotus (4.178–9), Pindar (*Pythian* 4.20–42), Apollonios (4.1548–53). In exchange for a tripod or mixing-bowl, the god not only enables the pilot Tiphys to steer the Argo to safety, but validates Greek (actually Spartan) possession of Cyrenaica, **892**. See I. Malkin, *Myth and Territory in the Spartan Mediterranean* (Cambridge, Cambridge University Press, 1994), 169–94. The Libyan place-names are authentic:

for the Kinyps (**885**), cf. Kallimachos (born in Kyrene) frag. 384.24 and
Virgil, *Georgics* 3.312, and for Ausigda, see *Barrington Atlas* map 38 C1.

897–908 Kassandra delays the identification of the shipwrecked Thessalians to
the end, not naming them, but alluding to their contingents in the Homeric
Catalogue of Ships: *Iliad* 2.734–59. They are Gouneus (Kyphaians, cf. **115–43**n.
for his name), Prothoos son of Tenthredon (Magnesians from Palauthra and
the area of the river Amphrysos), and Eurypylos (Tymphrestians, cf. **420**,
but Homer gave him four minor places, 2.734–6). The wolf of **901** was
petrified somewhere in Eurypylos' domain by the agency of Thetis, who
enjoyed especially intense cult in Thessaly; her motive for this is variously
given. There follows a long list of Thessalian places for which the men will
pine; for such pining or yearning, *pothos*, see **644–7**n.

909–10 Kassandra several times pauses to deliver short recapitulatory reflec-
tions; cf. **1087–9**, **1281–2** (**1409–11** is another such bridge passage, but is
anticipatory, see n. there). *Nostos*, 'return', is here used uniquely in the
poem, but see **1088** (in the next bridging section) for the negative form
anostos, 'of no return'.

911–29 We have already met Philoktetes, but indirectly: for Greek possession of
his bow as a condition for Troy's fall see **52–6**n. He was persuaded to leave
Lemnos, where he had been left in isolation because of a snake-bite, and join
the Greeks at Troy, where he killed Kassandra's brother Paris, the 'firebrand':
913. Homer (*Odyssey* 3.190) brought him home safe to Greece, and the Epic
Cycle agreed; for Sophocles' subtle handling of his *nostos* in the play about
him, see N. Lowe in *Returning Hero*, 190–2. For post-Sophoclean treatments,
including Lykophron's, see G. Bowersock, *Fiction as History* (Berkeley,
University of California Press, 1994), 55–76: Philoktetes' groans at his suffering were thought unRoman, see **927–9**n. He set off again because of civil
strife at home (cf. R. Fowler in *Returning Hero*, 49). Lykophron's likely contemporary the elder Cato knew a tradition which brought him to the Bruttian
region of S. Italy: *FRHist* 5 frag. 64, about Petelia; Virgil picked this up:
Aeneid 3.401–2. For archaeological evidence about Philoktetes (and Epeios,
930–50) in S. Italy, see G. Genovese in *Returning Hero* ch. 5. Kassandra
shows marked interest in Philoktetes, the wounded alienated hero whose solitary exile, and eventual Italian cult, resembled her own imprisonment, traumatic fate, and posthumous rehabilitation. That she makes Athena guide the
arrow which killed Paris (**914**) is not intended to lessen Philoktetes' achievement, cf. **404–7**n. He was eventually cured by either Machaon or Podaleirios,
sons of the healing god Asklepios, see **1047–55**n.

For the rivers Aisaros and Nauaithos, mod. Esaro and Neto (**911**, **921**),
cf. Theocritus 4.17, also 24, a poem set in the Kroton area. The Italian
river Krathis (**919**, named again at **1079**) was close to Sybaris: Herodotus
5.45. For an Illyrian Krathis see **1011–26**n.

916–18 Philoktetes lit Herakles' funeral pyre at Trachis: Sophocles, *Philoktetes*
801–3; in return, Herakles gave him his curved bow ('snake' and 'lyre'),
and arrows ('teeth').

919–26 Kroton was founded by Greeks from Achaia, one of whose centres was Pellene (**922**). For its refoundation as Roman Croton in 194 BCE, perhaps topical for Lykophron, see **1067–74n.** The Rhodians (**923–5**) whom Philoktetes helps are a surprise; Lykophron got this from Timaios: *On Marvellous Things Heard* 107, cf. **633–47n.** There is no good evidence for a historical as opposed to mythical Rhodian presence in Italy; perhaps Kassandra was right and they were ousted early by Achaian colonial rivals. Strabo knew a tradition about Rhodians at nearby Sybaris, 6.1.14, cf. 14.2.10, their alleged role at Naples. Like the Neapolitans, the Rhodians were friends and naval allies of the Romans in the time of both Timaios and Lykophron, so there is a topical aspect to these Italian Rhodians: Hornblower 2018 ch. 3. At **924** they are denied a return from Troy because they are blown off-course by a north wind (Thraskias, i.e. a 'Thracian')— a common motif in such colonial *nostos* stories: **1011–26n.** and Thucydides 4.120.1.

927–9 Kroton had been a celebrated medical centre (Herodotus 3.131), so the ulcerous Philoktetes is a suitable recipient of cult there, by a familiar religious dialectic of opposites (cf. **1126–40**, premarital cult for Kassandra herself).

The site of Makalla has not been securely identified, but it too was in the territory of Kroton (*On Marvellous Things Heard*, 107). The name suggests 'weakness' and this was explained in antiquity by Philoktetes' unmanly, unRoman complaints: Bowersock (**911–29n.**), 64.

930–50 Kassandra turns to another condition for Troy's fall (**52–6n.**): Panopeus' son Epeios built the Wooden Horse (**340–7n.**) with Athena's help; cf. **948–50n.** The opening compound designation 'Horse-builder' is otherwise found only in Kallimachos about, precisely, Epeios: frag. 197; it is surely likelier that Lykophron borrowed from Kallimachos than the other way round; if so, this has implications for dating our poem. Kassandra routinely denigrates Greek heroes as cowards, but here she hardly needed to, because Homer had already done the job so well. In Patroklos' funeral games, Epeios wins the boxing-match but confesses that he is a poor fighter (*Iliad* 23.690) and he cuts a laughable figure in the discus event (23.839–40); in Stesichoros (frag. 100) he is a menial water-carrier for Agamemnon and Menelaos. Despite all this, Kassandra allows that his technical skill was invaluable to the army (**945**): not negligible praise according to Greek values. For his failed *nostos* (he became separated from Nestor on the way home and founded Metapontion and Lagaria in S. Italy) see R. Fowler, and for the archaeological evidence G. Genovese (both as at **911–29n.**). Kassandra devotes more than half of Epeios' allotment of twenty lines to Panopeus' perjury, for which his son was divinely punished with cowardice (**932, 943**); for such inherited guilt see generally R. Gagné, *Ancestral Fault in Ancient Greece* (Cambridge, Cambridge University Press, 2013). Panopeus' perjury concerned retention of booty (here called 'sheep') contrary to an oath; a treacherous girl Komaitho (**934**) was part of this complex story. Panopeus quarrelled in the womb with his brother Krisos (**939–40**), like the biblical Esau and Jacob (Genesis 25.22–3). Panopeus was son of Phokos, so the story may be an aetiology for historical rivalry between Krisa and the Phokian town Panopeus for ascendancy at Delphi.

938 At **1410** Mamertos will again be coupled with Kandaon/Kandaios as designations for Ares. Mamertos was Oscan (local Italian) for the Latin wargod Mars; this is of great importance for Lykophron's identity, because it shows good knowledge of the non-Greek west (the Mamertines, third-century BCE Campanian mercenaries, took their name from Mamertos: Polybius 1.8.1 with *HCP* 1.52 on 1.7.2). This detail may indicate that Lykophron was bilingual (for this see also **1250–2n.**) or even multilingual. See further **1416–17n.** on the interesting feminine form 'Mamersa' for a warrior Athena.

943 The unusual Greek compound word for 'coward' is used once only by Homer, where Glaukos criticizes Hektor (*Iliad* 17.143); but that was angry rhetoric, and the echo here does not seriously endorse that sneer at Kassandra's brave beloved brother. Nearer the poet's own time, and more relevant, Kallimachos' poem about Epeios (**930–50n.**) used a closely related word.

948–50 Archaeological finds at Francavilla Marittima near Kroton may be relevant, see **930–50n.** Real-life workmen dedicated their tools to Athena 'goddess of crafts'. An epigram by Leonidas of (nearby) Tarentum lists the many tools supposedly offered by a man to this Athena: *Anth. Pal.* 6.205 = *HE* lines 1992–2001; Simias wrote an axe-shaped poem about Epeios' dedicated axe: *Anth. Pal.* 15.22.

951–77 Most of this is about Trojan settlement in W. Sicily, territory of the Sikans, an indigenous people (Thucydides 6.2.3). But since the opening line and a half refers to unnamed Greek settlers in E. Sicily, 'Sikans' denotes the 'three-necked island' (**966**) as a whole. Only then does Kassandra switch to Trojan immigrants. The Laistrygonians were in E. Sicily (**662–5n.**), so 'travelling west' to their land (**956**) must mean 'westwards from Troy'. The immigrants are Phoinodamas' daughters. For their fate see **468–78**, where however he was unnamed, just as the Laistrygonians are first named only here. One daughter is Hesione, the monster's dinner (**954**), but rescued by Herakles: **33n.** This passage resumes, from Menelaos' *nostos*, the theme of Elymian cities in the largely Phoenician west of Sicily: see **866–76n.**; but with a difference: as firmly Trojan foundations this time, the 'three places' of **964**, Eryx, Entella, and especially Egesta, connect the narrative with a greater Trojan foundation: Rome. The temple at **958–9** to Aphrodite ('Zerynthia'), mother of 'wrestler' Eryx (cf. **866–76n.**) was at Eryx the city; it was famous and depicted on coins: Polybius 1.55.8; C. P. Jones, *Kinship Diplomacy* (Cambridge MA, Harvard University Press, 1999), 86–7. Aineias made a dedication to his mother Aphrodite there: Diodorus 4.83. This Trojan connection was important to the Romans in the third century BCE: in their first war against Phoenician-colonized Carthage

(264–41), they used such myths to build alliances with Elymian communities like Egesta/Segesta (968–77n.); after their defeat by Hannibal at Lake Trasimene in 217, they built another temple to Venus Erycina, but at Rome: Livy 22.10.10; cf. E. Gruen, *Studies in Greek Culture and Policy* (Leiden, Brill, 1990), 8–14 and Erskine 198–205.

Aigeste, another of Phoinodamas' daughters (Hesione's sister), mated with Krimisos, a river-god in a dog's shape, **961**. Their son was Aigestes, Acestes in *Aeneid* 5, eponym and founder of Egesta, Latin Segesta. There is a double Trojan genealogy here: the 'bastard sprig' of Aineias' father Anchises (**965**) is Elymos, founder of Eryx: Dionysios of Halikarnassos 1.52; Strabo 13.1.53. Kassandra keeps Aineias himself out of sight for the moment, but other authors gave him a founding role in this region. She regards Aigestes as the founder of all three Elymian places. Thucydides (6.2.3) knew of only two: the third, Entella, was prominent only later: *SEG* 30.1117–23, third-century dossier of decrees. By Virgil's time it had an eponymous hero: *Aeneid* 5.387–422, Entellus.

968–77 Kassandra's opening cry of lament echoes herself about unhappy Troy at **31**. In 263 BCE, Egesta in W. Sicily (see map) threw off its Carthaginian allegiance and joined Rome, supposedly because of shared Trojan kinship: a crucial moment in the First Punic War: Cicero, 2 *Verrines* 4.72; cf. K. Galinsky, *Aeneas, Sicily and Rome* (Princeton, Princeton University Press, 1969), 173. The much-elaborated mourning by Egesta for its fallen Trojan fatherland emphasizes the kinship theme; but by the end of the poem Egesta's ally Rome, the new Troy, will rise again victorious.

These lines refer mainly to Troy ('its towers', **972**) and mourning for it by the citizens of Egesta; but Hellenistic Egesta was unhappy for an additional reason, the savage destruction of the city by Agathokles of Syracuse in 307 BCE: Diodorus 20.71. See Ciaceri, and A. Barchiesi forthcoming, in a festschrift.

978–92 Siris on the river Sinis was refounded in the 430s BCE as Herakleia, after a sixth-century disaster. It was visited by Menelaos (**856**); Kassandra now says the area was settled by 'many' other Greeks. The city's history is complex: *IACP* no. 69. The earliest inhabitants were indigenous 'Chonians' (**983**); then followed rivalry between Greek colonists: Ionians (**989**, also called 'Xouthians', **987**) from Kolophon in Asia Minor, against Achaians, who wiped out the Ionians with a sacrilegious violence from which Athena averted her gaze, cf. **361–2n.**: Kassandra's rape by Ajax. It is unclear whether Kalchas is the Homeric seer of **424–30** (Kolophon), in which case his Italian murder at **981** by Herakles (angry because he failed another sort of fig-test) is inconsistent with the earlier story; or whether Kalchas is a generic word for 'seer'; see N. Mac Sweeney in *Returning Hero*, 249 and n. 13. ('Sisyphos' here just means 'cunning'). Nor is it clear in what sense Siris resembles Troy ('Ilion', **984**), although this provides a neat thematic link with Egesta, above; nor whether either set of Greeks are to be thought of as having made a *nostos* from Troy.

991 'Whelp (son) of the priestess' is obscure. It has been suggested that this is a son of Kassandra by Agamemnon (Paus. 2.16.6–7, cf. the Dodona inscription at Fraser 2003 and C. Morgan in *Returning Hero*, 228–33), but for Lykophron she is the archetypal virgin.

993–1010 Narration of further Greek settlement in S. Italian Bruttium leads Kassandra to give an aetiology for S. Italian Kaulonia, which featured glancingly in Thucydides: 7.25.2, the invading Athenians stored ship-building timber there. The eponymous Kaulon was son of Klete, nurse of Otrere's daughter the Amazon Penthesileia (**997**). Penthesileia was killed by Achilles, who fell in love with her as she died, but Kassandra suppresses his agency (McNelis and Sens, 114); he also killed the ugly 'Aitolian pest' Thersites (for whom see *Iliad* 2.211–77), who had wounded her eye. Only in this indirect sense does she 'bring death' to him; the 'bloody spear' is that of Achilles: **1000–1**. Klete's myth is intriguing: she founds a dynasty of female (Amazonian?) rulers, all called Klete, which is overthrown by Greek arrivals from Kroton. Traditions of directly exercised female power are rare, but something like it is attested for nearby Italian Lokroi: J. Redfield, *The Locrian Maidens: Love and Death in South Italy* (Princeton, Princeton University Press, 2003). Laur(et)e was wife of Kroton, eponym of the city.

1008 For Tereina and the river Okinaros, cf. **722–31**n.

1011–26 These two Greek leaders are in the Homeric *Catalogue*: see *Iliad* 2.671–5 for Nireus of Syme island near Rhodes, the most beautiful Greek after Achilles, and 2.638 for Thoas, 'best of the Aitolians' at 15.282; cf. **779–86**n. Gorge was his mother; 'Lykormas' is the Aitolian river Euenos: **1013**. (For an important Aitolian Thoas, remarkably the only historical Aitolian of that name in *LGPN* IIIA, see *HCP* 3, 110 on Polybius 21.17.6: 190 BCE.) Excellence aside, the two have nothing obvious in common to explain their joint founding activity in places in Illyria (Epirus) via Libya: **1017–26**. This Krathis river (**1021**) can not be the Italian one (for which see **911–29**n.), but like the Mylakoi and Polai (**1022**) is in Illyria. For winds as thwarting a safe *nostos* (**1014–18**), see **919–26**n.

1022–6 These lines presuppose good knowledge of the Argonautic myth: cf. Apollonios (4.303–8, 507–91) and Kallimachos frag. 11 (for Polai at **1022**). Medea's father Aietes sent Kolchians in pursuit of her; some ended up at the Illyrian river Dizeros, **1026**. (Aietes had migrated from Korinth to Aia i.e. Kolchis, **1023**: see West 2003, 237). 'Bride-carrying' (**1025**) is an imposing, resonant word, used about Hellenistic princesses: Polybius 25.4.8, *Syll.* 639, Rhodians escort Laodike, bride of Perseus of Macedon, daughter of Seleukos IV.

1027–33 The word here translated 'Malta' is Melite, three syllables; the iden-tification is not quite agreed, but proximity to S. Sicilian places (**1029**, **1033**) is decisive; see A. Bonanno, 'Lykophron on Malta', in *Miscellanea Manni* (Rome, L'Erma di Bretschneider, 1980), 1.273–6. The difficulty is Adriatic Othronos (**1027**, cf. **1034**), which implies a very circuitous route from Troy. Malta (cf. *OCD* 'Melita') was seized from the Carthaginians and absorbed into the Roman province of Sicily in 218 BCE, near the start of the Hannibalic War: Livy 21.51.1–2. It had long been a Phoenician trading post. There is little hard evidence of a Greek presence before that date; from after it, cf. *IG* 12.600 (Greek-Punic dedication to Herakles/Melqart; J. N. Adams, *Bilingualism and the Latin Language* (Cambridge, Cambridge University Press, 2003), 200) and 953 (honorary decree for Syracusan), both late third century BCE.

1031–3 For Odysseus as 'Sisypheian', cf. **344**. For an 'Odysseian headland' near Cape Pachynos (**1029**, SE angle of Sicily) see the geographer Ptolemy 3.4.7; cf. **1174–88**n. For the river Heloros near Syracuse (**1033**, also at **1184**), cf. 'Helorine' at Thucydides 6.66.3.

1034–46 Elephenor led the Euboians in the *Catalogue* (*Iliad* 2.540). For Euboians as colonizing pioneers see Lane Fox, esp. 130 for Orikon in this region. The places named here are again (**1011–26**n.) in Illyria and Epirus, except that at **1035** Koskynthos must be a Euboian river, for which Elephenor feels an exile's 'yearning', *pothos* (cf. **644–7**n.), and for Ladon see **1040–1**n. Elephenor exemplifies another explanation for overseas settlement: homicide of close kin (for diversion by winds as an explanation, see **919–26**n.; the verse geographer Pseudo-Skymnos 441–13 explains the Orikon Euboians in this way). From myth, cf. Thucydides 2.102, Alkmaion after his matricide; in history, Timoleon of Korinth refounded Syracuse after killing his brother: Diodorus 16.65, 340s BCE. Elephenor killed his grandfather Abas, but beyond that the myth is obscure.

1040–1 Telphousia here designates one of the Erinyes or Furies. See **152–67**n. for Erinys as an Arkadian epithet of Demeter, who upheld justice, like the Furies. T(h)elp(h)ousa was an Arkadian city (*IACP* no. 300) and Ladon an Arkadian river.

1047–55 For Daunia see **30**n. Podaleirios and Machaon were sons of the healing god Asklepios: **1054** (*Epios*, 'kindly', is name-play on Askl-*epios*). They led Thessalians in the *Catalogue* (*Iliad* 2.731–2). Either or both healed Philoktetes' wound: **911–29**n. From the opening line we expect both brothers to feature, but only Podaleirios does so, for his Daunian incubatory cult (with 'helper' at **1055**, cf. **1205**: Hektor). Incubation (see *OCD*) is temple medicine: you slept overnight in a sanctuary, hoping that a dream-epiphany of a god or hero would tell you a cure. Inscriptions claim to record the cures (*iamata*): R/O 102, Asklepios at Epidauros; W. V. Harris, *Dreams and Experience in Classical Antiquity* (Cambridge MA, Harvard University Press, 2008), 107–8. The ramskins (**1050**) are an authentic detail: Pausanias 1.34.5 (Amphiaraos' sanctuary at Oropos in Attica), cf. Virgil, *Aeneid* 7.85–91; they establish contact between sacrificer and sacrificed. With Kalchas' Italian ('Ausonian') tomb at **1047–8**, cf. **980–1**.

The Daunian river Althainos (**1053**) derives from a verb 'to heal': Timaios frag. 56.

1056–66 The story of Diomedes and Daunia is resumed from **632**. Division of material in this way is a sign of its importance (cf. the widely separated treatments of the fates of Kassandra herself and her close family). The link with Podaleirios' *nostos* is Daunia. The Aitolian request for the 'acres of their king' (**1059–60**) presupposes the curse uttered by Diomedes at **619–24**. The grim Daunian response (they 'grant' the request by throwing the envoys into a pit) recalls Herodotus on the Greek treatment of Xerxes' heralds, who asked for earth and water as symbols of submission, and were thrown down a well, 7.133. Cf. Justin 12.2 about Brundisium (Puglia). This Aitolian attempt to vindicate their claim fails, but see **592–632n.**: possible later success of the Dasii.

1066 Athena promised immortality to Diomedes' father Tydeus. In the war of the Seven against Thebes he fought Melanippos. Tydeus, dying, ate his enemy's brains; Athena revoked her promise in disgust. The Epic Cycle told this myth: *Thebaid* frag. 9 in West 2003.

1067–74 These Phokian leaders are Epistrophos and Schedios (sons of Iphitos, grandsons of Naubolos), so named in the Homeric *Catalogue*, *Iliad*. 2.517–26. Tzetzes (see Introduction, *Difficulty*) thought Epistrophos died at Troy, but this was a mistake: the name means 'Returner'. Hipponion and Temessa (**1068**) were topical, if Lykophron wrote in the early second century BCE: both were refounded in 194 by the Romans as Vibo Valentia and Tempsa respectively: Livy 35.40 and 34.45. ('Tethys' is the sea, by metonymy; Lampete is Latin Clampetia, mod. Amantea). Tempsa was twinned with Croton, Greek Kroton (**1071**, cf. **919–26n.**). As Greek Temessa (**1068**, cf. **852–55n.**), it was home to an anonymous hero; see B. Currie, 'Euthymos of Locri', *Journal of Hellenic Studies* 122 (2002), 24–44. For 'yearning' (**1074**), cf. **644–7n.** on the colonial *pothos* theme.

1075–82 Setaia, a Trojan woman, was crucified for setting fire to a fleet, either Greek (in continuation of the war) or Trojan (to preclude any return). Dionysios (1.72) knew both versions; Kassandra seems to prefer the first ('your masters', **1078**). A similar story is told about a Trojan woman Rhōmē, eponym of Rome. For that and other myths of the type see *EGM* 2: 567. Virgil, *Aeneid* 5.604–63 has Trojan ships and anonymous Trojan women; the name Setaia is peculiar to Lykophron. The exact eponymous location, too, was variously identified (Strabo 6.1.14): it was near Sybaris and the river Krathis (**1079**, cf. **911–29n.** and **919–26n.**).

1083–6 An unusually obscure *nostos*: no clue is offered as to the identity of the 'others' (surely Greeks), and there is no modern agreement about 'Membles' or 'Kerneatid' (Sardinia? Aegean Melos?) The eventual destination is Lucania, mod. Basilicata. The name of the river Lametos (mod. Amato) survives in Lamezia Terme, site of the regional airport. For 'Tyrrhenian', see **712–37n.**

1087–9 For the recapitulation, and for *anostos*, 'of no return' (**1088**), cf. **909–10n.**

1090–8 For Nauplios' twofold revenge on returning Greeks for the death of his son Palamedes, cf. **384–5n.**, **768–78n.**, **1214–25n.** The 'hens' (**1094**) are their wives, whom Nauplios' deceptions usually cause to be unfaithful. Modern readers may be sorry that hedgehogs, Britain's favourite mammals, are here a metaphor for home-wrecking and deceit (1092–3). (But Greek *echinos* can also be a sea-urchin: Aelian *On animals* 6.54, with remarks on the craftiness of hedgehogs.) Kassandra's hatred for the Greek heroes inconsistently extends to their Greek killer (Nauplios was a 'viper' at 384). Methymna (mod. Molyvos) was one of the six cities of Lesbos. Philostratos (*Heroikos* 33.48) says Ajax and Achilles buried Palamedes on the mainland opposite Lesbos, of whose cities, however, only Mytilene and not Methymna possessed such a *peraia* (mainland territory of an island): Ellis-Evans (243–57n.) 157–8 n. 6. 'Methymna' is perhaps a kind of part for whole, meaning Lesbos as mainland as well as island.

1099–1107 The narrative of Klytaimestra's murder of Agamemnon and Kassandra derives from Homer, *Odyssey* 11.387–464; but much of the verbal detail echoes the Kassandra scene in Aeschylus' *Agamemnon*, 1076–1330, 1372–98, 1539–40; cf. also Pindar *Pythian* 11. There are, however, significant differences. Klytaimestra's lover Aigisthos is absent, despite his culpability for the murderous act in Homer (*Odyssey* 1.36, 4.535, 11.409–11, 24.97), and there is, naturally, no hint of Homer's contrast between Agamemnon's fate and Odysseus' ultimately happy *nostos*. See also next n.

1108–22 Homer's Kassandra dies with Agamemnon (*Odyssey* 11.423, followed by Aeschylus and Pindar). 'Who does not hear me' (1118) directly contradicts Homer, for whom Agamemnon does hear Kassandra's cries: *Odyssey* 11.421–2. This can be seen as part of a general and demeaning exaggeration of his helplessness (McNelis and Sens, 175), although already in the *Odyssey* he dies like an 'ox (castrated bull) at the crib': 11.411. In Homer (1.30, 40), Orestes avenges his father Agamemnon, but his victim is implied to be Aigisthos only, cf. 1099–1107n. The moral dilemma—should a son avenge his father if it means killing his mother?—is created by shifting the *active* role in the murder to Klytaimestra (at *Odyssey* 11.429 she *planned* it), and is explored in the last two plays of Aeschylus' *Oresteia* trilogy, *Libation-bearers* and *Eumenides*. The son's vengeance is foreseen by Kassandra in the first play: *Agamemnon*, 1279–83, including a magnificent line (1280) borrowed by Virgil, in virtual translation, for Carthaginian Dido's dying prayer that an avenger (Hannibal) would arise from her bones, *Aeneid* 4.625.

1122 The powerful word for (religious) pollution, *miasma*, is used here only in the poem, an indication of the episode's importance.

1123–40 For Agamemnon as Zeus (and vice versa), see 335–6n. For his joint cult with Kassandra at Spartan Amyklai, see 30n. Potsherds from Amyklai, some not fully published, are inscribed 'Agamemnon' and 'Alex[andra]', Kassandra's Spartan name: see again 30n., and for illustrations Hornblower 2015, fig. 2. Kassandra's Daunian cult is located near Salpe, port of Argyrippa (1129, cf. 592–3n.): Strabo 6.3.9, Livy 24.20.15 (Hannibal's base in 214/13 BCE). 'Dardanos' (1129) suggests Troy (69–85n., 1236–41n.,

1257, 1307), but this is an Italian city. It has not been located convincingly. Kassandra refused sex and marriage, but is the object of what looks like a premarital initiatory cult. This paradox makes anthropological sense: in rites of passage you often temporarily undergo a state opposite to that for which you are being prepared. For Hektor's flowing hairstyle (1133), cf. *Iliad* 22.401–2, and the vase-painting at Hornblower 2015, fig. 6. The (dark) female dress (1137–40) recalls Timaios frag. 55.

1141–73 In reparation for Lokrian Ajax's violent and sacrilegious assault on Kassandra in Athena's temple at Ilion i.e. Troy (348–72), the Lokrians must for a thousand years pay tribute to that temple (but see below); the tribute is not monetary but human, a maiden or maidens. The myth is conspicuously popular in literary sources, starting with the military writer Aineias 'the Tactician' in the mid-fourth century BCE (31.24, treating the tribute entirely matter-of-factly). But Lykophron's is the fullest, best, and most sinister literary account. It was a surprise when in the early twentieth century a lengthy but fragmentary early Hellenistic prose inscription from Greek (as opposed to Italian) Lokroi was published, giving details of what is almost certainly the ritual corresponding to the myth: for the only English translation, with commentary and Greek text, see Hornblower 2018: 180–6 and discussion at 154–66. The myth takes to a violent homicidal extreme what the civic ritual preserves in bearable form; for this pattern, see W. Burkert, in R. Buxton (ed.), *Oxford Readings in Greek Religion* (Oxford, Oxford University Press, 2000), 248, discussing a comparable myth-ritual pair from Lemnos; cf. 479–85n. Whereas Kassandra makes the maidens' penance last for life, and their entry into Troy beset with dire physical threats (so too the 'Tactician'), the inscription implies a temporary absence, probably as part of a premarital rite (cf. 1123–40n., Kassandra's Daunian cult), and deals prosaically with practical matters: expenses, clothing, and so forth. It is even possible that the usual annual destination of the maidens was not Troy proper but a local and epigraphically attested Lokrian shrine of Athena Ilias ('of Troy'); perhaps every few years some sort of symbolic civic deputation went across the Aegean to Troy, accompanying some selected maidens, but that is speculative.

The long, brilliant excursus on the Lokrian maidens has a clear literary function. So soon after the narrative of Kassandra's murder by Klytaimestra, it is a reminder of Ajax's earlier outrage against her (1143) and it resumes the recurrent theme of the evils to be inflicted on Greeks as a penalty for his assault: 365, 412, 910. The list of bereaved Lokrian places at 1146–50 (mostly taken from the Homeric *Catalogue*, *Iliad* 2.527–34) recalls the Euboian counterpart at 373–6, positioned straight after the rape. Kassandra has also (McNelis and Sens, 189–93) been thought of as acquiring cult honours—*kleos* (cf. 1126, albeit with the different Greek noun *sebas*, which has a cultic tinge) by her interference in the marital futures of young woman in both the west (Daunia) and east (Lokris; Troy) Mediterranean. That would contribute to the poem's larger message about the revival of Trojan glory, *kleos*: 1174–88nn. This is attractive—there are

thematic links between Daunian and Lokrian women (both initiatory)—but of those two female groups the text explicitly confines
Kassandra's cult to Daunian 'rod-bearing women', 1139–40.

1143 The 'Kyprian' is Aphrodite, so 'theft' of her is forcible sexual assault
by Ajax.

1148 Of the Lokrian places, little Naryx is of special interest because of the
publication in 2001 of an inscribed letter in Greek to Naryx from the
emperor Hadrian, saying that 'some of the heroes [i.e. Lokrian Ajax,
plural for singular] originated from your city', and that the Narykeioi were
mentioned by famous Greek and Roman poets, surely including the
author of the *Alexandra*: *SEG* 51.641. That Hadrian, himself a poet and
connoisseur of poetry, might have read the *Alexandra* was an inspired
guess by the novelist Marguerite Yourcenar, long before that inscription
was found: see *Memoirs of Hadrian* (London, Penguin Books, 1986
[French original, 1951]), 135.

1172–3 Poets cheerfully retrojected epigraphy into the heroic age, like the simple message 'in Doric dialect' at Theocritus 18.48, Helen's bridal song.
But it is by a particularly bold anachronism that Kassandra is made to
envisage a carved decree at Ilion granting advance immunity to killers of
the maidens. Such inscribed grants, usually to tyrannicides, were a feature
of the Classical and Hellenistic periods. One of the longest and most
informative is from, precisely, Ilion (Troy): *OGIS* 218 (280 BCE), with
D. A. Teegarden, *Death to Tyrants!* (Princeton, Princeton University
Press, 2013), 173–214. Had Lykophron seen it?

1174–88 The Hekabe section and the Hektor section which follows it
(1189–1213) form a Trojan triptych with the preceding narration of
Kassandra's own fate. The presentation reverses the order of the much
earlier prophecy about Kassandra and her family (307–64), where the
material about Hektor, Hekabe, and other members of Priam's family led
up to Kassandra's rape as climax. The lengthy *nostoi* section intervened.

For Hekabe's metamorphosis into a dog, and for the sinister three-
headed (1186) goddess Hekate whose canine attendant she became, see
330–4n. For the Sicilian promontory Pachynos and the river Heloros see
1031–3n. Here Odysseus leads the (Greek?) stoning of Hekabe (1188); at
331 the Thracian Dolonkoi alone stoned her.

The 'marked' word for Hekabe's fame or glory (1174) is *kleos*, used only
three times in the poem, always about Trojans, never Greeks: 1212
(Hektor) and 1226 (Kassandra's ancestors, whose *kleos* will be increased by
their Roman descendants).

1183–8 Hekabe's future cult is implied rather than asserted explicitly; contrast
Kassandra's (premarital) or Hektor's (healing relics), the other elements
of the Trojan triptych. But 1183 is a hint, because cults were often
established as a result of dreams: cf. *Syll.* 663 (Delos 200 BCE); Harris
(1047–55n.), 168. From the language used about the libations and sacrifice,
this cult looks 'chthonic' (dark, sinister, underworld-related).

1189–1213 Hektor's bones will, on the orders of an Apolline oracle (**1206–7**) be removed from Ophryneion in the Troy region and reburied at Boiotian Thebes, where they will have healing powers. This is in one aspect a hero-cult of relics, of a sort familiar from Archaic and Classical Greek history. Cf. the oracularly sanctioned transfer of the bones of Orestes, Rhesos, and Theseus (**1322–6**n.); see B. McCaulay, 'Heroes and power: the politics of bone transferral' in R. Hägg (ed.), *Ancient Greek Hero Cult* (Stockholm, Swedish Institute at Athens, 1999), 85–98. But Lykophron's is the earliest evidence for the removal, and for Hektor's Boiotian cult: there is no trace in what survives of Attic tragedy or the Boiotian poets Hesiod or Pindar, an astonishing silence given Hektor's importance in Greek myth. *After* Lykophron several literary texts attest the oracle, transfer, and cult (Aristodemos of Thebes, *FGrHist* 383 frag. 7, Strabo 13.1.29, Pausanias 9.18.5). An epigram attributed to Aristotle (frag. 640) knows the story, but is late Hellenistic, not fourth century BCE: Hornblower 2018, 151–3. So some special explanation and moment is needed for the late appearance of the tradition. It has been plausibly sought in the refoundation of Thebes by Kassandros in 315 BCE after its destruction by Alexander the Great in 335: A. Schachter, *Cults of Boiotia, Bulletin of the Institute of Classical Studies Supplement* 38, vol. 1 (London, 1981), 233–4; for the rebuilding see Diodorus 19.53 and *Syll.* 337 (new fragments at *SEG* 64.403, cf. Y. Kalliontzis and N. Papazarkadas, *Annual, British School at Athens* 114 (2019), 293–315). Kassandros hated the now-dead Alexander, who had posed in life as the new Achilles, so his choice of Hektor had malicious point, especially since Achilles had sacked another Thebes, in the Troy region, home of Hektor's wife Andromache. If this is right, Lykophron's source (here as elsewhere, cf. **799–806**n.) could well be the great historian Hieronymos of Kardia, who was governor of Thebes in the 290s BCE and was interested in Theban antiquities.

1193–1203 The excursus on Zeus' birth (at Thebes, in Kassandra's version, **1194**) is prompted by his 'throne of Ophion', who ruled Olympos with his wife Eurynome until they were overthrown by Rhea and Kronos, Zeus' parents: Apollonios 1.503–9. Rhea then prevented Kronos from eating Zeus by substituting a stone: Hesiod, *Theogony* 467.

1204–5 The word 'hero' (the English word derives from the Greek one) occurs here only in the poem, a token of Kassandra's special affection for the dearest of her brothers. For the Islands of the Blest, cf. **180–201**n.: Achilles. In the present section Kassandra talks up Hektor in ways which evoke Achilles: McNelis and Sens, 198. The word for 'helper' was applied to another mythical healing hero, Podaleirios, at **1055**. Historical individuals might enjoy posthumous cult as healers, like the fifth-century BCE hero-athlete Theagenes of Thasos: *Syll.* 36, Paus. 6.11.9.

1206 The whole Hektor passage is full of out-of-the-way synonyms for Thebes and Boiotia. The Sown Men are a Theban autochthony myth (cf. **479–85**n.): they sprang from the teeth of a dragon killed by Kadmos, founder of Thebes: Apollodoros 3.4.1.

1214–25 Kassandra has already noticed Idomeneus' tomb at Kolophon: 431–2n. In the *Catalogue* (*Iliad* 2.645–6), he led Kretans from Knossos and Gortyn. When he went to Troy he left his son-in-law Leukos in charge. Nauplios corrupted Leukos so that he killed Meda, Idomeneus' wife, also Kleisithera, his own wife and Idomeneus' daughter (and other children of Idomeneus): Apollodoros epitome 6.9–11. Idomeneus is another Greek victim of Nauplios (**1216**); this links him with Agamemnon (**1099–1107**). But the sequence is not immediate, and Nauplios' revenge does not take the usual form of making a wife unfaithful. A more proximate link is requital to Kassandra: 'my wretched calamity', **1214**. With this, cf. **1141–2**, grief caused to the mothers of the Lokrian maidens: McNelis and Sens, 94. The reference to Arkadian Onkai (**1225**) is difficult: it suggests Demeter, who in Arkadia was assimilated to the Furies ('Erinyes', cf. **152**), who policed crimes like those of Leukos.

1226–35 The Roman descendants of the Trojans at last make their appearance unmistakably—if indirectly, as usual; the city's name meets us very early because it is the same as the Greek word for 'strength' at **1233**: *rhōmē*. The pseudo-prophecy of Roman 'sceptre and kingship over land and sea' (**1229**) is the most famous line in the poem, and for political reasons has always been considered a grave obstacle to a composition date in the first half of the third century BCE, before the Romans had acquired a single overseas possession; see Introduction, *Authorship and Date*. An ancient commentator even believed a new author had taken over at this point. The 'miserable fatherland' is Troy; its fall will be redeemed by Rome's military might and its Mediterranean empire. For 'glory', *kleos* (**1226**), see **1174–88n.**; *kudos*, 'renown' (**1231**) has similar force.

1232–5 The 'kinsman' is Aeneias, son of Anchises (cf. **965**) and of Aphrodite; for their liaison, see the Homeric *Hymn* (5) *to Aphrodite*. Poseidon (*Iliad* 20.302, 307–8) had predicted that Aineias would survive and rule over the Trojans, as would his descendants. The 'twin [lit. 'double'] lion-whelps' are Romulus and Remus, founders of Rome. See Livy Book 1 and T. P. Wiseman, *Remus* (Cambridge, Cambridge University Press, 1995); the twins were depicted on silver coins circulating in Italy during the third century (Wiseman 156–7 and fig. 17 no. 3) and Lykophron could have seen these. Kassandra ignores the chronological difficulty: Rome was conventionally founded in the eighth century BCE, long after the fall of Troy and Aineias' flight westwards; see D. Feeney, *Caesar's Calendar* (Berkeley, University of California Press, 2007), 95–100. Aineias' characterization (**1235**) is Homeric: see *Iliad* 6.77–9: the seer Helenos, Kassandra's brother, says that Aineias and Hektor (in that order!) are best at fighting and thinking.

1236–41 The 'man who wanders to and fro' (**1239**) is Aineias. He will travel from Troy to Etruria via Macedonian or west Thracian places—a kind of *nostos*, except that he is Trojan not Greek (for this extension of *nostos* see *Returning Hero*, 27 and 36, and for the Trojans as 'returning' to Italy, from where their ancestor Dardanos had set out, see Virgil *Aeneid* 7.240–1 and 8.37). Behind 'settle' (**1236**) lies a tradition connecting him with Aineia, near Macedonian Thessaloniki: Livy describes a festival to Aineias there as *conditor*, 'founder' (40.4.9, 182 BCE; cf. Erskine, 93–8. By Lykophron's time, there was even an anti-Roman story that Aineias never reached Italy but died hereabouts, in Thrace: Erskine, 96; Hornblower 2018, 190; and M. Visscher, *Beyond Alexandria. Literature and Empire in the Seleucid World* (Oxford, Oxford University Press, 2020), 198. Kassandra naturally ignores this.) The river Lingeus (**1240**) is the Arno (or perhaps the Auser/Serchio (William Harris)). For Pisa (mod. Pisa in Tuscany, not the Greek Pisa near Olympia, cf. **152–67**n.) and Agylla (Caere, mod. Cerveteri), cf. **1355** and **1359**.

1242–9 For Odysseus as Aineias' 'frenemy', cf. **648–819**n. §4. He is a 'dwarf', *nanos*, at **1244** because he was relatively short of stature at *Iliad* 3.193, but there was also a Nanas who founded Etruria: Dionysios 1.28; Wiseman 1995 (**1232–5**n.), 51. Tarchon (eponym of Etruscan Tarquinii) and Tyrrhenos (eponym of Tyrrhenia/Etruria) are Mysians here, but at **1351–2** Lydians from further south in Asia Minor. For the myth about their father Telephos and Dionysos see **206–15**n., and, for the alliance of some Etruscan princes (including Tarchon) with Aineias, Virgil, *Aeneid* 10.153–6 with S. J. Harrison's commentary (Oxford, Oxford University Press, 1991), and R. Heinze, *Virgil's Epic Technique* (Berkeley, University of California Press, 1993), 146. Virgil may have drawn on Lykophron for this. The word for 'army' (*stratos*) at **1242**, and the ferocity of the descriptors used here for these brothers, imply that Aineias and his allies fought a war against indigenous peoples for possession of Italy; see further **1351–61** for Italian conquests by the two brothers, the 'falcons'. (At **852**, *stratos* meant 'people', but the more usual sense was military.)

1250–2 For 'there' see next n. Aineias and his entourage were told prophetically that before they could found their promised city, hunger would force them to 'eat their tables': Virgil, *Aeneid* 3.255–7 for the prophecy (attributing it to the harpy Celaeno) and 7.107–34 for its fulfilment (attributing it to Anchises; for the change as a deliberate 'deletion' of Celaeno see Pillinger, 156); cf. Dionysios 1.55. But these texts were not available for at least two centuries after the *Alexandra*, which stands at the head of the fully surviving tradition, and therefore has great importance. Timaios may have been Lykophron's source, but there is no hard evidence for this common assumption. The Latin for 'tables', *mensae*, also means flat cakes of a sacrificial sort, so when Aeneias' son Ascanius/Iulus cried at meal-time, 'hey, we are eating our *mensae*!', the prophecy was fulfilled and the Trojans settled there. There is no such ambiguity in *trapeza*, the Greek for 'table' (C. J. Fordyce, commentary on *Aeneid* 7 and 8 (Oxford, Oxford University Press, 1977), 84), so Lykophron's source, direct or via Timaios, must have been Italian, and Lykophron himself bilingual (cf. **938**n., **1409–10**n.). The hunger motif is typical of Greek colonization stories; see N. Horsfall, commentary on *Aeneid* 7 (Leiden, Brill, 2000), 110.

1253–72 Kassandra brings Aineias south from Etruria to Latium without actually saying so. But since his first foundation is in Latium (below), 'there' at **1250** must mean Latium—the area round Rome—not Etruria. The name

of the 'place' at **1253**, Aeneias' first Italian foundation, is uncertain, and
Lykophron is vague. He probably meant Lavinium in Latium, 20 km south
of Rome. Virgil (*Aeneid* 7.156–9) describes Aineias fortifying a camp, which
an ancient commentator says was named 'Troy', *Troia*: S. J. Harrison
(**1242–9**n.) on *Aeneid* 10.27 and D. Feeney, 'The reconciliations of Juno',
Classical Quarterly 34 (1984), 179–94 at 190 and n. 74 (= *Explorations in
Latin Literature* vol. 1, Cambridge, Cambridge University Press, 2021, 56
n. 69, tracing it back to Ennius). But if Lykophron knew it was a Troy he
would surely have found a way of saying so. Also in **1253**, the Aborigines
('indigenous people', Cato *FRHist* 5 frag. 63) are a people ruled by Latinos,
eponym of the Latins: Strabo 5.3.2. It is odd, therefore, that Aineias' evidently Latin settlement is said at **1254** to be '*beyond* the Latins' and
Daunians. Perhaps Lykophron located the Aborigines in far eastern
Latium, towards Daunia.

What follows is an idiosyncratic version of the mythical origins of the
thirty communities of the Latin League; see A. Alföldi, *Early Rome and
the Latins* (Ann Arbor, University of Michigan Press, 1965), 271–8. In
Virgil (*Aeneid* 8.43–5, cf. Dionysios 1.55), a white sow guided Aineias to
Alba Longa, somewhere SE of Rome (*alba* is Latin for 'white', but the
'Dark Poet' Lykophron prefers black, **1256**); for such guiding animals, cf.
29n. The thirty piglets are the League members. But Aineias' dedications
to Athena (**1261**) were at the sacred site of Lavinium (Timaios frag. 59),
'one of those [Latin] cities', **1259**; so the sow's guidance was from there,
Aineias' original settlement, to Alba Longa. For a possible hero-cult for
Aineias at Lavinium, see C. J. Smith, *Early Rome and Latium* (Oxford,
Oxford University Press, 1996), 134. Lykophron has Aineias bring the sow
by ship from Troy originally (**1256–7**).   ʼ

The 'ancestral gods' (**1262**) are the Penates (see *OCD*), the household
gods whose images Aineias brought from Troy via Samothrace (Kassandra
ignores that part of his itinerary). This was probably in Stesichoros. At
1263, the abandoned wife is Virgil's Creusa, but Lykophron probably
knew her as a Eurydike (not the same woman as in the Orpheus myth); the
abandoned children do not include Ascanius/Iulus (cf. **1250–2**n.), ancestor of the Julian dynasty. He went west with Aineias.

Aineias is already 'pious' (**1270**) towards the gods in Homer (*Iliad*
20.298–9). But when Troy fell, the Greeks allowed Aineias to take whatever
he wanted, because he saved his father, so giving evidence of his piety, in
the Greek sense which includes care for parents: for this concession see
Xenophon, *Kynegetikos* 1.15; Apollodoros epitome 5.21. There is some
illogicality here: he piously saves his father and is rewarded for this by
being allowed to save his father. Perhaps the reward was originally thought
of as for piety in the *Iliadic* sense, but the real motive for devising the
reward story may have been to explain his heavily burdened escape while
implicitly denying that he colluded with the enemy, like Antenor: **340–7**n.
Virgil later made piety, broadly conceived, central to his characterization
of Aineias. See Galinsky (**968–77**n.) 3–61.

It is surprising, given the poem's emphasis on Rome as a victorious reborn Troy, that the foundation of Rome itself is so muted in this Italian section, apart from the very general 1271–2 (Aineias will found a new martial and prosperous fatherland); and for the city's name see 1226–35n. Nor is the Tiber ever mentioned, despite Kassandra's marked liking for rivers. The focus is mainly on Latium and its chief city Lavinium.

1273–80 After the prophecy that Aineias will eventually found Rome (1271–2), the reader expects (cf. 1253–72n.) an elaboration of the Rome theme; instead, Kassandra lists other places situated—more or less—in Latium; the exception is the final item, the Sibyl's cave at Campanian Cumae (1279–80) away to the south-east. Pillinger (e.g. 141, 149, 164) argues attractively that Lykophron's Kassandra sees this Sibyl—there were several others in the ancient world—as her prophetic successor. For the Sibyl's cave, cf. Virgil, *Aeneid* 6.11, a passage indebted to Lykophron. See also 1451–60n. and 1461–74n.

Kirke is coastal Circeii (see *OCD*), mod. Monte Circeo. The harbour at 1274, originally founded by the Argonauts (Apollonios 4.661–3), is Virgil's Caieta, named for Aineias' nurse (*Aeneid* 7.1–4); for a link with a similarly aetiological woman called Prochyta in the early Latin poet Naevius, frag. 9, see A. Barchiesi, 'Aeneas in Campania: notes on Naevius as a model for the *Aeneid*' in *Habent sua fata libelli: Studies... in honor of Craig Kallendorf* (ed. S. Oberhelman and others) (Leiden, Brill, 2022), 19–33. Phorke is the Fucine lake in the territory of the Marsi, a central Italian people (*OCD*); the 'Titonian river' is the Pitonia (mod. Petogna), cf. Pliny, *Natural History* 31.41.

1281–90 For the recapitulation at 1281–2, cf. 909–10n., but this one does not summarize the immediately preceding lines. Instead it marks the end of the entire long *nostoi* section which began at 417 (for Aineias' wanderings as a *nostos*, cf. 1236–41n.; but he does the opposite of destroying his fatherland). For the remainder of the poem, its climactic and most explicitly historical part, Kassandra narrates prophetically the entire future conflict between Asia and Europe, and its eventual resolution. The poet leans heavily on Herodotus (mainly but not only his opening chapters), but with differences: (1) whereas Herodotus used the Asia–Europe conflict as an introduction to his Histories (1.1–5), Kassandra saves it for an extended closure; (2) she passes seamlessly and gradually from mythical to semi-mythical (colonization myths) and finally to fully historical events (the Persian wars and later conflicts), whereas Herodotus marked a clear methodological break at 1.5.3, moving explicitly from what he could not assert confidently to what he felt he knew. For other divergences and additions, see the individual notes.

Prometheus' mother was Asia (Apollodoros 1.2.3); Sarpedon's 'nurse' (mother) was Europe (Hesiod frags. 89 and 90; Hellanikos *FGrHist* 4 frag. 94). The divide between the continents is treated as the whole stretch of sea between Hellespont and Bosphoros (at whose northern end were the Symplegades or Clashing Rocks); for Salmydesos as the Black Sea, by

a typical part-for whole expression, cf. **186**. The Tanais (mod. Don) and
Lake Maiotis (Sea of Azov) develop the Black Sea theme. The question at
1283–4 looks at first purely rhetorical, implying the answer 'Asia and
Europe have nothing in common'; but it will be revealed later that they
will after all be reconciled: **1448**.

1291–5 Now begins the series of Asian and European abductions and counter-
abductions of women, in the sequence laid down by Herodotus (Io–Europa–
Medea, but Helen is postponed until **1362**). The Argive priestess Io featured
in two Aeschylean plays, *Prometheus* and *Suppliants*. Zeus had sex with her.
She was then turned into a cow by Zeus so as to deceive his wife Hera (the
usual version), or else (Aeschylus) by Hera as punishment, but Zeus evaded
this by turning himself into a bull and having sex with her again: cf. Aeschylus,
Suppliants 299–301 with A. Sommerstein's commentary (Cambridge,
Cambridge University Press, 2019); this metamorphosis may (cf. *OCD*
'Io') hint at female initiatory rites. The parallel with Europa (next n.) might
suggest that Kassandra preferred Aeschylus' version. See Herodotus 1.1 and
1.5 for Io's abduction from Argos to Egypt by Phoenicians (Lerna is in Argive
territory). Her marriage to a king of Egypt is not Herodotean; cf. next n.
Since Io was identifiable with Isis (Herodotus 2.41.2) the king might be
Osiris, and 'bull-maiden' (we expect 'cow-maiden' from the Greek version of
the myth) could refer additionally to Isis as the bull Apis' mother, or even to
Isis' hermaphroditic procreation of Harpokrates: S. West, 'Lycophron on
Isis', *Journal of Egyptian Archaeology* 70 (1984), 151–4; J. G. Griffiths,
'Lycophron on Io and Isis', *Classical Quarterly* 36 (1986), 472–7. But the
Greek tradition of metamorphosis is also clearly present, and with it the
divine rape, which Herodotus ignored, but which looks forward to Europa
(**1296**) and back to Kassandra herself; cf. McNelis and Sens, 96–7. This is the
only place where the poet may show genuine knowledge of Egyptian cults
and myths. In this he is unlike the Alexandrian Kallimachos.

At **1291**, 'sailor-dogs' translates two distinct Greek nouns separated by
other words, 'sailors' . . . 'dogs'. On this interesting expression ('sailors that
in their behaviour resemble dogs') see J. N. Adams, *Asyndeton and its
Interpretation in Latin Literature: History, Patterns, Textual Criticism*
(Cambridge, Cambridge University Press, 2021), 45.

1296–1308 Next in line is Europa, as for Herodotus (1.2), but again with significant divergences. Like Io, Europa fell victim to Zeus' lust, and this
entailed metamorphosis, but this time certainly of the rapist not the raped
(see previous n.): Zeus, in the form of a bull, carried her off from Phoenicia
('Sarapta') to Krete. The Hellenistic poet Moschos' 166-line poem on the
theme (the *Europa*) survives. For the abduction, Kassandra retains
Herodotus' exclusively human, specifically Kretan agency (Mt Ida at **1296**
is Kretan not Trojan, cf. **52–6n.**), but the ship's 'bull-shaped ensign' is
a clue to the divine rape; cf. Priestley, 180–1. The marriage to the local
king Aster(i)os at **1301** (cf. Hesiod frag. 89) is another non-Herodotean
parallel with Io. We are meant to remember Kassandra's own enforced
relationship with King Agamemnon.

The further reprisals at **1302–8** are not in Herodotus. Teukros (not the same as the brother of Telamonian Ajax, cf. **417–23n.**) set out from Krete and founded a place on the site of Troy, so that one of Virgil's names for Trojans is *Teucri*. An oracle had told them to settle where they were attacked by the 'earthborn', who turned out to be mice, who ate their bow-strings: Strabo 13.1.48, quoting the Archaic poet Kallinos. For the type of story (animals guiding colonists), cf. **29n.** The word for 'mice', *sminthoi*, is rare, but had recently been used by Kallimachos, frag. 177.16. These mice provided the aetiology for Apollo's Trojan cult-epithet Smintheus: Homer, *Iliad* 1.39 and Hellenistic inscriptions and coins. Arisba (**1308**) was Teukros' daughter and wife of Dardanos, ancestor of the Trojan kings (**69–85n.**); cf. *IACP* no. 768 ('Arisbe').

1309–21 For female abduction no. (3), Medea from Kolchis, cf. Herodotus 1.2.2–3, although Kassandra concedes, in a contradictory expression, that she was 'snatched' willingly (**1317**, 'self-invited crow'). This and other important details are—with chronological dislocations—taken from other sources, notably Pindar *Pythian* 4 and Apollonios. There were lost epics too: the legend of Jason (*tagos*, Thessalian for 'ruler') and the Argonauts was familiar, even in Homer's time: *Odyssey* 12.70, 'Argo known to all'. For the heroic quest for the Golden Fleece (**1310**) see **22n.**; modern interpreters view this in terms of initiation into adulthood. The rare word for 'one-sandalled' is a gesture at Pindar: *Pythian* 4.75. At **1318** events are telescoped: Medea killed her brother Apsyrtos on the way home from Kolchis, and only much later her own and Jason's children, as in Euripides' *Medea*. Again, 'chopped up in a cauldron' (**1315**) means Jason himself was rejuvenated, as in Pherekydes (*FGrHist* 3 frag. 113), but at Korinth, not—as here implied—Kolchis and its serpent and fire-breathing bulls.

1319–21 The Argo was a talking ship with a mind of its own: its keel was from the oracular oak at Dodona in Epiros ('Chaonia').

1322–6 This double Amazonian episode is not from Herodotus 1.1–5, but see 4.110 and 9.27.4. We have met Theseus already, as Akamas' father: **494–5**, using the same rock-and-sandals identifier. This is close thematic self-repetition; but here Kassandra elaborates on Theseus' career because he is himself the main focus. If Phemios is Poseidon, as is likeliest, Theseus son of Aigeus has double paternity, like some other males in the poem (**307–13n.**). His bones were taken from his death-place Skyros and reburied at Athens in the fifth century BCE (Plutarch *Kimon* 8); cf. **1189–1213n.** for such cults of relics. On 'too steep for goats' (**1326**), see Aeschylus, *Suppliants* 794 and A. Sens, *Hellenistic Epigrams. A Selection* (Cambridge, Cambridge University Press, 2020), 115.

1327–40 Hera hated Herakles whom she had suckled (**39n.**). He was initiated at Eleusis. 'Beast', a typical animal metaphor, may allude to his trademark lion-skin. He joined Theseus in invading Amazon lands (Themiskyra is on the Black Sea): they abducted an Amazon ('Orthosia' = Hippolyte or

Antiope), and stole a war-belt, ninth of his Twelve Labours. Other Amazons rode from Skythia and sacked Attica in reprisal: **1338–40**. See J. Boardman, 'Herakles, Theseus and Amazons', in D. Kurtz and B. Sparkes (eds.), *The Eye of Greece* (Cambridge, Cambridge University Press, 1982), 1–28. The Thermodon is from Herodotus (previous n.); it is not the Boiotian river of **647**. The 'land of Mopsops' is Athens, cf. **732–7**n.

1341–50 Ilos, second king of Troy, was Kassandra's great-grandfather. For a Trojan invasion of Thrace and the N. Balkans as far as the Thessalian river Peneios (cf. **1343**) see Herodotus 7.20. Eordaia was Ptolemy I's home canton. For Macedonian Galadrai (cf. **1444**) see Polybius 23 frag. 1 with *HCP* 3.253. For Herakles' sack of Troy, cf. **31**n. Hera ('Gorgas') finally relented towards Herakles and deified him. For the six ships of **1347** see *Iliad* 5.641. (At **1346**, the Greek word I translate 'Europe' just means 'she'.)

1351–60 These lines about the Italian invasion of the Anatolian princes Tarchon and Tyrrhenos reprise and expand on **1245–9**, but with two differences: (1) there they were sons of Mysian Telephos, while here they are Lydians, as at Herodotus 1.94; this contradiction may be down to mere authorial absentmindedness. More important (2), Kassandra does not here specify that they were allies of Aineias: her mind is on inter-continental reprisals. But the repetition from **1241** of Pisa and Agylla is a subtle hint. The important point is that this is further evidence that Aineias' Italian settlements were achieved by war, cf. **1356**. For Mt Tmolos and the gold-bearing Paktolos (**269–72**n.), see Herodotus 5.101. The lake (**1353**) is Gygaia, home of the giant Typhon: *Iliad* 2.865, Strabo 13.4.5–6, L. Robert, *Documents d'Asie mineure* (Paris, De Boccard, 1987), 296–335. His wife was Echidna, mother of the Chimaira: Hesiod, *Theogony* 295–322.

'Sithonian' (**1358**) means 'from Chalkidike' in N. Greece (cf. **103**n. for Sithone), home of the Giants. This is an Italian foundation myth of some sort.

1361 These problematic Salpians are surely the Etruscan Salpinates of Livy 5.31.5 (where the manuscripts have minor spelling variations): W. V. Harris, *Rome in Etruria and Umbria* (Oxford, Clarendon Press, 1971), 43 n. 7. (Holzinger had rejected this solution without argument.)

1362–8 For Paris as firebrand, because he provoked the Trojan War, see **86–9**n. For the 'last' Asiatic aggression of the series (not really last, see **1397–1434**, Midas, then Xerxes), Kassandra reverts to Herodotus' preface: 1.3.1–2. In both accounts, Paris is angry about the incursion of the Argonauts (the 'Pelasgians' i.e. Thessalians of **1364**, cf. **877–910**n.). The Argonauts passed by the mouth of the Rhyndakos, which flows into the Propontis: Apollonios 1.1165. The theft of Helen was described at **86–9**, and this time (contrast **1351–60**n.) Kassandra does not repeat herself. The fourfold European revenge for this abduction will receive far longer coverage than its cause.

1369–73 So far, the Asia–Europe material has been entirely mythical. 'Threefold, fourfold' (**1367**) may be more than poetic intensification: Greek aggression no. (1), the Trojan War myth, is qualitatively different from the three colonization stories which follow, nos. (2–4): these are only semi-mythical. The individual founders are figures of myth, to be sure. But historical families claimed legitimating descent from them (**1374–7**n.). And the migration patterns they signify are historical, in the sense that the three coastal zones of Asia Minor share the dialects of the Aiolian, Ionian, and Dorian Greeks who moved north-east, east, and south-east across the Aegean to settle those zones on parallel tracks from their homelands (cf. **479–85**n. on Arkado-Cypriot for another argument from dialect). See Colvin (again **479–85**n.) ch. 6 and map at fig. 6.1. For these migrations as catalysts for ethnogenesis, see R. Fowler in *The Returning Hero*, ch. 2. Kassandra emphasizes force, deception, and abuse of women in colonizing acts.

'Lapersios' (cf. **511**) is a Spartan epithet for Agamemnon, recalling his cult there (**1124**). At **1372–3** Kassandra explains how, though dead, she will know what she does: she will *hear* about it. This apparent passivity is puzzling given her prophetic powers, but perhaps she means she will hear her own prophecies in the underworld: Pillinger, 127.

1374–7 Orestes' father Agamemnon was killed in a net, **1101**. For Orestes as his father's avenger see **1120–2**. 'Polyglot' is a rough equivalent of Greek *aiolos*, 'varied', which in turn evokes 'Aiolian', 'Aiolid'. Much earlier, Kassandra had related a different foundation myth for the Aiolid (**232–9**n.). Such alternative traditions may reflect competing claims by rival clans, cf. Fowler *EGM* 2.597–602: a local family, the Penthilidai, claimed descent from Orestes' son Penthilos, see e.g. Sappho frag. 71.

1378–87 Kassandra moves south from the Aiolid to Ionia, a large coastal area, here represented by Miletos in synecdoche. Miletos, a mixed Ionian-Karian city, was rich in foundations myths: C. Sourvinou-Inwood, *Hylas, the Nymphs, Dionysos and Others* (Stockholm, Swedish Institute at Athens, 2005), 268–309. Kodros was an early king of Athens, whose son Neileos founded Miletos: Herodotus 9.97 (cf. 5.97, Miletos colonized from Athens). Kassandra packs three myths into a dozen lines, the first (1) expressed by a single compound word 'woodcutting'. The woodcutter is Kodros. An oracle (Fontenrose L49) told the invading Peloponnesians that Athens could not be taken if the king were killed. Kodros pretended to be a woodcutter, went to the enemy camp, picked a quarrel, and got himself killed. See J. Hesk, *Deception and Democracy in Classical Athens* (Cambridge, Cambridge University Press, 2000), 89–102. For such 'king must die' oracles, cf. Herodotus 7.220, Leonidas of Sparta.

The other two myths concern the foundation from Miletos by Athenians. In (2), another oracle (Fontenrose L70) led Kodros' son Neileos to deceive a Milesian ('Branchesian') girl to give him earth and water, a symbol of territorial ownership; cf. Herodotus 5.73. For powerfully symbolic clods of earth, see also Pindar *Pythian* 4.34–9, and, for their acquisition by trickery, Plutarch, *Greek Questions* 13 and 22.

The 'lewd daughter' of **1385–7**, myth (3), is intelligible only with the help of an ancient commentator, and then only partially. For the evidence see again Fontenrose, L70. The oracle at Delphi told Neileos to settle where his daughter showed him. At Athens she mysteriously uttered two hexameters which named Miletos. When the Athenians reached the future site of Miletos, she became promiscuous (cf. **1387**). Opening her legs, she struck her genitals, saying, 'Who wants to have sex with me?' Her father understood this to mean that he should settle at Miletos. With the utterance which turned out prophetic, compare **1250–2**n. (Ascanius and the 'tables'); and the girl's role has something in common with that of guiding animals, discussed at **29**n. The slaughter of the indigenous Karians is notable (**1384**); cf. **1369–73**n.

1388–96 The third and last area of Greek settlement is that of the Dorians, the 'descendants of Dymas': the south-west corner of Asia Minor (the 'Rhodian *peraia*', cf. **1090–8**n. for this term), and neighbouring islands, now the Dodecanese, the largest of which are Rhodes (cf. **923**), Kos, and Karpathos (cf. **925**). The places at **1389** are in central Greece, the region called Doris; for Kytinion see *SEG* 38.1476. The peninsula at **1391** is the Triopian, a finger of land with Hellenistic Knidos as its nail.

The myth at **1393–6** is the subject of Kallimachos *Hymn* 6, *To Demeter*, but Kassandra's version is closer to the Hesiodic *Catalogue of Women*, frag. 69, from a papyrus published only in the mid-twentieth century: Erysichthon or Aithon son of Triopas (cf. above for 'Triopian') offended Demeter ('Kyrita') by chopping down a sacred grove; inscriptions prohibit this, and cf. Thucydides 3.70.4. He was punished with insatiable hunger, which he gratified by prostituting his daughter Mestra; but Poseidon had given her the gift of shape-shifting, so she escaped her predators. This is the last metamorphosis of the poem (unless we count Midas' ears, **1402**), and the last of the poem's many unfortunate women who suffer for, and at the hands of, men. The implication of **1391–2** is not quite right: it was not Triopas, eponym of the peninsula, whom Demeter hated, but his impious son.

1397–1408 'Fraternal blood' is that of Agamemnon's victims, the Trojans. Midas is part historical, part mythical, and probably should be split into two: *OCD* 'Midas' nos (1) and (2), both mentioning a king of c.700 BCE whom the Assyrians called Mita. A Phrygian migration into Macedonia is a historical fact: N. Hammond, *History of Macedonia* vol. 1 (Oxford, Clarendon Press, 1972), 302–11. For the historical Midas (738–696 BCE) see Herodotus 8.138, the fragrant 'gardens of Midas' in Macedon, cf. 1.14, his alleged dedications at Delphi. The mythical Midas heard a music contest between Pan and Apollo but preferred Pan, and was punished for this folly by being given donkey's ears (**1401**). See Ovid *Metamorphoses* 11.90–193 for this and the rest of the entertaining Midas myth; but Lykophron includes, whether from some predecessor or his own black imagination, macabre details of amputation. At **1398** the 'land' is Europe because Europa was the mother ('nurse') of Minos, judge in the underworld: *Odyssey* 11.569.

1409–10 See **909–10**n. for such bridging passages, but this one looks forward not backwards: it covers all conflicts between Midas and Xerxes (see next n. for the Ionian Revolt). Kandaios/aon and Mamertos were epithets for

Ares the war-god at **938** also; see n. there for Mamertos as Oscan, and **1416–17**n. for the feminine Mamersa = Athena.

1412–34 After Midas, Kassandra jumps to Xerxes' invasion, 480 BCE. Asia was mother of both Prometheus (**1283**) and his brother Epimetheus. By passing from one Asiatic aggression to another with no intervening European one, Kassandra breaks the alternating sequence. She could have used the Ionian revolt of 500–494 BCE to restore the regular thematic oscillation. Greek (mainly Athenian) military help to that revolt against Persia of their Ionian and Karian subjects would neatly have fitted her reciprocal scheme: Herodotus (5.102) had expressly called Xerxes' sack of the Athenian acropolis in 480 a 'counter-burning' for Greek burning of the Persian satrapal capital Sardis twenty years earlier. But, as often, she scorns predictability.

This is the poem's fullest narration of a historical episode, and draws heavily on Herodotus from the start: at **1413** 'giant' for Xerxes takes to an extreme 7.187 on his height and beauty (compare **1244**, a mild Homeric hint turns Odysseus into a dwarf); and the notion that Perseus was ancestor of the Persians (**1414**, cf. **1435–50**n.) derives from 7.150. But Trojan Kassandra concentrates on Persian failure, and ignores Greek success.

Detail continues to be Herodotean: cleverly reduced, but with differences. A famous Delphic oracle (the 'seer' of **1419**, unexpectedly called servant of Hades) told the Athenians to trust their 'wooden wall', certainly their fleet not their fortifications: Herodotus 7.139–44, Fontenrose 124–8. But Kassandra cleverly juggles with the ambiguity, **1418–20**, **1432**; cf. McNelis and Sens, 24–6. In Herodotus, Xerxes had rejected a plan to sail home (8.118–19), but here he adopts it like a terrified girl, **1433**, assimilating him to the female naval abductions of Io, Europa, and Medea: so Priestley, 185. Otherwise, the paradoxes at **1414–15** are ingeniously generated from Herodotus on the canal cut through Mt Athos and the bridge over the Hellespont, 7. 22–3 and 33–6; the hunger and privations of the retreating Persian army (**1421–3**) from 8.115; rivers drunk dry (**1424–5**) from e.g. 7.43; arrows hiding the sun (**1426–8**) from 7.226, Thermopylai.

1416–17 Mamersa, like the equally warlike epithet Laphria ('goddess of spoils'), designates Athena, whose temple on the Athenian acropolis (a predecessor of the Parthenon) was burnt by Xerxes. For the male form Mamertos (Mars, Ares) see **938**n. and **1409–10**n.; Mamersa is an authentically Italic form. Mars' consort was a Sabine divinity called Nerio, who was identifiable with Minerva (Athena). All this suggests intimate acquaintance with Italic religion on Lykophron's part. For the scattered evidence see Hornblower 2018, 169–70.

1429 Lokrian roses are not known to have been proverbial for ephemerality; the allusion may be to a kind of rouge (Pollux 5.102). Lokroi is probably the S. Italian city.

1435–50 This is the prophecy's climax, much discussed for its important evidence of Greek awareness of and attitudes to Roman power. The poem's composition date depends in part on the identification of the historical individuals or groups designated by wrestling or animal metaphors. (But only in part: literary borrowings are the other main such indicator, cf. Introduction, *Authorship and Date*.) What follows are dogmatically asserted preferences.

The opening lines **1435–6** cover the packed century and a half of conflict between the end of the Persian wars (479 BCE) and the reign of Alexander the Great (338–323 BCE). **1437–8** is a flowery version of the familiar land and sea combination, cf. **1229**, **1448**; but the translation accepts emendations in **1437** to avoid the absurd 'on land and on land'.

The lion of **1439** is Alexander the Great of Macedon. For Alexander and his son Herakles by Barsine as 'born from Aiakos' (a figure from Greek mythology) see **799–806**n. Alexander was 'born from Dardanos' (for whom see **69–85**n.) because his mother Olympias claimed descent from Priam's son Helenos. So Alexander is both Greek and Trojan as well as Macedonian. Alexander's 'brothers' (**1442**) are the Persians, by shared descent from Perseus (Herodotus 7.150, cf. **1412–34**n.); the Achaemenid empire was overthrown by Alexander in a series of battles beginning at the Granikos river in 334. The fawning Argives (**1443**) are Greek politicians. 'Wolf-commander of Galadra' (cf. **1341–50**n.) is the king of Macedon at any given time: Alexander until **1445**, then Philip V (reigned 221–179 BCE), who is the 'him' of 'With him . . .'. Kassandra's kinsman-wrestler (**1446–7**) is the glamorous Roman proconsul Titus Quinctius Flamininus, who defeated Philip at Kynoskephalai in Greece, 197 BCE. See Introduction, *Authorship and Date*. The idea of the Romans as victorious wrestlers may have been in Ennius (see D. Feeney, *Explorations in Latin Literature*, Cambridge, Cambridge University Press, vol. 2 (2021), 350–1)—perhaps borrowed and adapted from Lykophron? For 'land and sea', cf. **1229**, clearly evoked here.

1448–50 On the view taken here, this reconciliation is the settlement after Kynoskephalai (Polybius 18.44), which left Philip his kingdom (cf. Livy 33.11.4, Flamininus tells Philip to be cheerful). 'About land and sea' goes with 'reconciliation' not 'spear-fight': see Hornblower 2018: 4 n. 7. Flamininus was indeed 'celebrated' (**1449**): he received actual cult in his lifetime. See Polybius 18.46.12 with *HCP* 2.613, and inscriptions, collected at Sherk no. 6, A–G. His 'friends' were the propertied upper classes in Greece. The reconciliation may be intended to recall that of Aineias—another kinsman of Kassandra—with his 'frenemy' Odysseus (**1242–9**n.): McNelis and Sens, 208–10.

1451–60 Kassandra ends with a lament, comparable to the second-century BCE Jewish-Greek hexameter poem the *Third Sibylline Oracle* (815–16): the Sibyl predicts that she will be called a mad liar. 'But why. . .?' (**1451**) echoes Kassandra's rhetorical question at Euripides, *Trojan Women*, 444. With 'twanging . . . empty noise' (**1453**), Pillinger, 227–8 aptly compares line 3 of A. E. Stallings' poem *Cassandra*: 'all my harping lies unstrung'. (*Hapax: Poems*, TriQuarterly, Evanston IL, 2006), 44.

Apollo (the 'Lepsian', **1454**, cf. **1207**) promised Kassandra the gift of prophecy in return for sex, but when it came to it, she refused him. He could not withdraw the gift of truthful prophecy, but he qualified it by ensuring that she would not be believed. The myth is first attested in Aeschylus, *Agamemnon*, 1208, 1212 (but at 1213 the chorus find her prophecies true enough). Kassandra was conspicuously beautiful and attractive (*Iliad* 13.365–6)—and so was Apollo: E. Kearns, 'Pindar and Euripides on Sex with Apollo', *Classical Quarterly* 63 (2013), 57–67 at 58. The meaning of **1458–60** seems to be that although Troy will fall, Rome will replace it, and then Kassandra's veracity will be vindicated—in a metaliterary way? That is, by the *Alexandra* itself?

1461–74 As we have seen (1–30n.), some factual details about Kassandra's imprisonment and the guard's own role are delayed until now, his final speech. The comparisons at **1464–5** are important: they pull together strands of Kassandra's implied self-characterization in the course of the poem. In pride of place is the Siren, about whom, and her sisters, much was said in **670–737**, but the actual word 'Siren' was withheld until now, **1463**. Melankraira daughter of Neso is a Sibyl, cf. **1279**; and 'Phikian monster' is the Sphinx, cf. **6–7n**. Here the technique is the reverse of that applied to the Siren: the plain words 'Sphinx' and 'Sibyl' were used on the earlier occasions, but now the denominations are indirect. The Klarian Mimallon is the only newcomer, but is perhaps meant to stand for Kassandra's prophecy as a whole, since Klaros was an Apolline oracular sanctuary in Asia Minor: Tacitus *Annals* 2.54; L. and J. Robert, *Claros* vol. 1, *Décrets Hellénistiques* (Paris, De Boccard, 1989). A Mimallon was some sort of bacchant, cf. Plutarch *Alexander* 2. The guard is no less a master of variation and surprise than Kassandra.

At **1466**, the word for 'twisted' is a metaphor from spinning thread, and may owe a debt to the programmatic opening of Kallimachos' *Aitia*, line 5 and ultimately to the earlier poet Erinna: see K. Gutzwiller, 'Under the sign of the distaff: *Aetia* 1.5, spinning and Erinna', *Classical Quarterly* 70 (2020), 171–6 at 182 n. 23. On 'crooked' at **1467** and the unusual word for 'messenger' at **1471** (derived from the verb 'run', cf. **13–15n**.) see Introduction, *Difficulty*: the 'Lykophron epigram' amalgamates the two into a *hapax* compound word.

1474 The closural prayer 'save the city!' is a device found both in literary hymns (*Homeric Hymn* 13 *To Demeter* 3, and Kallimachos *Hymn* 6 *To Demeter*, 134) and inscribed prayers and hymns (e.g. W. H. Buckler and D. M. Robinson, *Sardis* VII. 1: *Greek and Latin Inscriptions*, Leiden, Brill, 1932) no. 50 (first century BCE).

INDEX OF NAMES

Note: divine epithets or alternative divine names are listed (sometimes translated) after each god, with page references; they are also separately entered, with a cross-reference to the divine name, e.g. 'Kastnian see Aphrodite' or 'Tripper-up see Dionysus'

GENERAL INDEX

acorns, eating of 4
   and autochthony 18, 77
address, forms of 71
adultery 28, 41, 88, 90
aetiologies 64, 86, 91, 92, 95, 97, 107, 109
Aithiopis 65
alphabetization (of divine epithets) 67
altars 8, 11, 12, 22, 36, 43, 67, 72
animals *see* ants, bears, bitches, boars,
   bulls, crabs, deer, dogs, dolphins,
   donkeys, dragons, hedgehogs,
   heifers, lions, moles, monkeys, oxen,
   rams, seals, snakes, sows, wasps,
   whales, whelps, wolves *cf. also* fish
   helpful or guiding 60, 106, 109, cf. 64
   (Paris' bear-nurse)
   metaphors from/comparisons with 61,
   63, 65, 73, 109, 114
   naming of by Kassandra xiii, 64, 72
ants 7, 65, 76
arrows 3, 11, 24, 44, 52, 93, 113
authorship, of the *Alexandra* xxi–xxiii
autochthony myths 17, 77, 103
axes 40, 42, 95, 95
   Axe (pattern poem) 95

bacchants 115
bears 6, 64
bestiary, Kassandra's *see* animals, birds
Bible, biblical parallels 75, 95
bilingualism xxiii, xxx, xxxii, 95, 105
birds, bird-metaphors 26, 66 *and see*
   corncrakes, crows, cuckoos, doves,
   eagles, falcons, geese, hens, iynx,
   kingfishers, nightingales, quails,
   shearwaters, sparrows, swans,
   vultures, woodpeckers, wryneck
   guiding 60
   metamorphosis into xii, xv, 22, 65, 81
   'no-birds' place (Aornos) 86
   used in oracular discourse 61
bitches 2, 4, 11, 22, 24, 31, 38, 71
   (Maira)
black xxxii, 10, 20, 26, 36, 42, 43, 106
   and see dark, darkness
   dress for mourning 101

blind, blinding, blindness 15, 74–5, 85
   as appropriate punishment for sexual
   deviation 75
blood (in ritual) 25, 43, 85
boars 30, 37, 39, 47, 78, 90, 92
bones, cult of xviii, 103 (Hektor), 103
   (Orestes, Rhesos, Theseus), cf. 61
   (Pelops)
booty 94 *and see* index of names under
   Athena (booty, goddess of)
bows 6, 19, 21, 33, 49, 61, 93
boxing 13, 94
bream 14
'bride-carrying' 37, 97
bulls 21, 43, 48, 76, 109 *and see* index of
   names under Dionysos (Bull-god)
burial rites 18, 92 *and see* bones

cakes, sacrificial 105
cannibalism 24, 77, 84, *cf.* 99 (Tydeus)
Capture of Troy (Trifiodoros) xxxii
castration 88, 100
catalogue form xxiv, 112 *and see* index of
   names under Homer (*Iliad*,
   Catalogue of Ships)
cattle 24 (Herakles as Cattle-driver)
   of Geryon 86
   of the Sun 27, 88
causes xvi, xxviii *and see* aetiologies,
   guilt, requital, revenge
cenotaphs 13, 38, 43
censors (Roman magistrates) xx
centaurs 24, 44, 61, 74, 84
choruses (tragic) xxvi, xxvii, 115
chronology xvi, xviii, xxix, 66,
   104, 109
chthonic (underworld) 102
cleansing 32, 42
closure, narrative 89, 107, 115
clothes, clothing 22, 31, 44, 46, 72, 101
   and see dress
coins, coinage xxiv, xxx, 95, 104, 109
colonization xi, xvi–xvii, xix, xxix, 50–1,
   82, 85–6, 95, 98, 105, 107, 111–12
   and see earth and water
   Roman xxiii, 99

The Oxford World's Classics Website

www.oxfordworldsclassics.com

- Browse the full range of Oxford World's Classics online

- Sign up for our monthly e-alert to receive information on new titles

- Read extracts from the Introductions

- Listen to our editors and translators talk about the world's greatest literature with our Oxford World's Classics audio guides

- Join the conversation, follow us on Twitter at OWC_Oxford

- Teachers and lecturers can order inspection copies quickly and simply via our website

www.oxfordworldsclassics.com

American Literature

British and Irish Literature

Children's Literature

Classics and Ancient Literature

Colonial Literature

Eastern Literature

European Literature

Gothic Literature

History

Medieval Literature

Oxford English Drama

Philosophy

Poetry

Politics

Religion

The Oxford Shakespeare

A complete list of Oxford World's Classics, including Authors in Context, Oxford English Drama, and the Oxford Shakespeare, is available in the UK from the Marketing Services Department, Oxford University Press, Great Clarendon Street, Oxford OX2 6DP, or visit the website at www.oup.com/uk/worldsclassics.

In the USA, visit www.oup.com/us/owc for a complete title list.

Oxford World's Classics are available from all good bookshops. In case of difficulty, customers in the UK should contact Oxford University Press Bookshop, 116 High Street, Oxford OX1 4BR.

HORACE	The Complete Odes and Epodes
JUVENAL	The Satires
LIVY	The Dawn of the Roman Empire
	Hannibal's War
	The Rise of Rome
MARCUS AURELIUS	The Meditations
OVID	The Love Poems
	Metamorphoses
PETRONIUS	The Satyricon
PLATO	Defence of Socrates, Euthyphro, and Crito
	Gorgias
	Meno and Other Dialogues
	Phaedo
	Republic
	Symposium
PLAUTUS	Four Comedies
PLUTARCH	Greek Lives
	Roman Lives
	Selected Essays and Dialogues
PROPERTIUS	The Poems
SOPHOCLES	Antigone, Oedipus the King, and Electra
SUETONIUS	Lives of the Caesars
TACITUS	The Annals
	The Histories
THUCYDIDES	The Peloponnesian War
VIRGIL	The Aeneid
	The Eclogues and Georgics
XENOPHON	The Expedition of Cyrus